100 THINGS BLUE JAYS FANS SHOULD KNOW & DO BEFORE THEY DIE

Steve Clarke

The Library of Congress has catalogued the previous edition as follows:

Clarke, Steve, 1974–
100 things Blue Jays fans should know & do before they die / Steve Clarke.
pages cm
ISBN 978-1-60078-774-4
1. Toronto Blue Jays (Baseball team)—History. 2. Toronto Blue Jays (Baseball team)—Miscellanea. I. Title. II. Title: One hundred things Blue Jays fans need to know & do before they die.
GV875.T67C53 2013
796.357'6409713541—dc23
2012038284

This book is available in quantity at special discounts for your group or organization. For further information, contact:

Triumph Books LLC
814 North Franklin Street
Chicago, Illinois 60610
(312) 337-0747
www.triumphbooks.com

Printed in U.S.A.
ISBN: 978-1-62937-412-3
Design by Patricia Frey
Photos courtesy of *Toronto Star* unless otherwise indicated

To my amazing wife, Kasia, may we have many more long walks on the beach together, hand in hand. To my brilliant, beautiful, and hilarious daughter, Peyton, without whose loving attention this book would have been finished in half the time. To every kid out there with a glove and a dream. To C & T & M & D.

Contents

Acknowledgments

I might never have been inspired to pursue writing professionally, had I not received such tremendous support from my mom, Linda. She proofread the majority of the words you see before you. So, if you find any errors, you know exactly who to blame.

Thank you to my creative writing teacher, Mr. Hougham, for further fuelling my love of the art of writing. As I headed off to Western, it was his reassurance that drove me to begin writing for the school newspaper.

Without the kindness of Bryan Douglass, I might have never taken the next steps. Bryan took me on as a blogger for a pair of basketball-related sites and later connected me with Cory Elfrink of Fanball.com, who was kind enough to hire me for his site. Special thanks, as well, to Mark Healey and the rest of the crew at Going 9 Baseball for allowing me to both write for the site and make appearances on their SiriusXM radio program.

Sincere thanks to Jeff Fedotin, editor at Triumph Books, for his insight and advice throughout the writing process. Jeff is as sharp an editor as I've encountered with a keen eye for detail and a passion for quality. Even as deadlines approached, Jeff was incredibly encouraging, and he deserves a tonne of credit for helping me put this thing together.

I am humbled by the kindness and professionalism of the entire team at Triumph Books, an innovative and bold publisher. My most sincere thanks, in particular, to Tom Bast and Mitch Rogatz for giving me this opportunity.

As I began writing this book, I reached out to my favourite writer, the remarkably talented Jason Parks of Baseball Prospectus. I asked him how he would tackle a project like this, and he provided thoughtful and meaningful advice. His insight primarily centered on the fact that Toronto need not consider itself the also-rans of the American League East, and fans would be remiss if they didn't celebrate the accomplishments of a proud franchise. His insight, simple as it might seem, acted as a guide for me throughout this process, and I owe him much gratitude.

Lastly, I'd like to thank the individuals who took the time to speak with me, resulting in many of the quotes and stories in the book. Thanks to Joe Carter, Roger Clemens, Cito Gaston, Charlie Sheen, Julius Erving, Johnny Cardona, Jorge Arangure, Kevin Goldstein, and many others.

Introduction

Sadly, my introduction to baseball took place at Tiger Stadium, home of Detroit's baseball club. I say sadly, because for just one day in my life, my loyalty was directed to a team that would later become the archenemy of the Toronto Blue Jays. I should have known better, that day, than to clap my little hands and cheer for the vile gang of bandits who would cause so many problems for Toronto's teams in later years.

Maybe my father should have stopped me.

Maybe I should have known intuitively that this hooting and hollering I did in favour of the Tigers would someday haunt my dreams. Hand in hand, my father led me into Tiger Stadium. The grass on the field wasn't just green—it was the most insipidly vivid shade of green my young eyes had ever seen. (My father's lawn maintenance at home had instilled certain expectations for the colour of grass—brownish and peppered with little yellow flowers.)

Holding his meaty, freckled hand—I can still remember it now—we walked toward our seats. My young mind was numbed by the sheer mass of humanity gathered in the stadium. No, sir—this was not the Rogers Centre on a Tuesday night in April—this was a *crowd*. And it was brash…cheering with unbridled passion.

They lured me in. My five-year-old mind was seduced by the madness, and I let go of all my inhibitions. I cheered for the Tigers with all my might…a shame I'll never truly overcome. I've since decided to forgive my father for putting me in this situation and am (secretly) thankful for the experience of seeing my very first baseball game by his side. It wasn't his fault, damn it. It wasn't his fault.

Mercifully, his employer soon transferred him away from Tiger territory and closer to Toronto—where I would find comfort in the plush welcoming arms of BJ Birdy. Dad's lawn maintenance acumen improved along the way, perhaps just coincidentally, and much greener grass prevailed.

In those yards, my dad taught me how to throw and catch, spurring on my love of baseball. He coached my teams through childhood and has always had my back—both on and off the field—even to this very day. He sparked my love for the Blue Jays, a team we love to discuss and share opinions about, even while we have often disagreed about nearly everything else.

I became a Junior Jay superfan, dorkily wearing a worn-out Blue Jays hat to school and even saving up for an absurdly shiny mid-1980s replica team jacket. My friend, Colin, and I walked to the Stone Road fire station in Guelph, Ontario, to pick up their giveaway Blue Jays baseball card packs. Arriving home, I'd head up to my bedroom and study the stats on the back of the cards while listening to Tom Cheek and Jerry Howarth on my clock radio.

As if to compensate for that terrible day in Detroit, I worshipped at the altars of Ernie Whitt, Jesse Barfield, Fred McGriff, Jimmy Key, and Dave Stieb—and so many others. Mark Eichhorn, Jeff Musselman, Tony Fernandez…these guys were incredible.

I wanted to be a Blue Jay myself and could have been.

The market—at the time—was shamefully biased against max-effort, right-handed Anglo Saxons whose velocity topped out just north of 80 mph measured on a JUGS gun (which, for the uninitiated, is rumored to add a few mph to readings).

Undaunted, I took a chance—like many other young players—and attended a Blue Jays tryout camp in Cambridge, Ontario. I threw as hard as I could and ran as fast as my legs would take me. Ultimately, the baseball "machine" found no room for this particular flamethrower.

Thankfully, somewhere along the line, my mom sparked my love of writing and gave me all the encouragement I needed along the way. She's probably proofread 95 percent of the articles I've written for websites like Fanball, Going 9 Baseball, Comcast.net, and others. She's even suffered through the painful experience of hearing me use the word "tremendous"—upwards of 50 times in a 10-minute segment on one particular episode of the *Going 9 Baseball Show* on SiriusXM—something no mother should ever be forced to endure.

So, now, I find myself charged with the task of spelling out *100 Things Blue Jays Fans Should Know & Do Before They Die*—the key moments in team history and a list of must-dos for admirers of the ballclub. I hope the book accomplishes its mission. As you read though the collection of stories, I hope you take pride in the uniqueness of the Blue Jays fan experience. Toronto has a rich and exciting baseball history, and if this book accomplishes anything, I hope it makes you love and appreciate this team even more, while perhaps making you smile a couple of times along the way.

The time is ripe for Blue Jays Nation to step up and be proud of this franchise—a team which has almost always carried itself with an air of professionalism, a focus on player development, and an honest commitment to the community.

No, maybe we don't have the storied histories of the New York Yankees or the Boston Red Sox. There's no annoying Monument Park or Pesky Pole at our park. And maybe the Rogers Centre outfield walls aren't covered in ivy like Wrigley Field, and we don't have a mascot flinging himself down a waterslide every time our boys hit a home run, like that godforsaken yellow-beard in Milwaukee. We don't have a Miami Marlins-style seafood shrine in centre field, or a "too cool for school" manager who makes his team dress up in costumes like the Cubs, and we certainly don't have an Angels-style monkey showing up on the Jumbotron when we need a rally.

What we do have are the Blue Jays—*our* Blue Jays—a team with as rich a history as any in baseball since the late 1970s. This is a team of superstars, sluggers, and aces. This is a team with banners, and several of them.

Winners of the 1985, 1989, 1991, 1992, and 2015 AL East pennants and the 2016 AL wild-card.

Winners of the 2015 and 2016 ALDS.

Winners of the 1992 and 1993 ALCS and World Series.

So, what does it mean to be a Blue Jay?

It means committing to the "Blue Jay Way"—a code of ethics, in essence, adhered to almost from the team's inception. Granted, Toronto doesn't stuff it down your throat like other teams do with their contrived traditions. That fact alone makes it all the more exceptional. The "Blue Jay Way" has been carried out by leaders like Paul Beeston, Pat Gillick, Gord Ash, and Alex Anthopoulos. Treat players right. Treat your fans with respect. Treat members of the media like humans. Celebrate your history. Be creative with player personnel decisions. Scout like mad. Scout some more. Tap into international markets. Be proud and dignified in your actions. Be honest.

Don't ever forget that the Jays were one of sports' most admired and feared teams throughout much of the '80s and '90s—and don't think for a damned second that the Jays won't find a way to stay on top. Savour the team's recent accomplishments and those of the '80s and '90s and look with excitement toward the future. Take pride in the fact flags fly forever.

I hope you find this book to be a celebration of a proud sports franchise and I hope you share my excitement as we glimpse into the future of Toronto's men in blue. Baseball's alive and well in Toronto.

In the interest of full disclosure, I'll admit that I occasionally return to Detroit to check out a ballgame with my longtime friends, Tom, Craig, and Dave. I'll join them in indulging in all the trappings of a visit to Comerica Park, like pregame refreshments at the Hockeytown Café, Texas-style chili at Cheli's, and exhilarating walks through the city's downtown core, while the night air is filled with the soothing rhythms of N.W.A. and Tupac.

But I'll never again clap for those filthy Tigers. Never again.

1 The 1993 World Series

"*There's a swing and a BELT, LEFT FIELD... WAY BACK...*"

You could sense the exact millisecond announcer Tom Cheek realized that this ball—hit with one out in the bottom of the ninth—was headed into the seats. It was the same precise moment Blue Jays fans across Canada realized they were watching history, just the second time a World Series had ever been won with a walk-off home run.

"*BLUE JAYS WIN IT! The Blue Jays are World Series champions, as Joe Carter hits a three-run home run in the ninth inning, and the Blue Jays have repeated as World Series champions...*"

The country rejoiced as Carter leapt and bounded toward first base, arms extended in the air as far as they could reach. Cheek was aware of what this home run meant.

"*Touch 'em all, Joe! You'll NEVER hit a bigger home run in your life!*"

The Blue Jays had won 95 regular season games in 1993. Fuelled by the contributions of seven All-Stars (Roberto Alomar, Joe Carter, Pat Hentgen, Paul Molitor, John Olerud, Duane Ward, and Devon White), they won the American League East crown by that same number of games. Olerud had made a run at .400 this season, finishing with a .363 average. Teammates Molitor (.332) and Alomar (.326) finished second and third in the batting race—the first time in a century that the top three finishers in batting average played for the same team. Bottom line? This was hardly a gang of underdogs. "We've got a team of All-Stars," Carter said.

With this potent offence and a highly capable collection of pitchers, the Blue Jays headed into their second consecutive World

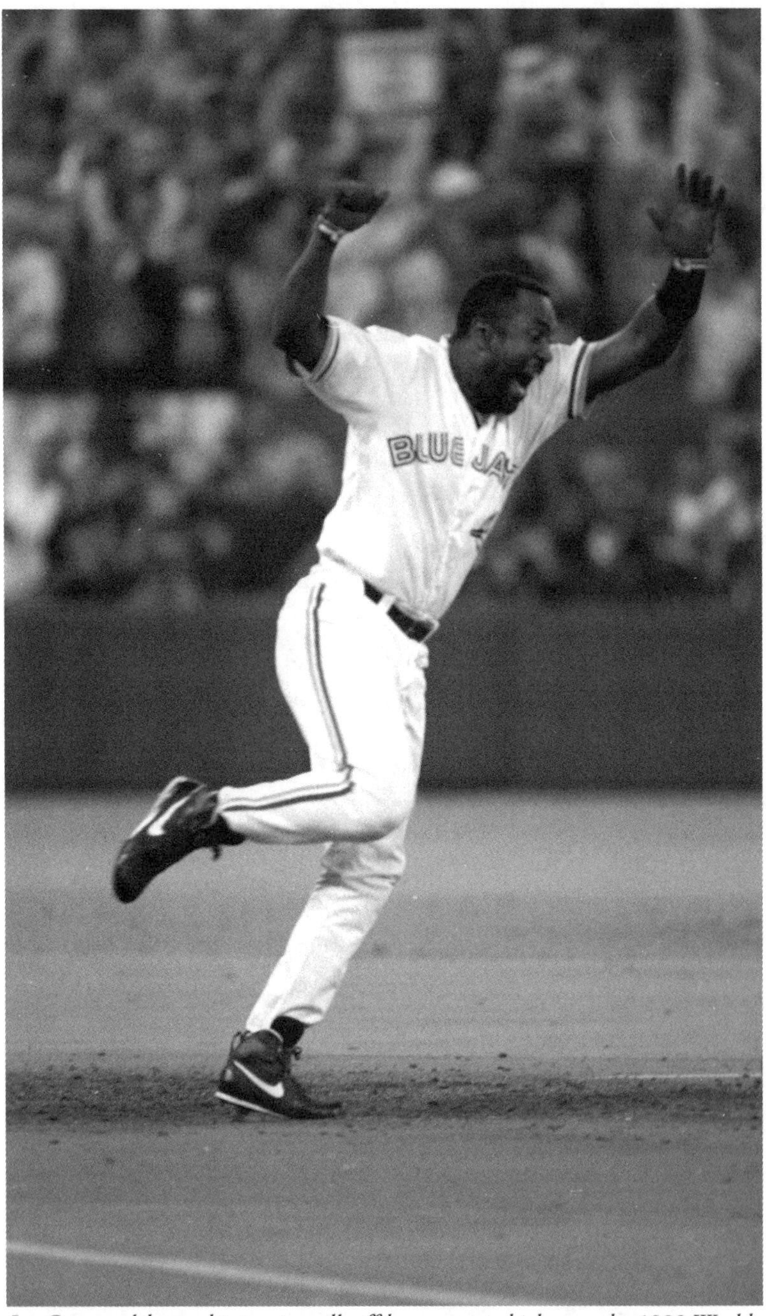

Joe Carter celebrates his iconic walk-off home run, which won the 1993 World Series for the Blue Jays.

Series, this time against a gritty gang from Philadelphia. The Phillies battled hard but suffered a critical blow in Game 4, as the Blue Jays overcame 12–7 and 14–9 deficits. Their relief corps was drained by the length of the match, which included an eighth inning in which 10 batters came to the plate. The Jays won that game in Philadelphia, swinging the momentum firmly in their favour.

But the memory that lingers in the minds of fans—both in Toronto and Philadelphia—is of Game 6 in Toronto, where the Blue Jays trailed the Phillies 6–5 entering the bottom of the ninth. Phillies closer Mitch Williams walked Rickey Henderson, which was followed by a Molitor single.

Then Joe Carter came up to bat.

With a 2–2 count, "Wild Thing" Williams delivered, and Carter smashed the pitch into the left-field seats in the SkyDome for a stunning three-run walk-off home run. Williams dropped his head and walked to the Phillies clubhouse. The stadium erupted while players spilled onto the field. Carter bounced around the bases. A swarm of bodies encircled Carter as he crossed home plate. Among the most emotional was Molitor, the eventual Hall of Famer who had joined the Jays prior to the season. "I've waited so long for this," he said while tears streamed down his face.

Henderson had experienced the championship feeling before, but he was equally thrilled. "I'll cherish this ring as much as the ring with Oakland," he said. Pitcher Dave Stewart had also won the 1989 World Series with Henderson on the Oakland A's, but even those talented A's squads could not repeat as champions, like the Jays did. "[Opposing] teams got close, we found a way to pull away," he said. "When we fell into second, we found a way to get back to first. We just did the right things at the right time."

Cito Gaston, manager of the team for its second straight World Series championship, said the win spoke volumes about the squads's focus. "Teams don't repeat because players aren't willing to go through the bull you have to go through," he said. "If you don't have 25 guys willing to go through all the hard work, the problems, the distractions, you're not going to repeat."

Asked if he painted the town red that night, Carter said his post-game celebrations were primarily limited to the clubhouse. Remarkably, his teammates didn't leave him—the man of the hour—any bubbly. "Unfortunately, we didn't have a chance to really celebrate after the game. Yonge Street was too crowded, and I had to go do about 10,000 interviews and I came back, and everyone had taken the champagne [from the clubhouse]," he said. "I didn't really get a chance to celebrate with the guys. I just went upstairs, grabbed a bite to eat, and went home to sleep, because we had a parade the next day. That was just about it."

Molitor, who played his previous 15 years with the Milwaukee Brewers, remained in the clubhouse in his champagne-drenched uniform until after 2:00 AM. His eyes were red and swollen from tears. His voice was raspy from hooting, hollering, and speaking with endless reporters. "I didn't want to say anything before, but now that we've won it I can say it's the best year I've had," he said. "It just all worked out."

2 A Championship for Toronto

Funny, isn't it, that the Blue Jays' first World Series victory is filed behind the second in the collective memory of Toronto fans? Dave Winfield, whose double down the left-field line against the Atlanta Braves might have been remembered for decades as the Blue Jays' greatest moment, has now become more of a footnote in team history when compared to Joe Carter and his headline-grabbing home run. The 41-year-old designated hitter had been searching for a World Series ring for each of his first 18 seasons in the big leagues and finally got his prize. If not for a bad pitch by Mitch "Wild Thing" Williams, the gentle giant's "Winfield Wants Noise" slogan might be remembered as the team's signature quote, rather than "Touch 'em all, Joe."

But regardless of whatever heroic feats would later rewrite the history books, the Blue Jays' very first championship is a historic tale of its own, considered by many to be one of the finest Fall Classics ever. More than 45,000 patrons filled the SkyDome in Toronto to watch Game 6—an astounding number, considering they were there to watch the game on television. Besides that crazy crowd assembled to watch the game on the Jumbotron, more than 4 million other fans would cross the SkyDome turnstiles in the 1992 regular season, setting a major league record.

The late-night victory in Atlanta marked the first time in history the World Series banner would fly north of the border. It was also the first time in the history of baseball that an African American manager would win the World Series, as Cito Gaston led his band of stars—formerly stigmatized as the "Blow Jays"—to postseason victory.

It was the first World Series victory for Winfield, one of baseball's biggest stars of the '70s and '80s, who was nearing the end of his career and looking to overcome a negative image foisted upon him during a turbulent tenure with the New York Yankees. "Winfield used one hit—one stinking little hit," *The New York Times* wrote, "to exorcise a decade of demons and heartache."

"When I played for the Yankees, a lot of disparaging things were said about me and done to me," Winfield said. "Things that hurt my career, hurt my life. It took a couple years to regain some of the things that were taken away. But now, tonight, everything is so good for me. Finally."

That one stinking hit capped a season filled with memorable moments in Blue Jays history. Earlier in October, Alomar collected the most timely hit in Blue Jays history (to that point, at least) against the Oakland Athletics. The Jays' All-Star second baseman belted a two-run home run off fireman Dennis Eckersley to tie Game 4 of the American League Championship Series, a blast which swung momentum firmly in Toronto's direction. Fans remember Alomar running to first with his arms raised in celebration, as the ball cleared the fence. The Jays closed them out two games later, winning the series in six games.

The next series took tension to an even higher level. The Jays dropped the first game but were redeemed by Ed Sprague's homer in Game 2. Equally notable was the bizarre start to that game, in which Canadian singer Tom Cochrane messed up his homeland's anthem and a member of the U.S. Marine's colour guard accidentally flew the flag of Canada upside down. Not to be outdone, Kelly Gruber infuriated the Atlanta fandom by mocking its Tomahawk Chop as he ran off the field. Toronto fans loved it. The Atlanta fans? Not so much.

Game 3 featured an infamous near triple play, and Alomar serving up a mock Tomahawk Chop of his own as he scored the winning run on a Candy Maldonado single.

The Blue Jays won Game 4 2–1 on a Jimmy Key gem against Tom Glavine. Catcher Pat Borders was the Jays' offensive hero, socking a third-inning homer, while Whyte scored Gruber for the winning run in the bottom of the seventh.

Game 5 wasn't much of a contest, as Lonnie Smith of the Braves crushed a grand slam off Toronto's Jack Morris in the Braves' 7–2 victory.

Then came Game 6 in Atlanta. The 11-inning affair featured a multitude of lead changes, but the Jays were primed for victory heading into the bottom of the ninth. Toronto brought in reliable closer Tom "the Terminator" Henke to close things out, but Atlanta shortstop Jeff Blauser got on base, and an Otis Nixon single scored him, sending the contest into extra innings.

It all came together for Toronto, though, in the 11th inning. With one out, Whyte was hit by a pitch, after which Alomar singled to centre field. Carter made the second out of the inning for the Jays. Then, with two outs, Winfield stepped into the batter's box. The veteran worked pitcher Charlie Leibrandt to a full count before making history. Winfield muscled a liner down the left-field stripe, scoring both Whyte and Alomar and springing the Jays into a 4–2 lead.

Fans in the SkyDome went nuts, jumping and embracing in celebration. But it wasn't done yet.

Key returned to the mound for the bottom of the 11th and allowed a run before being replaced by Mike Timlin with two outs. Nixon, a future Blue Jay, stepped to the plate, finding himself in position to potentially tie the game for the second time. Instead, Nixon's drag bunt was fielded by Timlin, tossed to Carter, and the victory was sealed.

The Toronto Blue Jays were world champions.

While fans celebrated in Ontario streets, the Jays closer spoke to the battle the Braves had fought in this epic Fall Classic. "Atlanta would not give up," Henke said. "This was great for baseball."

"People just don't realize just how hard it was," relief pitcher Duane Ward said. "We had the pressure of a country—not just the city of Toronto, but we had the pressure of the country—to produce and to win a World Series."

Winfield reflected on his game-winning double. "I'm just so pleased," Winfield said, as champagne rained down on him. "I said a couple of extra prayers going up there. Normally you rely on your own skills, but I had to look above for some extra help. I mean, nothing was falling. I had no luck—except buzzard's luck. But fortunately that one went in.

"I didn't care to be a hero or anything, because we've had so many guys to get us here, to get us through," Winfield said. After all the struggles he experienced in a Yankees uniform, Winfield was on top of the world. Asked to sum up the moment's significance to his body of work, Winfield called it "my biggest game, my best day in baseball." Pat Gillick, Toronto's general manager said, "Dave's a great human being who hasn't been treated in his career as well as he should have been. It was probably a little bit of redemption that his hit won this championship for us."

Carter was equally impressed. "That was awesome," Carter said. "It couldn't have come to a better end." Nope—a World Series couldn't possibly come to a better end, could it, Joe?

3 Joe Carter's Home Run—Differing Perspectives

It's one of baseball's most iconic moments.

When Joe Carter hit the second walk-off, World Series-winning home run in baseball history, a three-run shot off Mitch Williams to win the 1993 championship for the Blue Jays, it was euphoric for Toronto fans and gut-wrenching for Philadelphia Phillies fans.

Philadelphia:

"As soon as it left my hand, I knew I made the mistake."—Mitch Williams

"The moment after Joe Carter's home run was the first time I ever blatantly cursed in front of my parents. My emotional fifth-grade self took the Nerf Turbo football I'd been clutching like a stress ball throughout the game, hurled it at Carter's face, and yelled "Fuck!" as loud as I could before bursting into tears."—Carl, Phillies fan, Phillysportshistory.com

"I was in Atlanta, Georgia, with the Sixers [as a broadcaster] staying at the Marriott Hotel. A few of us were watching the game.

The Joe Carter Classic

Joe Carter has a magnetic personality. His smile is as big as it is genuine, and he has a warm disposition to match. There's little wonder why so many of sport's biggest celebrities join him at his Joe Carter Classic charity golf tournament in Toronto, an annual event since 2010.

Among the celebrity attendees in 2016 were Dan Marino, Barry Larkin, Bret Saberhagen, Tim Raines, Cito Gaston, and comedians Chris Tucker and George Lopez. Past guests include Charlie Sheen, Ozzie Smith, Vince Coleman, Bo Jackson, Kenny Lofton, Fred McGriff, Dave Stewart, and Kelly Gruber. Entertainer Alan Thicke and *Shark Tank*'s Robert Herjavec also attended past events, as did basketball's Charles Barkley, football's Marcus Allen, Jerome Bettis, and Jonathan Ogden.

Perhaps the most interesting guest at the 2012 event was Mitch Williams—the man who threw the pitch Carter crushed for the 1993 World Series winning home run. Williams put aside whatever pain he might have held and enjoyed himself at the charitable event. He and Carter shared a limo, along with Dr. J (Julius Erving), and drove to the golf course together.

Carter's foundation made a donation of $500,000 to the Children's Aid Foundation. "Access to education and supportive programs, like the ones offered by the Children's Aid Foundation, are essential to creating opportunities and breaking down barriers for at-risk youth and children," Carter said. "Our hope is to create a lasting legacy that encourages these kids to stay in school and provide the necessary support for their foster families and communities."

We saw the shot. We saw him run…we saw the gallop…we saw the leap. Poor Mitch."—Philadelphia 76ers Hall of Famer Julius "Dr. J" Erving

"[Mitch] Williams is supposed to be the Phillies closer, their firefighter. But instead of putting fires out, he often tosses hand grenades into them."—Dave Anderson, *The New York Times*

"Unfortunately, he just didn't get the job done."—Phillies manager Jim Fregosi on Williams' performance

"I said, 'There's no way we're losing this game.' Apparently, I lied to him."—Phillies first baseman John Kruk, on the conversation he had with Williams before he took the mound

"I was in the fourth grade—almost 10. At the conclusion of Game 6, I locked myself in the bathroom and cried for a half an hour."—Michael O, Phillies fan

"I wouldn't wish that on my worst enemy."—teammate and pitcher Curt Schilling, who raised the closer's ire by wearing a button on his cap after Game 4 which said "I survived watching Mitch pitch in the 1993 World Series."

"Mitch has been our whipping boy all year. What people don't realize is, without Mitch, we're not here. People can say what they want about him, but he's given us our share of thrills in this clubhouse, and we're not blaming him for anything."—Kruk

"As I told Mitch after the game, he's the one that got us here. He saved over 40 games for us. He's the guy. That's the situation I use him in."—Fregosi

"I was standing next to Mayor [Ed] Rendell, when Carter ended both the Series and the '93 Beaux Arts Ball. There had to be a 60-foot screen at the convention center. That ball goes out, and the party ends hours earlier than expected."—Bill, Phillies fan

"I stink. There is no other way to put it."—Williams

Toronto:

"CBS gave me a tape from every camera that was on that night... Sure, the home run was great, but to see the excitement on one, my teammates, two, the fans, listening to what people were saying, the sheer joy—that's what a player lives for in baseball. Me rounding the bases, I thought that was secondary to all the players' and the fans' responses. I thought about that probably the most. That's what comes to mind."—Joe Carter

"In the ninth inning, we were hoping for Mitch to come in. We know he has a tendency to be a little wild. We were hoping that he would walk a couple of guys and then throw one over and he did."—outfielder Rickey Henderson

"Every year I watch the World Series, not the first three or four games, but I'll always watch that last game of the Series and hope the home team does not win, because that way it can't end on a home run,"—Carter

"I cried like a baby. In fact, I still get emotional when I see replays. It was like a miracle."—Carson Loridan, a computer networking administrator in Windsor, Ontario

"You see the sheer joy and excitement that all the fans felt. I felt it, and they felt it, just as much as I did."—Carter

"It might have been the biggest moment in Toronto sports history."—Kasia S., a research and development specialist in Burlington, Ontario

While attending Carter's Toronto charity golf tournament in August of 2012, Charlie Sheen, a friend of Carter's, was asked where the home run ranks on the list of all-time greatest home runs. Sheen, standing beside Carter, said "Number one!" But, when Carter turned away, Sheen leaned into the microphone and whispered, "Okay—it's tied for number one. Gibby [Kirk Gibson]…Game One…1988."

"Every single day someone asks me about the homer. Not a day goes by. I never get sick of it. It's one of the great moments in all of sports—especially in Canada, where it ranks up there with Paul Henderson's goal, and Sid the Kid having that goal in the Olympics. It ranks at the top."—Carter

4 The Blue Jays Are Hatched

The 1977 Blue Jays were as fresh as the driven snow. The snow, that is, that was driven off the Exhibition Stadium field by a Zamboni prior to their first regular season game.

But before they kicked off the regular season in blustery Toronto, the expansion Toronto Blue Jays spent weeks gathered together for the first time as a unit, preparing for the season in their sunny preseason home of Dunedin, Florida. Their roster was largely composed of cast-offs—players unwanted or unneeded by their former teams. Most arrived via the expansion draft, a roster-filling exercise held just months earlier, which left the team with little more than table scraps. Their total team payroll was $750,000—less than half of what the Blue Jays gave first rounder D.J. Davis as a draft signing bonus in 2012.

On March 11 Toronto's very own team took the field dressed in pajamas-style uniforms—an unfortunate trend in sports at the time—for its first spring training game, a matchup against the New York Mets. Sam Ewing, a little-known outfielder snared from the Chicago White Sox with the 57th expansion pick, doubled home the winning run as the Jays took care of the Mets 3–1. Almost as obscure as the offensive hero, a pitcher by the name of Dennis DeBarr was credited with the win in his first game as a major leaguer.

Spring training progressed, and the new team notched a couple of victories against their Canadian rivals, the Montreal Expos, while also taking down the world-champion Cincinnati Reds in another exhibition match. As the preseason drew to a close, the Jays headed north, full of excitement and optimism for the days ahead.

But not everyone was excited that the American League East had a new participant. A Boston-area news report lamented the arrival of the Blue Jays, fearing the league expansion would ruin the natural rivalry between the Boston Red Sox and New York Yankees. Of course, it would have the opposite result. An arms race between the two teams would escalate in the coming decades.

But, for the Blue Jays and their sub-million-dollar payroll, it was a season full of firsts, as one might expect from a baseball team in its infancy. Bill Singer threw the first regular season pitch for

1977 Opening Day Roster

Pitchers
36 Jerry Garvin
26 Steve Hargan
24 Chuck Hartenstein
34 Jesse Jefferson
44 Jerry Johnson
23 Dave Lemanczyk
48 Bill Singer
30 Pete Vuckovich
33 Mike Willis

Catchers
8 Alan Ashby
9 Rick Cerone
4 Phil Roof

Infielders
25 Doug Ault
6 Ron Fairly
38 Pedro García
10 Jim Mason
39 Dave McKay
29 Hector Torres

Outfielders
1 Bob Bailor
3 Steve Bowling
5 Sam Ewing
11 John Scott
19 Otto Velez
20 Al Woods
35 Gary Woods

Manager
7 Roy Hartsfield

Coaches
31 Bobby Doerr
43 Don Leppert
15 Bob Miller
42 Jackie Moore
41 Harry Warner

Toronto's team, a fastball for a strike. Outfielder John Scott was the first batter for the Blue Jays.

Toronto's first win came in its first game, a 9–5 defeat of the Chicago White Sox. First baseman Doug Ault became the team's fan favourite that day, hitting the team's first home run and adding another later.

Outfielder Otto Velez won the franchise's first Player of the Month Award after his strong April. Ron Fairly became the Jays' first All-Star, hitting .279 with a team-leading 19 home runs and 64 RBIs on the year.

The season also introduced an announcer named Tom Cheek to the Toronto region, as the smooth talker was teamed up with Early Wynn for radio broadcasts. The television work was done by Don Chevrier and Tony Kubek.

When all was said and done, the Jays finished with a 54–107 record under manager Roy Hartsfield, placing them last in the seven-team AL East. The team, however, drew 1,701,052 fans to Exhibition Stadium, fourth-best in the AL for attendance.

While their record was less than desirable, this ragtag bunch proved to be scrappy. They might not have featured the talent of other teams in the division, but they had more than their share of fight. As much as anything, 1977 was a formative year in the development of a couple of players who would have significant roles with their pennant-contending teams of the future. Ernie Whitt accumulated at-bats as a call-up, while Jim Clancy, a Texas Rangers cast-off, got his first shot to pitch in the majors and never looked back.

The results weren't pretty, but it really didn't matter in the grand scheme of things. What mattered most, as play-by-play man Jerry Howarth might have said, was that "the Blue Jays were in flight!"

5 The Bat Flip

On a night when the spectrum of emotions had been stretched to its furthest limits, this was the motherloving climax. There were two out, and the Blue Jays and Texas Rangers were tied 3–3 in Game 5 of the five-game 2015 American League Division Series. Even between pitches the Rogers Centre crowd noise held at a steady roar, perhaps the loudest it had been in 22 years. Blue Jays players lined the dugout wall. Nearly every fan in the stadium was on their feet.

Bautista pulled Sam Dyson's first pitch foul. The former Blue Jays pitcher's next offering was a fastball, which was taken outside for ball one. Bautista stepped out of the box, took a practice half-swing, and then readied himself back in the batter's box.

Then it happened.

Jose Bautista, the guy opposing baseball fans love to hate, tattooed a 1–1 Dyson pitch off the facing of the left-field stands and into the history books. Every particle of oxygen was sucked out of the Rogers Centre for one glorious millisecond. Every anxiety and frustration of earlier disappointments was tossed to the side in one incredible moment. It was as if 100 bazillion atom bombs exploded in that moment. It was pure, unadulterated euphoria.

OMFG.

Those fans that had been lucky enough to attend the game danced with elation in their seats. The ones who weren't at the game let out shouts celebratory screams from their living rooms, pubs, and restaurants. They jumped, high-fived, and embraced. Leaping out of the Jays dugout were teammates Russell Martin, David Price, and R.A. Dickey. Marcus Stroman flexed as if auditioning for *Monday Night Raw*.

New Brunswick Farmer Pays Tribute to the Bat Flip

As a tribute to the Blue Jays' 40th anniversary, Chip Hunter and his family decided to create a unique work of art at their farm in Florenceville-Bristol, New Brunswick. They carved the image of the legendary Jose Bautista bat flip to create a massive corn maze. "It's one of the most iconic images associated with the Blue Jays," Leigh Hunter said.

The family worked with a local surveyor to plot out the design layout, planted the crop in a six-acre area, and rolled the field flat. The engineer marked the area with paint and flags to indicate which corn needed to be removed to shape the image. And then the corn did the rest of the work, growing to a height of over 12 feet and forming a fantastic likeness of Joey's bat flip.

In an amusing sidenote for the benefit of anyone who followed the antics of Trevor Bauer during the 2016 American League Championship Series, the family uses a drone to monitor the growth and take photographs.

And while we're swimming in hyperbole, it might not be entirely crazy to suggest that this home run shook the Earth off its axis. Or, at least we can say that camera operators had to do their best to stabilize their equipment as the raucous crowd of 49,742 rattled the stadium with eardrum-bursting noise. Those shaky cameras cut from Dyson to a dejected Cole Hamels, who looked like a kid who had just been informed by his parents that he was not getting an iPhone for Christmas.

There was a low five to Ryan Goins, a secret handshake with Josh Donaldson, a high five to Edwin Encarnacion, followed by a chest bump to Marcus Stroman, a hell-yeah hand slap with Russell Martin, a hug with Chris Colabello, a butt smack by R.A. Dickey, and an endless flurry of high fives with David Price, Ezequiel Carrera, Dalton Pompey, Aaron Sanchez, Dioner Navarro, and coaches. Bautista hopped through the Jays dugout in a fashion that reminded some fans of the last historic home run in Blue Jays history. Martin raised his hands in Drake-like prayer hands, as if to thank a higher power for bailing him out for an earlier throwing error that had put the Jays behind to start the top half of the inning.

For those who think Blue Jays fandom is limited to the Greater Toronto Area, this moment was a reminder that this notion couldn't be further from the truth. Haligonians went berserk. Fredericton danced in the streets. Winnipegers were jubilant. Calgarians went completely apeshit. Vancouverites rejoiced. Even Montrealers celebrated. A Saskatoon resident named Bud Jorgenson gave perspective to what Bautista's home run meant for Jays fans. "Joey Bats' home run brought the entire country together," Jorgenson said. "This is pure joy from coast to coast."

When the celebration calmed from a fever pitch to mere pandemonium, Fox television coverage revealed a moment that television viewers hadn't yet witnessed—the bat flip. Viewers who saw the insanity that occurred after the ball left Bautista's bat had been unaware of his trademark reaction.

They soon saw that after crushing Dyson's inside pitch, Bautista came to a dead stop. He stood and watched with defiance as the ball went into the stands, doing nothing more than swishing his mouthpiece. Then he launched his bat a country mile into the air with his left arm—in perhaps the most epic bat flip of all time—and took off to circle the pillows.

Leading a chorus of party poopers, Fox sportscaster Tom Verducci took exception to the celebration, and across social media, opposing fans (many of whom were jealous, dumb, and Texan) seethed at the display of excitement Joey Bats unleashed in the heat of the moment. It was a disgrace, they said—an affront to the grand old game of baseball. But while singing "JOSE, JOSEJOSEJOSE" at a volume never heard before, Toronto fans didn't give a flying Louisville Slugger about the feelings of Tweeters, Texans, or priggish announcers.

For us this was a spectacular moment in Blue Jays history. Perhaps sportswriter Joe Posnanski said it best: "I understand there are traditionalists and purists and whatever-ists who think that flipping a bat after you hit a home run is bad form, or disrespectful, or something. I disagree. I think it's awesome, frankly, and if you can't enjoy Joey Bats, who had that crazy itinerant baseball life and then found a home in Toronto, and who is the soul and beating heart of this team...if you can't enjoy Joey Bats flipping his bat toward his own dugout in a badass and life-affirming and glorious yawp of baseball excellence after hitting a home run in that situation, then I feel bad for you."

6 Trader Pat vs. Stand Pat

A gifted scout by trade, Pat Gillick had more than just a remarkable eye for talent. Almost immediately after his promotion into the role of Blue Jays vice president of baseball operations, "Trader Pat" began to use his skills of player evaluation toward player extraction—stealing talented youngsters from unsuspecting opponents. He took on a roster with limited star power and wasted no time reshaping the team as he saw fit.

In his first year, he leapt into action, making six trades involving 16 players. Among other contributors, he landed Roy Howell, a young third baseman who became an All-Star just a year later.

In 1978, he bumped up his trading activity, completing eight such deals. Those transactions brought Alfredo Griffin, Rick Bosetti, and Tim Johnson—a man who would later manage the Jays for one notorious season—to Toronto. During the next four years, the pace of Gillick's trading activity was only slightly less prodigious and proved to be crucial in building the team's foundation. He stockpiled Damaso Garcia, Buck Martinez, Rance Mulliniks, and Cliff

Johnson in mostly lopsided deals. The skilled negotiator topped it off by acquiring Dave Collins, Mike Morgan, and Fred McGriff from the New York Yankees for Tom Dodd and Dale Murray.

For clarity, that's Murray...not Murphy. The righty served up an ERA of 4.73 for the rival Yankees and won just three games in as many seasons. Collins, on the other hand, set the Blue Jays season record of 60 stolen bases, which still stands. Morgan finished his career with 141 wins, though none were earned in a Toronto uniform.

McGriff's accomplishments were on a different level entirely. His 493 career homers, three Silver Slugger Awards, and bevy of other hitting accomplishments prompted 23.2 percent of Hall of Fame voters to select him on their ballots in 2012...well ahead of the 14.5 percent who voted in favour of Atlanta Braves legend Dale Murphy.

Taking little time to savour that heist, Gillick's pilfering spree resumed in 1983, as he stole plump young first baseman Cecil Fielder from the Kansas City Royals, shipping them light-hitting outfielder Leon Roberts in exchange. Fielder became a favourite in Toronto, not only amongst fans, but also to steakhouse owners throughout the region.

Gillick's trades had been resounding successes, and, in addition to Rule 5 creativity, served to shape a talented young roster. But, suddenly and unexpectedly, the trading frenzy came to a slowdown.

Gillick made just one move in 1984, adding Bill Caudill from the Oakland A's for Collins and Griffin. Largely satisfied with the roster he had built, the pace of trading slowed to a crawl. By the end of the 1980s, it seemed that the legend of "Trader Pat" had drawn to a close. The better the team did, the less he tinkered.

In 1988, he didn't make a single trade.

Local media anointed him with a new nickname—"Stand Pat"—the polar opposite of his early moniker. Radio talk shows were filled with critical Torontonians, urging an end to his newfound conservatism. The *Toronto Sun* even published a chart tracking the number of days since Gillick's last trade.

Suffice it to say, Gillick reversed his reputation by pulling off a pair of historically significant deals in 1990. It started with a ripple on December 2, when he landed Devon Whyte (then known as White) from the California Angels for little more than a bucket of baseballs. Fans were thrilled with the arrival of Whyte, a talented hitter, speed merchant, and one of the best defensive outfielders of his generation.

But if the Jays/Angels deal was a ripple, what happened on December 5 was a tidal wave. In a move now known throughout baseball as "the Trade", Gillick swapped aging shortstop Tony Fernandez and McGriff to the San Diego Padres for an RBI-producing outfielder and a slick-fielding second baseman. As history would prove, the incoming players—Joe Carter and Roberto Alomar—would serve as keys to the Jays' back-to-back World Series victories in 1992 and 1993.

Gillick rounded out his days with the Blue Jays with several other significant trades. He picked up the uniquely talented Rickey Henderson for the paltry sum of Steve Karsay and Jose Herrera and added veteran Candy Maldonado for obscure minor leaguers Rob Wishnevski and William Suero.

Gillick often says the best trade of his career was the acquisition of David Cone during the pennant race of 1992. He came at a significantly higher price than most. The Jays gave up rising star Jeff Kent and a minor leaguer, but Cone played an essential role in helping the Jays to their first championship.

He didn't win every trade—just the overwhelming majority of them. With a resume like Gillick's, it comes as no surprise that some teams were hesitant to enter into trade talks with him. Take the Yankees, for instance. For the early part of Gillick's time at the helm in Toronto, the Jays and Yanks exchanged players with regularity. But with every passing trade, George Steinbrenner reportedly became more and more furious with the Jays GM's talent swindles.

The last straw for the feisty Yankees owner came when his team sent young pitcher Al Leiter to Toronto for a past-his-prime Jesse Barfield. Although it took a subsequent departure from Toronto for Leiter and his infamous blisters to develop into the successful left-hander we all remember, the Yankees never again consummated a trade with a Gillick-led Toronto team. In fact, it took six years and a change in management for the Bronx Bombers to swing another deal with the Jays.

Gillick left the Blue Jays in 1994, taking his trade wizardry to the Baltimore Orioles, Seattle Mariners, and Philadelphia Phillies. Under his tutelage, the Mariners went to the playoffs in back-to-back years, accomplishing the remarkable feat of winning 116 games—tied for the all-time best regular season record in baseball history.

In 2005 Gillick made the ironic jump to Philadelphia—the same team whose hearts had been broken by his trade acquisition, Carter, back in 1993. He spent the next few years shaping the team into one of baseball's best through trades, drafts, and free agency. When the 2008 Phillies team won the World Series, just as his Toronto teams had in the 1990s, Gillick walked away from the game as one of the greatest general managers in baseball history.

He was enshrined in the Baseball Hall of Fame in Cooperstown, New York, in 2011, alongside Alomar, one of his prized acquisitions. Gillick's speech was typically humble, deferring praise onto others. "For a baseball person, [working for the expansion Jays] was a dream come true," he said. "Imagine...being able to build a team from scratch in a city where everyone was excited about finally having a major league team."

7 The Dome Is Born

Toronto's new stadium, the SkyDome, was hailed as "the Eighth Wonder of the World," Coming from Exhibition Stadium, a nightmarish blend of wind, rain, cold, seagulls, and uncomfortable seating, nearly anything would have been an upgrade, but this shiny new facility was something special.

Overhead was an incredible engineering marvel, a 19 million-pound roof that could open and close in mere minutes. The lid covered eight acres and still folded away neatly to allow the park to feel like an open-air facility. The revolutionary ballpark engineered by Ellis-Don Limited of London, Ontario, was so well designed that the electrical bills associated with shifting the enormous roof amounted to little more than $100 Canadian.

The multi-purpose stadium was designed to host both the Jays and Toronto Argonauts of the Canadian Football League with roughly 50,000 relatively comfortable seats available for baseball and some impressive amenities. The stadium had snazzy new restaurants, lounges, and a hotel overlooking the field. For the well-heeled crowd, skyboxes were plentiful and luxuriously appointed, and a big-ass Sony Jumbotron overlooked the field. At the time the 35-by-115 foot screen was three times larger than any other display screen in the world.

Although projections made in the early planning stages pegged the anticipated cost of constructing the stadium at around $150 million, the final tally was believed to exceed $600 million. Roughly $60 to $70 million of that was to come from public funds and land grants equally divided between the province and the city.

Opened in 1989, the SkyDome was the first stadium to feature a retractable roof. The Blue Jays still play in the facility, though it has been renamed the Rogers Centre.

Endless hours of planning and construction took place from 1985 until 1989, meticulously designing the structure and its novel roof. Finally believing the roof was properly installed, renowned architects Rod Robbie and Michael Allen prepared for a test run. They were confident in their construction but weren't about to risk embarrassing themselves when they tested the lower panel. "They decided to move it at night when no one could see it," Allen said. "So at 2:00 AM in the morning, they started to move it and they moved it mechanically…and it worked just fine. The big fear was, is it going to hit something? But it really worked fine."

Already two months behind schedule, local media began to speculate the SkyDome wouldn't be completed in time for the first game on June 3, 1989. Instead it was full steam ahead, as an excited crowd assembled in the downtown core to view the team's new home. This dome was something unique, and its opening game was an international spectacle, featuring extensive media coverage, and a gala celebration which carried ticket prices ranging from $125 to $250. The world marveled at the incredible retractable-roofed megaplex. *The Baltimore Sun* called it "the Taj Mahal of entertainment palaces."

Robbie said, "I'd like people to walk in and notice the personality of the building. It's a fun place, a homey place." Allen added, "I hope people get a feeling of intimacy; that's important." (How'd that work out, fellas?)

During the facility's 20th anniversary, Paul Godfrey, who helped bring baseball and the new stadium to Toronto, said that the ballpark design was far from perfect, but that he still considers it an overall success. "If you were doing it now, would you do it differently? Sure. But it's just like houses," he said. "The houses they build now are a lot different from the ones they built 20 years ago." Blue Jays president Paul Beeston was more pointed in his words when asked if the building was still a viable home for the Blue Jays. "I've read too much about this being a bad place, it's got no personality, it's just a mass of concrete," Beeston said. "Fact of the matter is it's in downtown Toronto, the roof works 20 years later, and you can visualize 20 years more here. Is it Camden Yards or PNC Park? No. Does it have the history of Fenway Park or Wrigley Field? No. But it's ours, the roof works, we start our games at 7:07 or 1:07 and we play every day we're supposed to play." Rain or shine.

8 The Discovery of Dave Stieb

On May 3, 1978, the Jays dispatched renowned scouts Bobby Mattick and Al LaMacchia to a college game in Charleston, Illinois. The pair arrived at the Eastern Illinois ballpark with the primary purpose of checking out a young outfielder on the visiting Southern Illinois Salukis.

At the time, it was a big deal for talent evaluators such as Mattick and LaMacchia to travel such a long distance to check out a college kid. They made the trip largely based on rave reviews this particular player had received from their colleague, Don Welke, along with the fact the youngster was hitting .394 at the time of the visit. As the game played out, the scouts sat along the first-base line at the smallish stadium, looking to validate Welke's words.

Innings passed, and they became increasingly flummoxed.

They saw the kid make a few plays in the field and studied him closely in the batter's box. At best, they thought, maybe he could develop a bit of power, but the total package just wasn't all that impressive. And Mattick knew how to evaluate hitting talent. After all, this was the guy who signed Hall of Famer Frank Robinson. LaMacchia had scouting chops of his own and he also knew there was little to be excited about in the young outfielder.

The scouts could hardly have been blamed if they gave up and headed for the exits, undoubtedly spending their return trip cursing Welke's name.

But late in the game, an odd thing happened.

"Itchy" Jones, the Southern Illinois coach, summoned the outfielder to the mound to provide some relief for his tired bullpen. As it turned out, the young man the Jays scouts had come to see was occasionally used as an emergency arm for the Salukis squad, and he was needed that day.

And with that, Dave Stieb stepped on the mound and delivered a virtuoso performance. "Stieb knocked our eyeballs out," Mattick told *Sports Illustrated* in 1983. "He was absolutely overpowering. We hadn't liked him as a hitter, but he sure as hell opened our eyes when he started pitching. We decided to draft him." His fastball popped the catcher's glove, and his breaking ball was incredibly advanced for a young man who hadn't pitched a single inning in Little League or high school. The Jays scouts knew this was a young man they'd need to select early in the draft.

Those aware of Stieb's reputation for…well, confidence… wouldn't be surprised to find out he insisted the Jays draft him as an outfielder. He was adamant that he should be given every opportunity to play an offensive position. Mattick and LaMacchia, among others, knew that the best—maybe only chance for Stieb to contribute at the major league level—was from the mound. The team threw Stieb a bone during his first pro season by allowing him to split time between the outfield and designated hitter on the days he wasn't pitching.

In this first season in rookie league at Dunedin, Florida, he hit a paltry .195 with a slugging percentage of just .253. On the mound, however, he was dominant. He began to turn heads, registering a WHIP (walks plus hits per inning pitched) of 0.92 to go along with a 2.04 ERA.

Stieb followed Mattick's advice—with some resistance, of course—and became a full-time pitcher. Within a year he went from riding the buses in the low minors to pitching on the sport's biggest stage. He won eight games in the majors as a 21-year-old and never looked back.

The proud owner of a slider almost as impressive as his moustache, Dave Stieb carved out a career with the Jays which included seven All-Star appearances. He became Toronto's first homegrown baseball star and the undisputed leader of the upstart pitching staff. More importantly, his performance on the mound helped transform the Jays from lovable losers to one of the most feared teams in the league.

9 WAMCO

The Blue Jays lineup in 1993 was a starting pitcher's worst nightmare. Before the first inning was over, he'd have to face speed demon Devon Whyte (formerly White), dynamo Roberto Alomar, and the great Paul Molitor. If any of them got on base, he might have to contend with slugger Joe Carter, followed by smooth-swinging John Olerud.

Whyte, Alomar, Molitor, Carter, Olerud…in order.

Two Hall of Famers and three next-tier legends. This top-of-the-order collection of stars was glued together in the 1992 offseason, as the team experienced significant turnover after their first World Series victory. "We lost a lot of guys from one year to the next year," manager Cito Gaston said. In fact, 20 players who saw regular season action for the Jays in 1992 team weren't on the 1993 roster. The list of the departed included nine different players who had made the cut to play on the team's World Series roster, most notably Dave Winfield and Candy Maldonado.

The mass exodus necessitated a bit of a philosophical change. Whereas the 1992 team involved contributions from a number of different bit players, the team took a new approach for 1993. "We had a pretty balanced team in 1992, but in '93, we pretty much just overpowered people," Gaston said.

The Jays signed longtime Milwaukee Brewers star Molitor to a three-year, $13 million contract to plug the hole left by Winfield. Planted in the middle of speedsters Whyte and Alomar and protected by Carter and Olerud, Molitor was the final ingredient the roster needed.

A clever Toronto fan wisely observed that the first initial of each of their last names made for the convenient acronym of "WAMCO." The name evocatively represented what the lineup was—a powerful five-man company. And it was a corporation that produced hits and runs in large quantities.

The new kid in town, Molitor, would hit .332 on the season. Alomar's hitting was nearly as prodigious, with a .326 average. Olerud trumped them all by hitting .363 and collecting an American League batting crown.

Molitor, Carter, and Olerud each collected more than 100 RBIs. All but Carter scored in excess of 100 runs. Alomar stole 55 bases, Whyte 34, and Molitor 22. Oh, and each WAMCO member was selected to the 1993 All-Star Game. Every single one of them. With the help of a solid pitching staff and exceptional managing, the WAMCO boys led the Blue Jays to a 95–67 record, en route to their second consecutive World Series victory.

Asked if any team in baseball will ever replicate such an imposing lineup, one through five, Carter said, "I'm sure they'll try, but it sure won't be as good."

10 The Drive of '85

The 1985 Blue Jays were bold, brash...and maybe even a little bit cocky. Late-season pickup Steve Nicosia said of his new teammates, "These guys have a lot of self-confidence, almost to the point of overconfidence." Players like George Bell, Tony Fernandez, Dave Stieb, and Doyle Alexander gave the team a league-wide reputation for a collectively elevated self-esteem, but they had the game to back it up. Behind a combination of speed, power, defence, and pitching, this Blue Jays squad beat opponents 99 times in the regular season. Only the St. Louis Cardinals won more regular season games that year.

And, on October 5, they finished what they started. Toronto left fielder Bell caught a fly ball off the bat of New York's Ron Hassey and crumpled to his knees to celebrate the final out of the Jays' 5–1 division-title-clinching victory. Bell clutched the ball in his mitt with an expression of pure joy on his face, while Tony Fernandez sprinted out from shortstop to embrace him.

In just the ninth year of their existence, the Blue Jays were AL East champions.

The players headed down to the clubhouse, and the party began. They sprayed each other with cheap Ontario-made Chateau-Gai champagne but kept aside a stash of fine French Dom Perignon to savour. Perhaps fuelled by a mix of that expensive French champagne and the thrill of the moment, some Blue Jays players all but proclaimed that day's starter Doyle Alexander as the second coming of Cy Young. "Doyle is the best pitcher I've ever seen," said closer Tom Henke. "He gets guys out and makes them look bad even without much speed on the ball." Willie Upshaw was almost as effusive. "Doyle's our money man," he said. "He's Mr. Clutch," Jesse Barfield added.

Offered a glass of the fancy champagne, Alexander said "I ain't drinking that crap," and cracked open a beer.

While the players celebrated, fans carried their own party into the downtown core, honking and hollering, but keeping their rowdiness in check. "We didn't have a single arrest for rowdiness that we could connect with baseball," said police staff sergeant Mel Duffty. The headline of the next morning's *Toronto Star* sports section read, "THE CHAMPS". The Jays held a rally outside City Hall, where thousands of adoring fans gathered to honour the team.

General manager Pat Gillick, a key architect of the team, was proud of the team's accomplishments, and appreciative of the fans. "People were very patient with us...when we were losing 100 games a year," Gillick said. "We've got great ownership here, and they've been very patient with our game plan."

The expansion team headed into the playoffs as odds-on favourites to win the American League Champion Series against the Kansas City Royals. And things seemed to go just as predicted, as Toronto took a 3–1 series lead. Kansas City, though, became only the fifth club in major league history to overcome such a deficit to win a postseason series. The Royals upset the Jays in seven games.

It was a painful ending to a terrific season, and at the time there was very little consolation for the Blue Jays and their fans. In retrospect the team's performance and pennant were incredible accomplishments and ones which laid the foundation for a string of success that would extend well beyond the Drive of '85.

11 Cito Gaston and the Kindness of Strangers

It wasn't easy being black and poor in San Antonio in 1961. Discrimination and segregation would colour the lives of too many young black men growing up deep in the heart of Texas. Granted, San Antonio was generally more progressive than other big cities in the Southwest throughout the '50s and '60s. It was one of the first southwestern communities to integrate its school system, a transition made easier by its Mexican American population which almost matched that of whites and helped to blur racial lines.

But San Antonio circa 1961 was still a city divided, literally and figuratively. Black residents were relegated primarily to the eastern part of the city—a rapidly decaying, overcrowded community.

Life was often tough for a black kid from the east side. If he saved enough pocket change to watch a show at the downtown Majestic Theatre, he'd be asked to enter the building through a separate entrance, away from white ticket holders. If he drank a little too much root beer during the show, he'd certainly not be allowed to use the white folks' restroom, let alone order a burger from a whites-only lunch counter on the long walk home.

The career path for a kid from the east side of San Antonio was basically predestined. Regardless of his skills or talent, his prospects were largely limited to manual labour for menial wages. He could be a handyman, a day labourer, or a garbageman.

But one garbage collector from the east side—Clarence "Cito" Gaston—proved that it was possible to break the cycle.

Gaston would eventually become a productive major league outfielder, a legendary hitting instructor, and a World Series-winning manager. But none of it might have happened without the kindness of a stranger.

"In 1961 people told me about this guy that was hitting the cover off the softball out in the woods—in the country," said Johnny Cardona Sr., the San Antonio welding shop owner who sponsored the Cardona Welders amateur baseball club. For more than 30 years, the Cardona Welders played Sunday baseball against opponents such as the San Antonio Black Sox—the equivalent of a Negro League minor league team.

When Cardona witnessed the raw talent of Gaston in person, he recruited him to try out for the Welders. The skinny young outfielder asked what he should bring to the first tryout. "All you've got to do is furnish your glove and your spikes," Cardona said. But Gaston shrugged his shoulders in response. "He said, 'I can't play for you, because I don't have a job and I don't have any money to buy spikes. All I have is an old glove.'"

Not willing to let this equipment issue get in the way, Cardona persisted with the 17-year-old, finally convincing him to give it a shot. Gaston showed up the next day at Woodlawn Lake Diamond, the tree-lined ballpark where the team practiced. His clothes exemplified his meagre upbringing, especially his shoes...or lack thereof. "When he showed up, he had nothing. [Here was] Cito Gaston—barefooted," Cardona said.

The majority of players on the team were less than impressed with the new arrival. They began to grill Cardona in frustration. "They asked me, 'Who the hell is this skinny guy? He ain't got no business being here!'"

Cardona, in his warm way, told the team to give the new kid a chance. But ultimately, Gaston's actions would serve to silence the sceptics. "Cito came up to bat during batting practice," Cardona said, noting that a few players stood around to watch the greenhorn. "[Gaston] started hitting the ball out of the park—into the lake!" Heads began to turn. "No one had ever hit the ball out into the lake—nobody," Cardona said. "And Cito hit almost all the balls that were pitched into the lake."

The cynics on the Welders, who had initially doubted Gaston, quickly changed their tune when they saw him hit. "They started asking, 'Where did you find him? Goddamn, this guy can hit the ball,'" Cardona said. Cito stunned them with his speed around the bases. Cardona recalled that his arm caught their eye as well. "During outfield practice, he threw the ball from the outfield to home plate. They said, 'My God, where did you find this guy?'"

But all that talent couldn't pay for a proper pair of baseball cleats, and Gaston's family was more concerned with paying for life necessities than an impractical thing like spikes. It ultimately took the kindness of a stranger—or at least a new acquaintance—to properly equip young Cito. Cardona, in a moment of quiet generosity, pulled his new player aside. "Look, I'm gonna do something for you. You go to the sporting goods store, where I buy the team equipment," Cardona said. "And you go up there and tell them to try you out for spikes."

Rudy, the store salesman, called Cardona on Monday morning after Gaston visited the shop. "Hey, Johnny," Rudy said, "since *when* are you buying spikes for the ballplayers? I know you buy bats and balls, but you've never asked me to measure a guy for shoes!" Cardona explained to the store salesman that this was a bit of an exceptional circumstance. "I told Rudy not to say anything to the rest of the team," he said, "just measure him up and keep it quiet from the other guys!" Cito wore his new footwear with pride.

Cardona's kindness didn't stop there. He contacted a Milwaukee Braves scout, who lived nearby, and hounded him to watch one of Gaston's games. "I called up Al LaMacchia and told him I had a guy on the team who plays good baseball," Cardona said, "and he should come see him. Of course, he didn't show up. But I kept calling. Two or three times later, I told him, 'Al, come see this guy—he's good!'"

LaMacchia finally relented, partly due to Cardona's persistence and partly due to a miserable forecast. Instead of risking a wasted

Two of the main leaders behind Toronto's championship seasons, Cito Gaston (left) and general manager Pat Gillick (right), endorse the announcement of Gaston as manager.

drive through bad weather to another game he was planning to scout, LaMacchia figured he'd stay close to home and check out this Clarence Gaston kid. He was instantly impressed. Donning those new spikes, Cito ran from home plate to first base in 4.2 seconds. During his impromptu audition, his cannon of an arm and power bat also wowed the scout.

LaMacchia approached Cardona. "John, I'm gonna take this guy from you."

Later that night, LaMacchia headed to the Gaston home, where Cito and his mother, Gertrude, sat upon the family's couch. She was no pushover, and wanted what was best for her son. She told LaMacchia that the Colt .45s had some interest in Clarence and let him know quite clearly that she wouldn't be easily swayed. But by the time the sun went down, LaMacchia won Gertrude over, convincing her that her son would have a bright future with the Braves. With a few strokes of the pen, Cito Gaston went from shagging flies for the Cardona Welders to becoming property of the big league Milwaukee Braves.

Before his 11-year playing career was over, he'd make an All-Star Game appearance (in 1970) and finish in the top three in assists among all National League centre fielders each year from 1969 through 1971. His biggest contributions to the game, though, came much later, when he earned a reputation as the game's best hitting coach of his era and one of the greatest managers of recent times.

Toronto fans remember him as the man who worked tirelessly with hitters like Jose Bautista, George Bell, Cecil Fielder, and many others, tweaking their swings to maximize results. Few hitting coaches in recent memory have helped batters achieve better results from their natural abilities.

Of course, the most lasting element of Cito's legacy in Toronto was managing the first and second World Series teams in Blue Jays history. Along the way, he became baseball's first African American manager to win a World Series.

Cardona's life might not have been as lustrous, but he built a strong legacy of his own. He worked diligently at his welding shop until handing over the reins to his son, Johnny Cardona Jr. To this day, Cardona Welding remains a successful operation at the corner of South Brazos and Merida in San Antonio.

Gaston remains close with Cardona, now in his eighties. During his final year as the team's skipper, Gaston flew the retired welder out to the Jays' spring training camp in Dunedin, Florida. It was a subtle way to thank a man who knows how a simple act of kindness can change a life.

12 Paul Beeston

He was the Blue Jays' first employee. In fact, his connection with professional baseball in Toronto predated the announcement of Major League Baseball's expansion to Hogtown. An ownership group bidding to bring the San Francisco Giants to Toronto hired Paul Beeston, an eclectic accountant from Welland, Ontario, to crunch the numbers. His job, he said, was to "set up the accounting, set up the financing, set up the taxation, and then it kind of evolved into the business side. The ticketing, I knew nothing about that."

While drawing attention for his quirky habit of not wearing socks, Beeston performed admirably in his role and almost always with a happy-go-lucky attitude. Herb Solway, a colleague of Beeston's, reflected on his start with the Jays. "If you had asked me then if I thought Paul would achieve what he has achieved, I would have said no. He was such a good guy and he was so much fun, that you tended to overlook his abilities. You thought a guy who is that much fun to be with is unlikely to be a serious businessman. But he turned out to be a very serious businessman and he is still as much fun to be with," Solway said.

Sockless and often with a cigar dangling from his mouth, Beeston served in a number of different roles as the Blue Jays transformed from a meagre expansion club to a baseball powerhouse. He assumed the role of president and chief operating officer in 1989 and president and chief executive officer in 1991. Along the way, he became a highly respected member of the baseball community, in large part due to his optimistic and personable nature. He was, and still is, admired by his own staff and other baseball executives, managers, and players alike.

This nearly league-wide respect eventually drew Beeston away from Toronto, as he was hired by Major League Baseball commissioner Bud Selig to serve as president and chief operating officer of the league, a position he held from 1997 to 2002. In addition, he was selected as a member of the board of trustees of the National Baseball Hall of Fame in Cooperstown, New York, and appointed a Member of the Order of Canada.

But his days in Toronto were not done. Beeston returned to the role of interim president and CEO of the Toronto Blue Jays in 2008 and wasted no time showing he meant business. He fired much-maligned general manager J.P. Ricciardi and replaced him with an unknown kid named Alex. The two then teamed up to trade Roy Halladay, reinvigorating the Jays' minor league system.

Just as he did with Pat Gillick throughout the '80s and '90s, Beeston has collaborated with Alex Anthopoulos to rebuild the team's scouting and player development. They placed a higher priority on obtaining draft picks, while consorting on trades and signings. "I think another partnership is forming with Alex Anthopoulos," said Phil Lind, vice-chairman of Rogers Communications.

But until Beeston's title of interim president changed, the threat remained that he might ride off into the sunset and retire, or be hired away by another club. Fortunately, Beeston agreed to remove the interim label from his job title and commit to the team as the president and CEO. "We are thrilled that we were able to convince Paul Beeston to take on this role," said Tony Viner, president and CEO of Rogers Media, which owns of the team. "Paul's background with the club, his credentials in the baseball world, and his enthusiasm for this sport will be incredible assets." Beeston agreed to a three-year contract but dismissed the significance of the deal. "I have never had a contract [before]. I never wanted a contract," Beeston told *CAmagazine*. "I never really believed in contracts. I have never read it. I know what is in it. I know what my job responsibilities are—if they are not happy, just sayonara, good-bye."

Regardless, Beeston was enthusiastic about the opportunity. "I'm happy working with these guys, because they're a good group of guys. The two luckiest guys in the world are [senior assistant and original Jays employee] Howie [Starkman] and me. We're veterans. We're working with a group of young guys that let us have fun too," said the 67-year-old Beeston.

And the Anthopoulos/Beeston combo worked toward building a team that would provide the Toronto market with lasting success. "We are very close and because of the philosophy [of building with] draft choices and everything, we are close enough that once this gets going, it could be 10 years sustainability of being an elite team in an elite division," Beeston said. "We have an advantage that very few have, and everyone in sports should want, and a lot of people in Toronto are afraid of. That is, we have the Yankees and Boston as one-quarter of our schedule." In other words, playing good teams is a major draw for fans.

Firmly entrenched as one of the sporting world's foremost executives and one of the Blue Jays' most beloved figures, Beeston retired from the Blue Jays at the end of the 2015 season.

13 The Trade

It's known by two simple words: the Trade.

On December 5, 1990, the Toronto Blue Jays and San Diego Padres stunned the sporting world, when the respective teams agreed to exchange stars Fred McGriff and Tony Fernandez for Joe Carter and Roberto Alomar. Two All-Stars for an All-Star and an up-and-coming star—an almost unprecedented swap.

The seeds of the Trade were planted when Blue Jays general manager Pat Gillick approached Padres general manager Joe McIlvaine to discuss the Jays' surplus at first base. The Jays were eager to allow young hitter John Olerud a chance to fulfill his potential by playing every day at the position, but he was blocked by the established McGriff. Although they considered using Olerud in left field, they preferred acquiring a more established outfielder instead. The idea of a McGriff for Carter trade was floated. "I said no," said McIlvaine on the day of the Trade. "We weren't trying to trade Carter. He's such a quality player. Then we got together yesterday afternoon, and when the big gun started coming out of the holster, you started thinking about it."

Gillick said he'd be willing to move his superstar first baseman, but only if the trade was expanded.

"Then they brought up Alomar and then Fernandez," McIlvaine said, shortly after agreeing to the deal. "I had no intention of trading Alomar, but I've always liked Fernandez. Today at two or 2:30, we agreed. You kind of catch your breath. You know the magnitude of it."

Gillick and McIlvaine kept the transaction quiet as they worked on its parameters. Unlike so many baseball trades—real and fake—which are leaked by unnamed sources, this deal snuck up on the media with ninja-like secrecy. When sportswriters did discover the Trade, it became an international news story. Beloved Jays McGriff and Fernandez were heading to Cali. Alomar and Carter were bound for Toronto, a team that needed an injection of youth and an outfield overhaul.

The savvy Jays GM had started the process of rebuilding the Jays a few days prior, acquiring Devon Whyte (formerly White) to patrol centre field. His arrival, combined with Carter's, marked a departure from the Jays teams of the 1980s, and the introduction of a new era in Toronto baseball. "Sometimes you need a recharge," Gillick said.

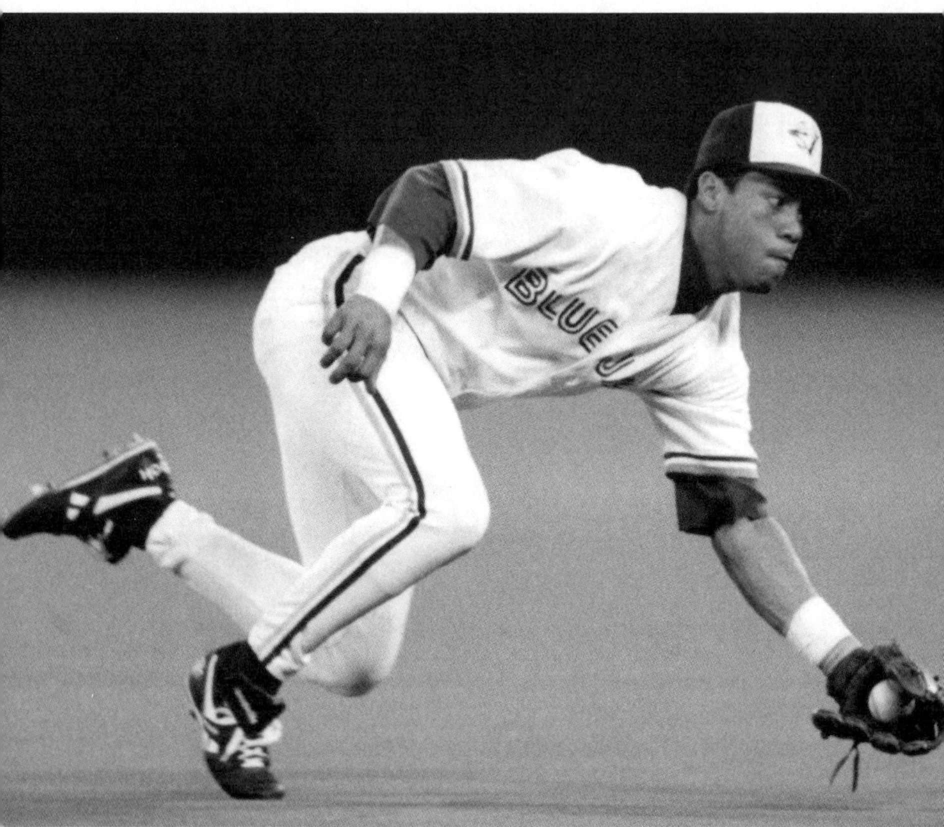

Because of Roberto Alomar's (above) defensive skills and all-around play, netting him and Joe Carter paid off for the Blue Jays, even though they had to give up Tony Fernandez and Fred McGriff in one of the most significant trades in baseball history.

Doris Gillick, Pat's wife, wasn't a fan of the deal, however. When he phoned her from the winter meetings to excitedly detail the megadeal, her response wasn't quite what he expected. "Will you get home before you screw up the team any further?" she said.

But Gillick's scouting instincts were deadly accurate. Alomar played out a string of incredible offensive and defensive seasons in Toronto, which placed him in the Hall of Fame and into the conversation of the all-time greatest second basemen. His numbers were gaudy, but it went a lot deeper than that. "He did so many things that did not show up statistically—the feel, the instincts, the anticipation he had for the game," Gillick said. "I don't know hockey that well, but Wayne Gretzky seemed to be the same way, always in the right place at the right time, anticipating where to be. It seemed like Robbie had a feel for where everybody was on the field—where the runners were, where the rest of his teammates were—and he did things without hesitation, without thought. It was one of those attributes you had to be born with, or maybe he acquired it from his dad. But it was unbelievable."

Jack McKeon, who managed Alomar during his Padres days, agreed. "Robbie had the greatest instincts of any player I had," McKeon said. "He was very unselfish. He didn't need a base coach. He had eyes in the back of his head." McKeon has never held back in condemning the Padres for letting Alomar slip away. "If he had stayed, it would have been a toss-up between him and Tony Gwynn as the most popular San Diego Padre ever.... It might have been the worst trade San Diego ever made."

McIlvaine still defiantly contends that the Padres received fair value in the deal. "You can debate that one for hours and hours, who got the better of it," said McIlvaine, now a senior advisor for the Baltimore Orioles. "Do Alomar and McGriff belong in the Hall of Fame? Absolutely...McGriff's numbers stand up with all the great first basemen, and Alomar was the best for 10 years at his position."

What can't be debated is the fact the Trade still stands up as a memorable moment in baseball history. "One trade changed so many things," McIlvaine said. "That trade happened so long ago, but people keep talking about it like it happened yesterday. A trade of that magnitude, involving four All-Stars—it's got to be one of the biggest trades in the last 34 years."

Fred McGriff summed it up succinctly, "It was a trade for the ages."

14 The Toronto Giants?

At last, they thought. Toronto finally had a Major League Baseball team to call its own. Paul Godfrey and members of a Labatt Breweries-led consortium celebrated the acquisition of Toronto's new ballclub with a mix of excitement and trepidation. Opening Day of 1976 was less than 90 days away, and the group faced a massive challenge. With this tight time frame, they knew they had long workdays ahead, not to mention mounds of planning, to put a big league club on the field.

But wasn't it all worth it?

Owning a MLB team was a reward of its own. And the satisfaction would be that much sweeter when the group could gather in the owners' box, pop open a few Labatts, and watch the stadium fill for the first big league baseball game in Toronto.

No doubt these Opening Day visions danced in their heads. Just imagine. An enthusiastic, half-frozen crowd would soon gather at snowy Exhibition Stadium to welcome Major League Baseball to Ontario's capital. John Montefusco would step on the mound and deliver the first major league pitch in Toronto history. When it was Toronto's turn at bat, Toronto's new play-by-play man, Tom Cheek, would make a historic call. "This one's well hit! Forget about it—it's a home run. First baseman Willie Montanez has electrified the crowd at Exhibition Stadium. A tremendous shot and the first player on the Toronto Giants to hit one out!"

Yes, the Toronto Giants.

Not only was it possible that Toronto's Major League Baseball team would be the Giants, it was probable. Just a few months prior to Opening Day of 1976, the San Francisco Giants would be purchased by the Toronto group and began preparations to make their way north. The timing for a move to Toronto couldn't have been better. The Queen City stood as the next logical market for professional baseball, while San Francisco looked to be on the way out.

Recognizing that the Giants were at financial crossroads in the mid-1970s, the Labatt group smelled blood. They monitored the situation closely, knowing the team had lost $1.7 million in 1974 and roughly the same in 1975. It came to light that the National League attempted to bail out the struggling team with a $500,000 loan, but the Giants failed to repay the debt by the December 1, 1975 deadline.

It didn't help that the Oakland A's set up shop just across the Bay Bridge in 1968, chipping away at the Giants' already-dwindling attendance numbers. Oakland won three consecutive World Series from 1972 to 1974, further hammering the Giants' already weak gate receipts. In addition, the Giants played in one of the game's most dismal home ballparks—Candlestick Park—which may have repelled more fans than it attracted.

The situation became so dire that the team couldn't pay the rent, a modest sum of $125,000, for the 1975 season. The city of San Francisco owned the stadium, and the team had agreed to lease it until the 1994 season. Attendance in San Francisco was just 519,000 in 1974 and barely improved to 522,000 in 1975…or less than 7,000 seats sold per game.

Horace Stoneham, owner of 51 percent of the Giants' parent company, decided it was time to cut his losses. On January 9, 1976, he called a press conference to make a stunning announcement. "Directors of the National Exhibition Company have agreed in principle to sell the baseball franchise, the Giants, to Labatt Brewery of Toronto," said Charles Rupert, executive vice president and secretary-treasurer of the Giants.

Spearheaded by local politician and businessman Godfrey, the Toronto group was comprised of owners from Labatt, Vulcan Assets Ltd., and the Canadian Imperial Bank of Commerce. They

Almost from the Bay Area to Tampa Bay

In an ironic twist for observers of the American League East, Bob Lurie—the San Francisco Giants' former saviour—later became overwhelmed by the financial struggles of the club and agreed to sell the team to a Tampa Bay group headed by Vince Naimoli in 1992.

The National League nixed this particular deal, forcing Lurie to sell the club to Safeway magnate Peter Magowan for $100 million to keep the team—once again—in San Francisco.

It wouldn't be long before Tampa Bay was granted an expansion club of its own, beginning a AL East rivalry with the Blue Jays.

were more than willing to meet the deal's financial conditions. "The price was $13.25 million, of which $5.25 million will be retained in a fund to meet certain possible obligations with respect to the transaction," Rupert said. "After the satisfaction of any such obligations, sums remaining in the fund will be distributed to the National Exhibition Company shareholders."

The "obligations" referred to the lease on Candlestick Park, which extended into 1994. Any party buying the team was required to agree to terms with the city of San Francisco either to assume the lease or buy out the contract. To indemnify the city, $5.25 million of the purchase price paid by Toronto was to be placed in escrow.

During a more jubilant press conference north of the border, Godfrey announced that the new Toronto Giants would play at the "revamped" Exhibition Stadium, starting in April 1976. The field now had a seating capacity of 40,000 for baseball and 55,000 for football, along with newly laid artificial turf.

Excitement reached a fever pitch in Toronto, but Godfrey threw a bucket of cold water upon the revellers. The deal, he said, was far from complete. "I do want to emphasize that conditions still exist, and we are still some distance from having a ball team in metro," Godfrey said. "But the agreement in principle reached today means we are visibly closer to Major League Baseball for metro Toronto."

However, San Francisco mayor George Moscone wasn't going to sit back and let those Canadian mercenaries rob him of a big league club without a fight. The very next day, January 10, Moscone filed an injunction request at the Superior Court. Behind the scenes, he worked the telephones and pressed the flesh with wealthy locals to assemble a new proposal to purchase the team from Stoneham. Satisfied by Moscone's progress, the court issued a preliminary injunction, blocking the sale of the bankrupt team to the group from Toronto on February 11, 1976.

But the injunction in and of itself was meaningless to Toronto's bid. Godfrey and the Toronto consortium still stood in position to win the right to buy the Giants. They had proven the financial wherewithal to satisfy all parties, and time was running out for Moscone. If, as the Toronto group hoped, the deadline would pass without new buyers, they would presumably be awarded the rights to the team and could proceed as they had planned.

Optimism abounded in Toronto, while residents of San Francisco braced to lose their Giants, one of America's oldest professional sports teams.

With little more than an hour remaining until the expiration of the injunction, Bob Lurie, a local businessman, and Bob Short, the former owner of the Washington Senators/Texas Rangers, stepped forward. Placing an offer almost identical to Toronto's bid, they teamed up announce their intentions to purchase the Giants and keep them in San Francisco. Justice John E. Bensen officially blocked the sale to Toronto and pushed through the sale to Lurie and Short.

Toronto's group fell short, and disappointment enveloped the burgeoning baseball community. But within only a few months, Toronto got its wish. The city was granted an American League expansion franchise—later to be named the Blue Jays. Rather than inheriting a stale roster, staff, and scouting network, Toronto would have a chance to build its own team from the ground up. It all worked out rather well.

15 The Seventh Inning

In a crucial situation, an All-Star catcher inadvertently throws a ball off a batter's hand, the go-ahead run scores from third base, normally civil fans litter the field with beer cans (at least one of which misses its target and hits a baby), a manager protests the game, typically solid defenders make three consecutive errors, and an angry dude with a beard crushes a go-ahead homer to send a nation into unbridled ecstasy—all within one inning.

Just another day at the ballpark, right? *Hardly.* In fact, it was arguably the most insane inning in the history of baseball.

With the score tied 2–2, young Aaron Sanchez came into the game in the top of the seventh inning to replace counterpart Marcus Stroman. Rougned Odor lined a single to left and then advanced on a bunt by Chris Gimenez. Delino DeShields grounded out on a tough play by Josh Donaldson with Odor taking third base on the play.

Shin-Soo Choo stepped up to the plate. Putting aside the pressure of the go-ahead run, Sanchez brewed up his best stuff. He hurled a 98 mph fastball in Choo's craw, and the Korean fought it off. It was followed by another fastball—away. Another 98 mph heater was fouled away. The crowd grew louder and more anxious. And then the improbable happened.

It was a play made thousands of times each year by catchers like Russell Martin. It was nothing more than a return throw to a pitcher, but it wasn't routine this time. Martin's throw glanced off the hand of Choo, who had chosen to stay in his place in the batter's box. The ball rolled toward the third-base line. Odor scrambled home. It was a once-in-a-lifetime miscue by Martin, who would later say he had never seen anything like it.

At first blush, home-plate umpire Dale Scott ordered Odor to return to third and invalidated the run. He then conversed with others in the umpiring crew, and the call was overturned. Odor's run indeed counted. Toronto fans were incredulous, but history would show that the call was correct. Rule 6.03 (a) (3) states that: "if the batter is standing in the batter's box and he or his bat is struck by the catcher's throw back to the pitcher, and, in the umpire's judgment, there is no intent on the part of the batter to interfere with the throw, the ball is alive and in play."

When word came down that the umpiring crew validated Odor's run, Toronto fans fumed and reacted in a very un-Canadian way. Showering the field with beer cans and litter, the fans seethed at what they collectively believed to be an unjust ruling. They had waited 22 years for some sort of playoff satisfaction, and it seemed to be close to slipping away due to a technicality.

The beer shower—a feeble-minded attempt at vigilantism—made a stunning situation turn into a source of embarrassment for the fanbase. In a rare moment of lucid commentary, Fox broadcaster Harold Reynolds described the situation. "These people got to stop throwing beer cans out of the upper decks. You're hitting people down below."

It's one thing to be loud and passionate fans. It's a whole other thing to be complete assholes. "I've seen some crazy baseball shit in my time, but nothing like the current Blue Jays-Rangers game," author Stephen King tweeted. "Who said Canadian fans were polite?"

Sportswriter Joe Posnanski wrote that the Fox broadcast, "ceased to resemble a baseball game. There were just long shots of the crowd, and stadium security, and moms clutching young children. It was surreal. At that point, it looked like the Texas Rangers were going to win the series based on this insane play, and then Canada was going to invade America."

Order was restored, and any plans of invasion were put on a momentary hold. The grounds crew scrambled to clean the debris scattered over the field. The Rangers held a 3–2 lead heading into the bottom of the seventh inning, and the clock was ticking on the Blue Jays' season. Making things worse, the bottom of the Jays' order was coming up, and the Rangers' bullpen was making preparations to close out the series.

What happened next was even weirder than the prior events. Martin hit a grounder to short. From his childhood to this moment, Elvis Andrus made that play tens of thousands of times. The normally strong defender watched as the grounder skipped off his glove for an error. Martin took first, as the crowd roared.

Up next was Kevin Pillar, who grounded the ball to Mitch Moreland. The first baseman fired to second to get the leadoff man but threw the ball in the dirt. Martin was safe at second with Pillar at first. Inexplicably, the Rangers had made consecutive errors on completely routine plays. The Rogers Centre grew louder in response to the team's unlikely good fortune. Dalton Pompey pinch ran for Martin, sending the catcher to the bench for the remainder of the game.

With runners on first and second, up came the Jays' No. 9 hitter, Ryan Goins. The light-hitting second baseman was 0-for-the-series, prompting manager John Gibbons to call for him to bunt. Rangers third baseman Adrian Beltre fielded the bunt cleanly and went for the force at third base with Andrus covering. Andrus dropped the routine flip. The crowd went wild. Was it the intensity of the crowd noise, or were the baseball gods just having a little bit of fun?

There was a brief respite to the insanity. Ben Revere grounded into a force play, as Moreland fired home to beat the speedy

Pompey. Sam Dyson was summoned from the pen and given the honour of facing Donaldson. More ridiculousness ensued. Donaldson popped up toward Odor, who staggered backward to attempt to catch the weakly hit ball. Once again, beyond the limits of belief, a Rangers infielder flubbed a makeable play. Pillar scored the tying run from third.

The crowd noise neared a deafening pitch as the events unfolded. Then, some guy named Jose Bautista came to the plate. You probably know what happened next: Bautista smashed Dyson's offering into the left-field stands to put the Jays ahead. He stood in defiance at home plate and tossed his bat skyward. It was bliss in the Rogers Centre and across the country. Delirium. Ecstasy. And an iconic bat flip that will outlive us all.

The flip wasn't premeditated. "I can't really remember what was going through my mind, to be quite honest with you," Joey Bats said. "After I made contact, I just, you know, I didn't plan anything that I did and I still don't honestly know how I did it. I just enjoyed the moment, rounded the bases, and got to the dugout."

Teammates greeted him with unbridled excitement, while Dyson stewed on the mound, unimpressed by Bautista's celebration. "That's not acceptable, regardless of what level you're at," groused the vanquished Rangers reliever. "I just saw him stand there."

In the moment Blue Jays fans could be excused if they didn't give a rat's ass about Dyson's feelings. But Martin spoke in defense of Joey's antics. "I think it was just instinctual," Martin said. "It was an epic home run and it was an epic bat flip."

In the midst of the pandemonium, Edwin Encarnacion came to the plate and waved his arms to urge Jays fans (or the morons amongst them) to stop throwing objects on the field. Dyson seemingly misinterpreted the gestures as something inflammatory and approached him from the mound. The benches cleared. Idiots threw more objects onto the field. Order was finally restored at the urging of members of the Blue Jays.

The inning didn't end until two more hits were recorded by the star-studded Toronto lineup. Even the final out came with a twist. Troy Tulowitzki popped out on a foul ball to Gimenez and headed to the dugout to grab his glove. Along the way Dyson tapped Tulo on the butt. Tulowitzki, perhaps the only person in the Jays dugout more intense than Bautista, was not amused. Pleasantries were exchanged between he and Dyson, and the benches once again cleared. Dyson would later argue that he meant no harm by the gesture. Tulo didn't care either way.

In the end a 53-minute roller-coaster ride led to a Toronto ALDS victory. "[It was] the craziest, silliest, weirdest, wildest, angriest, dumbest, and funniest inning in the history of baseball," Posnanski wrote.

16 One Mother of a Catcher

Growing up in southwest Ontario in the 1980s, few things brought as much pleasure as an Ernie Whitt Special from Mother's Pizza. We didn't need iPhones or MacBooks to make us happy—no, sir. All we needed was a gooey cheese and pepperoni pizza served up at one of the restaurant's locations partly owned by the Blue Jays catcher.

Whitt invested in the beloved pizza conglomerate in 1983, using his status as one of the most popular players on the Toronto Blue Jays to sell pizza pies by the dozen. The chain quickly became a local sensation and expanded into markets throughout the province with its trademark Old West décor and stained glass lighting (placed at *just* the right height for patrons to smack into when getting up from the table).

The Jays' 1985 All-Star catcher frequently appeared at the restaurants, taking time to speak with fans and signing autographs by the dozens. Mother's Pizza was heaven on earth for any kid. A Three Stooges movie would play in the background, tasty pizza would be served, a massive root beer float would be imbibed to wash it down, and their baseball hero—the man whose at-bats were greeted with chants of "ERNIE! ERNIE ERNIE!"—would even take time out of his day to talk a little baseball.

The early returns were quite positive for Ernie, and teammates Lloyd Moseby and Rick Leach decided they wanted in on the venture. Each purchased shares in the investment group known as the Bayswater Partnership. But the pizza chain hit a snag in the late-1980s, supposedly due to over-expansion and the sale of corporate stores to inexperienced managers. The ballplayers and other investors abandoned ship. Former employees say their once-stable organization became a rudderless vessel, and food quality began to suffer. The ship sank in 1992.

Whitt's playing days had a similar arc to the life of Mother's Pizza. Both got their start in the late 1970s, reached their peak in the mid-1980s, and were out of their respective games by the early 1990s.

Selected by the Red Sox in the 15th round of the 1972 Draft, Ernie Whitt's path to the majors was blocked by fan favourite Carlton Fisk. The Sox weren't entirely convinced the catcher had much of a future in the big leagues, anyway. "Your hitting is okay, but you can't throw or catch," Boston scout Frank Malzone told Whitt.

The rest of the Sox brain trust apparently felt likewise, as they left Whitt available for either Seattle or Toronto to nab in the 1976 Expansion Draft. The Mariners joined the detractors, leaving him available for the Blue Jays to pick with the 34th selection.

Roy Hartsfield, the Jays manager for their first three seasons, wasn't much of a fan either. He played Ernie sparingly, preferring

Known for Cars...and Pizza?

There's a strange allure of the pizza business to baseball men—and particularly those from the state of Michigan. Ernie Whitt and Rick Leach were both proud Michigan natives, joining Tom Monaghan (founder of Domino's Pizza and former owner of the Detroit Tigers) and Mike Ilitch (founder of Little Caesar's Pizza and current owner of the Tigers) as baseball-obsessed pizza barons.

the catching tandem of Alan Ashby and Rick Cerone. While they enjoyed the trappings of big league life, he shuffled back and forth to Syracuse, New York, in his 1972 Monte Carlo.

Almost ready to give up on the game after a wasted year in Triple A at the age of 27, Whitt stuck with it at his wife's urging. Not long after, the team dismissed the notoriously crusty Hartsfield and replaced him with the slightly-less-crusty Bobby Mattick. Fortunately for Whitt, the new manager saw his potential and appointed him to the role of starting catcher.

What followed were a couple of pretty mediocre seasons, which could have served as the ultimate demise of his career. But like a pizza parlour overcoming early struggles, Whitt showed he was far better than he originally let on. In 1982 he slugged 11 home runs in just 105 games. A year later, his output increased to 17 in 123.

Whitt followed that with an All-Star season in 1985, hitting .245 with 19 home runs and 64 RBIs. Although he didn't start for the American League team, he was subbed into the game in the sixth inning. In an ironic twist, it was Carlton Fisk, the man who once blocked Whitt's ascent to the majors, who was pulled, allowing the Jays' catcher to receive pitches from teammate Dave Stieb.

Whitt later made headlines and caught the attention of the umpiring community by offering some rather harsh words about a few of baseball's officials in his 1989 autobiography, *Catch: A Major League Life*. He referred to Durwood Merrill as "a showboat," Ken Kaiser as "a big dorky-looking guy," and Joe Brinkman as "incompetent."

Needless to say, the comments weren't exactly helpful to Toronto's relationship with umpires in general. Brinkman's crew ejected Jays players with regularity, and his disdain spilled over into future seasons.

That winter, the Jays shipped Whitt (along with Kevin Batiste) to the Atlanta Braves to make room for a pair of young catchers, Pat Borders and Greg Myers. In return, they received Ricky Trlicek, a young right-hander. Whitt was only slightly less valuable to the Braves than Trlicek was to the Jays. He hit .172 with two home runs and 10 RBIs, while Trlicek was limited to a pair of meaningless relief appearances.

Whitt made one last attempt at a comeback in 1991 with the Baltimore Orioles but struggled again, hitting .242 with no home runs and just three RBIs in 35 games. Like a pizza parlour fading into foreclosure, Whitt finally had to admit that the party was over.

A year after Whitt's baseball career finished, Mother's Pizza shut its doors as well. To this day, local entrepreneurs have flirted with the idea of revitalizing the brand, and websites have even surfaced hinting at its possible return.

Whitt, on the other hand, experienced his own revival, taking the position of manager on Canada's national baseball team. He guided Team Canada to a fourth-place finish at the 2004 Olympics in Athens and a gold medal at the 2011 Pan-American Games. He held coaching positions with the Blue Jays from 2005 to 2008 and now serves as an instructor in the Philadelphia Phillies system in addition to his role as Team Canada's field boss.

Fond memories of tasty Mother's Pizza, combined with Whitt's leadership of the national men's program have done nothing but strengthen the profile of the man who might very well be the most beloved player in the Blue Jays' history.

17 Rembrandt of Rule 5

Like the artist who artfully manipulated light and shadows to create some of the world's most memorable images, Pat Gillick deftly plied his craft. Recognizing that teams were holding major league calibre-talent captive, Major League Baseball created the Rule 5 draft. Unlike the amateur draft held annually in June (also known as the Rule 4 draft), the Rule 5 draft was designed to allow teams to select players who had been left off other teams' rosters.

For a relatively small sum of cash (currently $50,000) the chosen player would become the property of the team selecting him. That new team was required to keep the drafted player on its major league 25-man roster for the entire season or risk giving him back to the original team. Gillick shrewdly seized the opportunity to acquire major league-ready talent at a minimal cost, and in doing so shaped the Blue Jays into a perennial playoff contender. Just days after taking on the role of vice president of baseball operations in Toronto, Gillick began working his magic. He inherited full player procurement responsibilities for the yearling franchise in 1977 and made his first strike in December, grabbing an unheralded first baseman from its American League East rival, the New York Yankees, as a Rule 5 pick.

At the time, that young hitter, Willie Upshaw, was mostly known for being a cousin to six-time NFL Pro Bowler Gene Upshaw. But as a former member of the Yankees front office, Gillick knew Upshaw was more than just a baseball player with NFL bloodlines.

In fact, the two were more than familiar. Gillick had scouted Upshaw and convinced him to eschew a bevy of attractive football offers and sign with the Yankees instead. Given Toronto's player development plan, he suspected the lean athlete was just the right addition to an expansion team. While the Yanks were anxious to see quick results, Gillick's blueprint for the Jays focused on patience. The Rule 5 acquisition paid off, as Upshaw eventually blossomed into a stalwart at first base for the 1980s Jays.

One of general manager Pat Gillick's best Rule 5 acquisitions, George Bell, looks on from the dugout during the 1989 American League Championship Series.

During Gillick's induction into the Hall of Fame, Atlanta Braves president John Schuerholz noted that the Blue Jays' architect built his resume with a mix of headline-grabbing trades and a unique ability to mine previously untapped talent from other teams. "Under the surface of the big, dynamic deals," Schuerholz said, "was the constant, deep, effective, and very creative management of the organization. Take, for example, the Rule 5 draft. He was the guy who set the standard for taking unprotected minor leaguers off of rosters and turning them into major league players."

Not long after the Upshaw swindle, Gillick made one of the definitive moves of his Hall of Fame career via the Rule 5 draft. The opportunity came when the Philadelphia Phillies, fresh off their 1980 World Series victory, left outfielder George Bell off their 40-man roster. Gillick swooped in to nab the slugger from San Pedro de Macoris in the Dominican Republic.

Just as they had done with Upshaw, the team patiently eased Bell into his role. He made a breakthrough of his own in 1984, crushing 26 dingers to go along with a .292 average, a .498 slugging percentage, and 11 stolen bases.

Bell finished his career with 265 homers, three All-Star appearances, and the 1987 AL Most Valuable Player Award. But many Toronto fans remember him celebrating the team's first division title win in 1985 by jubilantly buckling to his knees in Exhibition Stadium upon clutching the final out in his glove.

The Jays' 40-man roster of that 1985 team featured another native of San Pedro de Macoris, Manny Lee. Gillick had worked his magic again in the 1984 Rule 5 draft, grabbing the young infielder from Houston, believing he could develop into major league talent. "Manny was on a Class A team at the time. So now he's drafted by the Blue Jays and he's on their major league roster," Schuerholz said. "Fast-forward to the upcoming spring training, and Manny Lee goes to Houston and plays against the Astros that day. He goes 4-for-4 and hits two triples, and the Houston brass and ownership go berserk, 'How did this guy get away from us?'"

In the end, Lee didn't develop into much of an offensive force, but his range and defence were the perfect complement for a Jays team already loaded with bats. He had his best year in the field in 1990, registering a .993 fielding percentage in 549 total chances.

The slick-fielding spark plug, though, had the dubious distinction of striking out 107 times without hitting a single home run in 1991—a record which has never been matched in baseball history.

Yet another member of the 1985 roster acquired via the Rule 5 was the handsomely coiffed Kelly Gruber. The crafty Gillick acquired Gruber from the Cleveland Indians in the draft of December 1983, and he was called up for a handful of games during the Drive of '85.

His best days were ahead, though, as he established himself as one of the league's premier third basemen of the late 1980s and early 1990s. Known for his flowing blond mullet, Gruber went on to collect a Gold Glove and a Silver Slugger Award to go along with several MVP votes for his 1990 season.

Ironically, Gillick was passed over Executive of the Year honours during his entire tenure in Toronto, an odd footnote considering the fact he and his talent evaluators saw something in these players that their original teams did not. Recent changes have diminished the relevance of the Rule 5 draft, leaving Gillick entrenched as perhaps its most clever exploiter.

While Hollywood cast Brad Pitt to act out the perceived genius of Billy Beane in the film *Moneyball*, there will likely never be a movie made about baseball architect Pat Gillick. The Jays leader was vigorously exploiting market inefficiencies when Beane was just a snot-nosed kid clinging to his mother's apron. Gillick's creative strategies of acquiring talent resulted in different rewards—a Hall of Fame induction and two Toronto World Series championships.

18 Why the Celtics Despise the Blue Jays

It's rare for a feud to develop between an NBA team and a Major League Baseball club. Such a dispute is about as likely as Larry Bird hitting an upper-deck home run, or Ernie Whitt draining a three-pointer.

But the unlikely collision of the two sports worlds took place in June 1981, leading the Boston Celtics and Toronto Blue Jays into a memorable legal battle. The subject of the dispute was Danny Ainge, as the teams' fates oddly intersected on a warm June 9 evening.

That night in Chicago, Ainge took the field for the Blue Jays. The versatile youngster set up at shortstop, manning the middle of the field behind right-hander Luis Leal. Ainge was struggling with the bat, hitting just .181 at the time, and he seemed a bit distracted in the batter's box that night, finishing 0-for-3 on a pop-up and two weak fly-outs to centre field.

Meanwhile, in New York City, basketball executives convened for the 1981 NBA Draft. The Blue Jays had issued a letter to all of the NBA's 23 teams, requesting that they abstain from drafting Ainge, even though his basketball skills made him one of the sport's top prospects. Ainge, they said, was committed to baseball, and any attempt to select him would be a waste of a time and resources.

But cigar in hand, Celtics general manager Red Auerbach ignored the Jays' warning. He announced to commissioner Larry O'Brien that Boston would select the feisty shooting guard with the eighth pick of the second round.

The immediate reaction of Blue Jays management was limited to hushed internal chatter. After all, Ainge had maintained his intention to stick with baseball and had signed a three-year contract just a year prior.

Aware that Ainge was a baseball, football, and basketball star during high school, the Jays chose careful wording for the contract offered to him in 1980. Specifically, he was given a $300,000 bonus for agreeing "not [to] engage in or play professional basketball" for the duration of his contract. But the lure of playing for one of the NBA's most legendary teams began to call Ainge's name.

Complicating matters was the fact the Major League Baseball Players Association voted to strike just two days after Boston drafted him. Ainge was growing more and more disenchanted by the game of baseball, and visions of Celtics green began to dance in his head. So he approached Jays general manager Peter Bavasi to inform him of his decision to embark on a basketball career. According to court testimony, a stunned Bavasi replied, "You have to do what you have to do." Ainge went on to discuss his intentions with Jays coach Bobby Doerr and vice president Pat Gillick that day, and both made similar remarks.

Ainge's name continued to be written into Blue Jays lineups after the strike ended in August, while he and the Celtics commenced negotiations on a basketball contract. That month the Jays were on the hook to pay him $120,000 as part of his signing bonus. Their bonus baby, meanwhile, was aggressively flirting with his NBA ambitions. Bavasi would later say the Blue Jays were like "an ailing wife being left behind by her husband for some blonde floozy from Boston."

After Bavasi and the rest of Toronto's frustrated management team met with their legal counsel, they filed a federal court suit against the Boston Celtics on August 25, seeking an injunction to prevent the basketball team from negotiating with Ainge until the expiration of his baseball contract in 1983. Boston's legal counsel countered by filing a separate suit in the U.S. District Court, requesting a temporary restraining order against the Jays. They argued that Toronto was interrupting contract negotiations and urged the court to allow them to complete a deal with Ainge.

The Blue Jays were granted their injunction, halting Ainge's contract talks with the Celts. In district court, Judge Lee P. Gagliardi and a four-man, two-woman jury dismissed Boston's claims. They determined that Toronto's contract, signed in September of 1980, had never been rescinded by Bavasi or Gillick, as Ainge had claimed. The signed contract was still valid. The jury also established that the Celtics were guilty of contract interference for negotiating with Ainge while his rights were contracted to the Jays.

The Blue Jays maintained, publicly at least, that they hoped Ainge would reconsider departing for the NBA. Never the shrinking violet, Bavasi mocked Auerbach and his bullheadedness as the trial drew to a close by lighting a cigar of his own. "As far as I'm concerned, Danny Ainge is a member of the Toronto Blue Jays, and until I'm absolutely convinced he's not, I'm not speaking to Auerbach or anyone else in their organization," Bavasi said.

When the dust settled, however, the Blue Jays reportedly received about $500,000 from the Celtics as compensation. Ainge, on the other hand, would go on to reap the financial rewards of a successful NBA career, and later assumed Auerbach's former leadership role with the Celtics.

The feud between the Celtics and Blue Jays will likely never be rekindled. That is, unless Brett Lawrie develops a jump shot.

19 Why Joe Brinkman Hates the Blue Jays

Even in the formative days of Major League Baseball, a discordant relationship between the umpires and the rest of the baseball world began to fester. In *The Bill James Historical Baseball Abstract*, the author details verbal and physical assaults on umps in the late

1800s, many of whom required police protection to make it home in one piece. In 1914 New York Giants Hall of Fame pitcher Christy Mathewson said, "Many fans look upon an umpire as a sort of necessary evil to the luxury of baseball, like the odor that follows an automobile."

From the very first pitch at Exhibition Stadium, the Blue Jays, like other teams, began a somewhat acrimonious relationship with the men in slacks. They had their favourites and they had umpires they weren't thrilled to see officiate their games.

Then there was Joe Brinkman.

In his autobiography, *Catch: A Major League Life*, longtime Blue Jays catcher Ernie Whitt didn't mince words when describing the relationship the team had with the umpire. "Brinkman hates our ballclub," he said.

The umpire, himself, told media he didn't exactly enjoy calling games which involved Toronto. After one particularly ugly game, Brinkman said, "If I had to work every game like these [with Toronto], I'd quit and go home."

Whitt wrote, "umpires hold grudges" and that "there are a few crews that just don't like the Jays." He opined that Brinkman's disdain for Toronto had a long history—going all the way back to the team's first couple of seasons. "Joe's attitude actually goes back to when Bobby Mattick was managing," he said. "All the umpires hated Bobby." The trend continued even after Mattick was replaced as Blue Jays manager. "Joe had his run-ins with Bobby Cox, too."

Brinkman carried on his revulsion for Toronto's squad throughout managerial changes. "Now he hates Jimy Williams...and he's thrown Jimy out a few times over situations that were absolutely nothing. Every close call with Brinkman and his crew goes against the Jays," Whitt said.

Whitt's comments assailed the ump for a perceived lack of impartiality in games involving Toronto's team. "I thought he was pretty fair until the last couple of years, then I think he took on

Also on the Brink

The Jays weren't the only team to experience Brinkman's wrath. Kansas City Royals outfielder Willie Wilson found himself on the ump's bad side after he argued heatedly with him about a blown call. "I could write him up [in a report to the league office]," Brinkman said, "but I'm not going to because he'll be going [thrown out] every night when I see him anyhow. Whenever he looks at me cross-eyed, or just looks at me. If he apologizes, I'll run him. I just don't care if the man ever plays a baseball game when I'm on the field ever, ever again."

an attitude of 'I'm going to get you guys,'" Whitt said. "He's gone downhill as an umpire. And the scary part of it is he runs an umpiring school."

When asked to clarify his words, Whitt didn't back down. "It's not that I don't like him. I have nothing against him," the catcher said. "I hope he improves...I never called him a cheater. He's not. He's just not a good umpire."

Whitt's harsh assessment of Brinkman was reminiscent of legendary manager Leo "the Lip" Durocher's thoughts about umpiring. "I've never questioned the integrity of an umpire. Their eyesight, yes," he quipped.

Once Whitt's book was published, and the cat was out of the bag, the Blue Jays certainly didn't seem to get the benefit of the doubt on close calls in games involving Brinkman. Williams' replacement, Cito Gaston, complained openly about the fact his team couldn't catch a break when Brinkman was on the job. Gaston escalated the situation even further by suggesting Brinkman's anti-Jays grudge might have racial undertones.

The Jays cut ties with Whitt soon after, but Brinkman continued to carry a chip on his shoulder when the bluebirds hit the field.

How could Brinkman get over this long-standing hatred of the Jays? Gaston had an answer. "Why doesn't he just go to Detroit and beat Ernie Whitt up and get it over with?"

While this particular scenario would never be played out, Brinkman hung up his mask and uniform following the 2006 season. To this day Brinkman remains the principal at the Joe Brinkman Umpire School in Cocoa, Florida.

Aspiring umpires attend the facility to learn the ins and outs of major league umpiring. Participants are put through drills which might make an Army sergeant wince. Missed calls aren't tolerated, and heaven forbid a wannabe ump who dares to bark out "ST-EEE-RIKE!" with the wrong pitch or tone. In addition to the bootcamp drills, the training centre educates prospective umpires on the nuances of the life of the professional umpire. Brinkman, speaking from experience, passes on his wisdom to the pupils.

"Never park in the space marked 'umpire,'" Brinkman cautions each graduating class, warning that some unhappy folks will resort to primitive means of voicing their displeasure. Others may even write nasty things about you in their books.

20 Watch a Game From the Stadium Hotel

The recently remodelled Renaissance Toronto Downtown Hotel, formerly known as the SkyDome Hotel, is nothing if not distinctive. The *Chicago Tribune*'s Randy Curwen once called it, "the only hotel in the world with a stadium built in. Basically, the rooms are skyboxes with hotel rooms attached," Curwen said. "Located along the outfield wall, they are not the prime viewing locations—you are a long, long way from the batter—but it's hard to beat the amenities."

Since those viewing areas overlook the field, the stadium hotel has become somewhat notorious. According to a Canoe sports article, since the hotel opened in 1989, there have been at least three incidents where guests were caught in their most intimate of moments in plain view of thousands of fans. That includes a May 1996 Red Sox game, when a couple put on what reporters dubbed a "20-minute sex show" for the 31,000 fans in attendance.

As a result of these…uh…indiscretions, the stadium installed one-way glass in spots, and guests must sign a code of conduct waiver at check-in. The Associated Press obtained a copy of the contract guests sign when booking into a field-view room. The restrictions include:

- No throwing, dropping, dangling, or holding anything out the window
- No placing or resting anything on the ledge
- No carrying on "any activity not considered appropriate in public"
- No being "in a state of partial or complete undress."

The stadium hotel features 70 field-view rooms with floor-to-ceiling windows and electronic drapes. The rooms are arranged so that a viewing room overlooks the field. The smallest rooms sleep two but allow game seating for six, and the biggest rooms sleep four with game seating for 20.

More than 270 other rooms look out onto the streets surrounding the stadium. Fans with those "city-view" rooms can watch a game from some great seats with a view of centre field in the Lobby Lounge for free. The lounge serves up local flavour, with appetizers and beverages reflecting Toronto. The lounge is like a team owner's private box. Even folks who have just come to town for the day can pull up a chair, grab something to eat, kick back with a pint of beer, and watch the game action.

Curwen, who stayed in a room with a field view, said there's more to watch than just games. In fact if you snooze, you'll miss out on a chance to get an insider's view of the park "Why do that when you can see the intimate workings of a ballpark at any time of the day or night? From your room you also can see midday batting practices and other unscheduled game-related activities, after-game cleanups with giant Zamboni-like machines, and fans pouring in from early morning until shortly before gametime for tours of this wonder of the sporting world," he said.

Another benefit of watching a game from the room is that guests are welcome to bring in their own food and refreshments—perhaps something of a higher grade than stadium fare and at a fraction of the price. Hotel employees told the *Toronto Star* that many guests have brought to their rooms many...um...treasures. "In a single season, the housekeeping staff has collected as many as 34,000 beer cans and bottles from the rooms," the *Star* wrote, "not to mention dentures and inflatable dolls." (Staff could not confirm whether the dolls were included in team's attendance figures.)

Despite those interesting artifacts, the hotel has taken a turn toward a higher level of sophistication after being purchased by Marriott and being rebranded as a Renaissance Hotel. While the décor and service quality have been tweaked, the core quality of the hotel remains the same. It's simply one of the most fascinating places in the world to watch a game of baseball.

If you stay there, just remember to keep your private moments private—not in the interest of decency—but because the Blue Jays are just 2–3 when hotel guests are caught in compromising positions.

21 The Redemption of Augie Schmidt

The list reads like a who's who of modern baseball.

Winners of the Golden Spikes Award—given annually to the top amateur baseball player in the United States—include Stephen Strasburg, Bryce Harper, David Price, Tim Lincecum, Jered Weaver, Mark Prior, Jason Varitek, Robin Ventura, and Will Clark.

Many of the award's recipients fulfilled their projections, reaping the financial rewards of big league stardom. Most went on to play several years in the majors with many making millions of dollars in career earnings.

But some Golden Spikes winners' careers went in a different direction. Former Blue Jay Augie Schmidt is one example. An All-American shortstop out of the University of New Orleans, Schmidt won the award in 1982.

On the flight home to Milwaukee from the award presentation, the trophy was broken into pieces. He packaged it up in a shipping box and mailed it off to be repaired, but he didn't take note of the receiver's address. Now, not only was his trophy shattered, but it also was lost. As Pete Jackel of *The (Racine, Wisconsin) Journal Times* wrote in 2005, the trophy became a "metaphor" for Schmidt's career.

The Blue Jays selected Schmidt second overall in the 1982 Amateur Draft—just behind Shawon Dunston—and three picks ahead of Dwight Gooden. Schmidt's performance was little more than adequate in his debut with the Jays' Single A affiliate in Kinston, North Carolina, and he was promoted to Double A to start the 1983 season. Again, he put up mediocre numbers, and even though he made 29 errors and had a paltry slugging

Toronto's Other Golden Spikes Draftee

Augie Schmidt wasn't the only Golden Spikes winner selected by the Blue Jays. In 1985 the team drafted Jim Abbott in the 36th round but were unable to agree to terms with him on a contract. Instead, Abbott attended the University of Michigan, and was then picked eighth overall in 1988 by the California Angels. He's best known for winning 87 major league games and no-hitting the Cleveland Indians—despite being born without a right hand.

percentage in the mid-.300s, the team fast-tracked him to Triple A in Syracuse, New York, by the middle of 1984.

The Jays' player development staff began to quietly question the skills of their former first rounder, while others in the organization hoped his production would increase with more seasoning. What little hope remained began to fade when Schmidt hit .201 with just five extra-base hits in 46 games for Syracuse. He was a bust.

Gord Ash, director of player personnel at the time, was quick to defend the scouts who recommended the team draft Schmidt. He said Schmidt was every bit the player they saw in college—he just didn't improve with time. "You look at a player. You try to estimate where he'll be in a few years with training and coaching," Ash said. "But Augie didn't make that progress. That's an unusual circumstance."

Looking to rid themselves of all the frustrations associated with a failed draft pick, the Jays jettisoned Schmidt to the San Francisco Giants in January of 1985. Schmidt's performance with the Giants' minor league squads was equally anaemic, and they cut him loose, as well. The college hero took one last shot with his hometown Kenosha (Wisconsin) Twins. Playing in front of friends and family, the local legend they had bragged about was reduced to a weak-hitting error machine.

Don Leppert, his manager with the Single A Kenosha team, said it was a tough homecoming for Augie. Not only was he trying to survive in one of the lowest levels in the professional game, his struggles also were magnified by playing at home. "You're disappointing not only you and your team," Leppert said, "but Joe down at the tavern and Charlie down at the barbershop." Schmidt echoed Leppert's sentiment. "It was kind of coming home," Schmidt said. "Well, I was kind of embarrassed."

His production on the field in Kenosha only made things more humiliating. His offence was just as meagre as his previous seasons, despite the four- or five-year age advantage he had over many of his opponents.

He retired after the 1986 season.

But soon after, Carthage College in Kenosha offered him an assistant coaching job with its baseball team. Schmidt knew the Division III team well; his father had managed the squad from 1962 to 1980. Schmidt was revitalized in the job and was promoted to the head coaching role in 1988. He quickly became known as one of the top coaches in America, leading Carthage College to multiple D-III World Series and many players to professional baseball careers.

When *The Journal Times* published the story of Schmidt's lost Golden Spikes trophy in 1994, Carthage's sports information director, Steve Marovich, read the sad details and decided the baseball team's coach deserved better. Carthage commissioned a replica of Schmidt's Golden Spikes Trophy to be constructed at the school's expense.

Then, during an awards dinner on campus, a shocked Schmidt was presented with the award and to thunderous applause. Cheering him on, his Carthage family hoped this trophy might undo some of the pain of his professional failure, which hung over the beleaguered Schmidt for so many years. "I think that trophy represented so many different emotions over the course of time," Schmidt said. "Obviously, I was excited and honoured when I got it, and then when I started struggling in pro ball, it almost became an embarrassment. To win that award and not make it to the big leagues is almost embarrassing."

The trophy now sits in a case outside his office in the athletic centre. "It's more of a source of pride now," Schmidt said. "I walk by it now and I don't cringe. I don't think back to what could have been. I'm older now. The other day, I walked through there. I was all by myself and I just smiled and laughed. I was like, 'Wow, I'm sitting here laughing looking at this trophy.'"

Carthage College's baseball stadium called Augie Schmidt Field in honour of both the former Jays farmhand and his father opened in 2013.

22 Roberto Alomar Is Enshrined

It might surprise you to learn that Robbie Alomar spent just five of his 17 major league seasons in Toronto. He got his start as a San Diego Padre before joining the Blue Jays and later plied his trade with the Baltimore Orioles, Cleveland Indians, New York Mets, Chicago White Sox, and Arizona Diamondbacks. But the legacy of Roberto Alomar Velasquez has endured beyond his relatively brief tenure with the Blue Jays.

In fact, forget about his other stops. The T-dot was where he earned his reputation as one of the greatest second basemen in the history of professional baseball, and is the place he still considers his baseball home.

He arrived in Toronto via a blockbuster trade between the Blue Jays and Padres on December 5, 1990, along with Joe Carter. In exchange, the Jays shipped shortstop Tony Fernandez and first baseman Fred McGriff to San Diego. "I was looking for a right-handed hitter and was interested in getting Carter," general manager Pat Gillick said, "[Padres executive] Joe [McIlvaine] said he wanted McGriff. There was an age differential there. I asked him if he'd throw in Alomar. He asked me, 'Well, if I throw in Alomar, would you throw in Fernandez?'"

A Hall of Famer in his own right, Gillick couldn't accept the offer quickly enough. He knew Alomar well, meeting him first when he was just seven years old. He had pushed hard to sign the young Puerto Rican as a teenager but was outbid by San Diego. His acquisition was thrilling.

But not everyone was excited with the transaction. "I remember driving along the freeway when I heard the news," said Jack McKeon, the former Padres manager. "I almost drove right off the road. I never would have traded Robbie. Never. He had the best instincts of anyone I've managed. Even at 19, you knew he was a future Hall of Famer."

The San Diego front office, though, was happy to cut ties with Alomar, considering him immature and unfocused. They were frustrated that Alomar refused to transition to shortstop and quickly consummated the deal.

The trade was an unquestionable victory for the Blue Jays. Carter's heroics aside, Alomar established himself as the slick-fielding, smooth-swinging infielder Toronto hoped he would become. He hit .295 in his first season with the Blue Jays, while stealing 53 bases and socking 41 doubles. All the while, he dazzled fans with highlight-reel defensive plays.

A year later, he led the team to victory in the 1992 American League Championship Series, putting up ridiculous offensive numbers along the way. During Alomar's 1993 season, he batted .326 with 17 home runs, 109 runs, 93 RBIs, and 55 stolen bases.

How incredible was Robbie Alomar? He holds the all-time record for Gold Gloves by a second baseman (10), and won four Silver Slugger Awards, which places him second all-time among second basemen. He made 12 All-Star teams, collecting an All-Star Game MVP Award along the way, and was also selected MVP of the 1992 ALCS. He is a member of the Level of Excellence, a distinction the Blue Jays use to recognize their biggest stars by displaying their names on banners on the Rogers Centre's 500 Level.

He's also the only player ever to have his jersey number retired by the Blue Jays. "Today I felt like a little boy," Alomar said after the jersey retirement ceremony. "I've been blessed that I had the chance to play for this organization. I always say it's my second home. I'm proud to be Puerto Rican and now I always say I'm half Puerto Rican and half Canadian."

Blue Jays President and CEO Paul Beeston took it a step further. "There's going to come a time when a young generation of fans come into the ballpark, and they're going to see that No. 12, and they're going to ask their parents, 'What does No. 12 mean?'" Beeston said. "And they're going to say, 'Why, that's the number of Robbie Alomar, the greatest second baseman who ever played the game.'"

23 Doug Ault, Overnight Hero

"The odds are against me," Doug Ault said. "I love it." The 27-year-old was just one of many vying for a spot on the Blue Jays' first Opening Day roster. He came into the competition with better credentials than most, sporting a .300 career batting average—albeit in the tiniest of sample sizes—just 20 at-bats for the Texas Rangers the year prior.

To be fair, he wasn't battling Eddie Murray or Willie McCovey for the job with the Blue Jays. His competition consisted of Nate

Colbert, Doug Howard, and an aging Ron Fairly. But he still needed to bust his butt to make the team. "I've set a goal to make it," Ault said. "I was given a chance [when picked up in the expansion draft]. I knew I was good enough to play in the big leagues."

The Blue Jays agreed. They named the first baseman to their roster and headed north with Ault and a motley crew of newbies. It wasn't long before Ault found his way into Blue Jays history. He was penciled into the No. 3 slot in the Jays lineup for the opening game of the 1977 season—the very first regular season tilt in team history.

In front of a crowd of 44,649, Ault and his teammates watched the visiting Chicago White Sox take their swings in the top of the first inning at snowy Exhibition Stadium. Ralph Garr led off for Chicago and drew a walk from Bill Singer, Toronto's starting pitcher. Garr eventually advanced to third and scored on a Jorge Orta sacrifice fly. Richie Zisk added another run for the White Sox by hitting the first home run off the new Blue Jays team.

With the bad guys ahead 2–0, the Jays came up for some at-bats of their own. Left fielder John Scott was the first batter in Blue Jays history. Ken Brett, pitching for the Sox, obviously wasn't feeling too nostalgic about the significance of the moment. He mowed down Scott for a strikeout. The crowd wasn't thrilled with the way the game was going. "Everybody was booing." Ault said.

Up next was another relatively obscure player in team history, Hector Torres. The shortstop faced an identical fate to Scott, as Brett, brother of Hall of Famer George Brett, struck him out, too. The crowd was less than enthused. "The boos really got loud, and I'm on deck thinking, 'My gosh, I'm next!'" Ault said. With an awkward sense of tension in the ballpark, Ault stepped up to the plate. The first pitch came in from Brett. Much to Ault's chagrin, it was a called strike. "Then they *really* started booing," Ault said. "They're thinking, 'Oh, three strikeouts in a row.' I'm thinking, 'I've gotta swing the bat.'"

And he did.

With that swing, Doug Ault—a 27-year-old rookie who'd struggled to earn his way onto a big league roster—became a Blue Jays legend. He smashed the 0–1 pitch deep to left-centre field and over the fence for the first home run in team history. The crowd transformed from a miserable bunch to an ecstatic, joyous gang. Ault was already cemented in team history, but he didn't stop

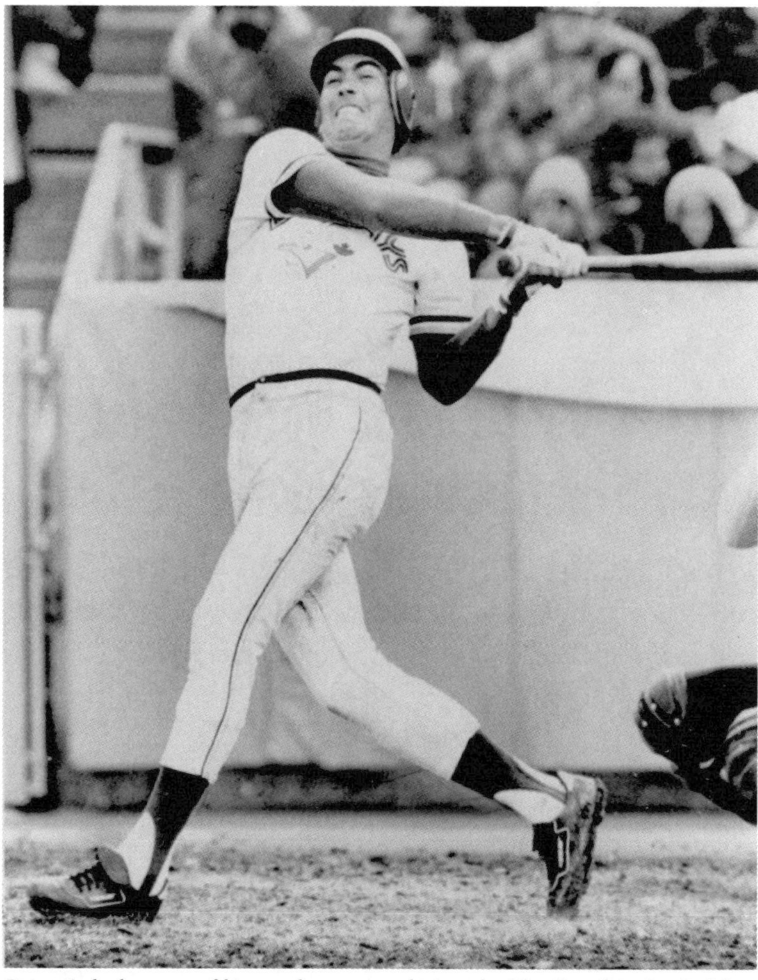

Doug Ault slugs one of his two home runs during the Blue Jays franchise's debut in 1977.

there. In his second at-bat, he took Brett deep for the second time in as many at-bats. This shot scored Torres and moved the team into a 4–4 tie with the Sox, heading into the fourth inning.

Coming up for his third at-bat, the crowd greeted their new hero, Ault, with raucous applause. But he showed himself to be a mere mortal, grounding into a double play. His offensive outburst, though, wasn't over. In the bottom of the eighth inning, Ault collected his third hit of the day, a single. The hit scored Scott, putting the Jays ahead 8–5.

The Blue Jays had their first hero. In one day, Ault made himself almost as well known across the country of Canada as Paul Henderson, the hockey hero of the 1972 Summit Series. Although Ault passed away in 2004, his memory lives on in the minds of Blue Jays fans.

24 Opening the World's First Retractable Roof

Perhaps rightfully so, Toronto fans complain that their stadium, the Rogers Centre, is sterile and lacks the warmth of other ballparks. But, if there's one element of the stadium which is beyond reproach, it's the dome itself—the world's first fully retractable ballpark roof.

For most of the Blue Jays' history at the Rogers Centre/SkyDome, Lee Brennan has been the man behind the roof's control panel. Unlike most of the retractable-roofed stadiums which came along after Toronto's stadium, the operation of the roof isn't simply an automatic, computerized process. That is, Brennan is able to manipulate the movement of the panels of the roof—even by a few inches—through a giant control panel. Like something out of *Star Trek*, the panel features a number of levers and buttons, which Brennan operates with precision.

Oh, and he's not the one to blame if the roof is closed on a perfectly sunny day.

The people responsible for weather tracking at the Rogers Centre are Dave McCormick, the engineering supervisor for Rogers Centre, and his roof operations team. They utilize the Weather Network's Pelmorex satellite weather tracking system to predict approaching weather systems and identify storms well before they happen. The satellite camera is located on Toronto Island and allows the team to make a judgment call on whether to open or close the roof (which takes roughly 20 minutes).

No such decisions need to be made once the end of October rolls around. At that point they keep the roof firmly shut until April, protecting the stadium's interior from a cold Toronto winter.

In fact, fans who complain about the Rogers Centre would be advised to take a quick trip to the site of Exhibition Stadium in early April. There they can fondly reminisce about the rain, snow, swirling winds, and swarms of seagulls they experienced in that crappy facility.

Or they can reminisce about Exhibition's 1982 Grey Cup and its terrible November weather, which caused the Canadian Football League championship game to be remembered as the "Rain Bowl." The fans chanted, "We want a dome!"

Say what you want about the Blue Jays' stadium…the roof is still pretty damn cool and will allow you to stay warm despite the sometimes inclement Toronto weather.

25 The Arrest of Dave Winfield

The team's official anthem, "OK, Blue Jays" famously features the lyrics "Is it a fly ball…or is it a seagull?" Those fowls are a part of lakeside life in Toronto and have a tendency to be quite annoying. They're loud, messy, and mischievous devils. Some call them beach chickens, flying rats…even shithawks.

Anyone who has spent time near the old Exhibition Stadium in the summer knows of the swarms of gulls that descend upon the area on a warm summer day, waiting to swoop in for dropped french fries, discarded hot dog buns, and the moist remains of an ice cream cone. They poop on us. They caw like mad. They steal our food and generally irritate the crap out of us. But despite their many faults, they don't deserve to die at our hands.

On August 4, 1983, Dave Winfield of the Yankees crossed that line.

As his Bronx Bombers took on the Blue Jays, he was put off by the bird infestation at Exhibition Stadium. Gulls flapped around and squawked during batting practice and throughout the early innings, plundering anything and everything they could find in the bleachers while occasionally resting on the playing field to digest their stolen booty.

In the middle of the fifth inning, Winfield completed his warm-up tosses and threw the ball firmly to a batboy. The ball accidentally hit a seagull in its path on the head, killing the bird instantly. Winfield mocked the incident, holding his hat over his heart, as it became apparent this particular gull wouldn't live to eat another ballpark nacho. Fans went from shocked to angry, as the slugger laughed off the bird's death. Catcalls rained down on him.

Winfield spoke with media after the game, claiming he didn't mean to hit the bird. "All I can say is that it is quite an unfortunate incident because one of the fowls in Canada is now no longer with us," Winfield said. "I had finished playing catch with [left fielder] Don Baylor and turned and whipped the ball to the batboy, and the seagull happened to be there and caught it in the neck. It's unfortunate, but it was an accident. It wasn't intentional." But fans and team authorities who observed the incident felt Winfield's throw was not an accident.

Toronto police, too, believed Winfield intentionally hit and killed the bird. The carcass of the bird was turned in as forensic evidence. A warrant was issued for Dave Winfield's arrest, and he was booked with bail set at $500. Winfield cooperated throughout the process, aware that he could face six months in jail.

Winfield's manager, Billy Martin, was quick to defend his star—in his typical facetious manner. "They say he hit the gull on purpose," Martin said. "They wouldn't say that if they'd seen the throws he'd been making all year. It's the first time he's hit the cutoff man."

Thankfully for Martin and Winfield, the charges were dropped the next day, and Dave Winfield was a free man. But fans didn't forget the action, and they continued to show their disdain for Winfield during his future visits to Toronto. He said the fans, "were on my case and threw things at me and tried to hit me."

Although he never fully admitted his intent in the incident, Winfield showed remorse, returning to Toronto to donate paintings for an Easter Seals auction and helping raise more than $60,000 for the charity.

Winfield, of course, eventually became a Blue Jays fan favourite and Toronto sports legend when he was acquired by the Blue Jays in 1992. During the 1992 World Series versus the Atlanta Braves, it was that remorseful slugger—once despised in Toronto—who raked a Charlie Leibrandt change-up down the left-field line. That double scored the winning runs in the 11th inning of Game 6, giving the Jays their first World Series title.

He spoke about his Toronto redemption in *Sports Illustrated:* "I've been thinking about this," he said. "If my career had ended [before Toronto], I wouldn't have been really happy with what baseball dealt me. I would have had no fulfillment, no sense of equity, no fairness. I feel a whole lot better now about the way things have turned out."

26 Take a Tour of Epy Guerrero's Training Complex

Young ballplayers travelling by bus to Epy Guerrero's training complex couldn't be blamed if they felt a bit queasy. The road ahead had more twists and turns than their likely life path, which might lead to the major leagues, or, more likely, back to the fields to cut sugarcane.

Seated next to other wannabe baseball stars, they'd travel past shoddily built shacks and farmland before the bus arrived at its destination outside Santo Domingo. Hidden amongst tropical vegetation in the outskirts of the Dominican capital, Guerrero's complex is a fascinating place. While visitors speak of the complex's obscure location, this place wasn't the least bit mysterious to the boys on the bus.

They'd heard the stories of Blue Jays like Tony Fernandez and Carlos Delgado, along with other Dominican stars who went on to play for other Major League Baseball teams. Their parents told them tales of their instructor's scouting heroics. They were aware he'd literally climbed mountains and dodged death threats to find raw talent and make it translate to professional baseball contracts for his protégés.

They came to Complejo Epy Guerrero de Villa Mella with hopes of becoming the next Fernandez. In this economically troubled country, a lottery ticket like this might be a Dominican kid's best chance to change his life and the lives of those around him. Many of these youngsters came from 100 miles away—some even farther. Several of the 12- and 13-year-olds had never spent a night away from their families, slept in their own beds, or had the good fortune of eating three meals a day.

They came here to learn and to play baseball. In the morning, they'd hit the field to sharpen their baseball skills, and at night they'd hit the schoolbooks to further their education. They'd put in long hours and wake up the next day for more of the same. Epy left no room for distractions. That's why he built the facility in the boonies—well outside bustling Santo Domingo. "Epy didn't want to have kids close to the capital city," said Jorge Arangure Jr. of ESPN. "He wanted kids committed to the game of baseball and didn't want to have kids who partied in the city. He wanted baseball players."

Guerrero bought the 18-acre facility for $9,000 from a man with mounting gambling debts and a messy divorce in progress. Guerrero served as his own general contractor, clearing out the palm trees to make room for a pair of baseball diamonds and oversaw the construction of the concrete-and-cinderblock stadium. When it was time to level the playing field, he hopped in the tractor and did it himself. The facility is a relatively modern—yet simple—place to learn the game of baseball. "The kids stay in a dorm environment you might see in college, with two sets of bunkbeds to a room," Arangure said.

The athletes typically chow down on a chicken breast, rice, and vegetables for dinner, giving them sufficient energy for the busy day ahead. After dinner, Arangure said, they typically relax in the television room or blow off steam in the weight room.

Forget about what you may have heard about filthy living quarters and harsh treatment of youngsters by *buscones* (agents). Arangure said MLB's executives intervened in 2010 to push for a higher standard of treatment for the young players. "MLB's No. 1 intent was to improve the facilities in the D.R.," he said. "They mandated that teams had to have a certain set of standards, and now most facilities are pretty state of the art."

Guerrero's camp is one of the best. His son, Patrick, named after former Blue Jays general manager Pat Gillick, now oversees operations. Epy passed away in 2013 at the age of 71, but Blue Jays fans know him as one of the most successful scouts in baseball history. He brought slick-fielding Fernandez to the team, along with Delgado, Kelvim Escobar, Junior Felix, Nelson Liriano, and Silvestre Campusano.

His contribution to Toronto baseball might have been even larger, had the Jays' Mel Queen concurred with his assessment of one particular—and diminutive—young pitcher. Queen travelled to Villa Mella to have a look at the 16-year-old but left without signing the player. Guerrero gave the Jays first right of refusal, but they decided not to pursue the opportunity "He's already as good as he's ever going to be," Queen reportedly told Guerrero. Instead, the Los Angeles Dodgers signed the young pitcher—Pedro Martinez.

27 No Beer for You

It's stunningly ironic. Some might even call it tragic.

The expansion Blue Jays, owned principally by the Labatt Brewery, couldn't sell beer at their home stadium.

"WE WANT BEER! WE WANT BEER!" chanted fans at the Jays' inaugural game at Exhibition Stadium. The target of their ire? Bill Davis, the premier of Ontario, whose government prohibited the sale of alcohol, was in attendance at the game. The sober masses thoroughly disapproved of the strange restriction and let him know about it.

At the time, every other team in Major League Baseball willfully doled out brews to thirsty fans in their stadiums. And it seemed only fair that fans suffering through a first-year expansion club's 107 losses could wash away their pain with a couple of Labatts. Hell, the team was named the *Blue* Jays.

Plus, the beer could have had medicinal applications, alleviating the sharp neck pain fans experienced by sitting in those misaligned Exhibition Stadium seats. Anyone who ever sat along the baselines at the Ex will recall being forced to twist their head at a roughly 90-degree angle to watch infield-area activity...such as pitching and hitting. (But if they wanted to see what Al Woods or Otto Velez were up to in left and right field, respectively, they could simply look straight ahead.)

But a small group of anal-retentive teetotalers ruined the fun for the other 99 percent of the crowd who wanted to tip back a brew or two at the game. They organized the "No Booze in the Ballpark Committee" and successfully petitioned the provincial government to keep alcohol away from the stadium. If beer was sold at the ballpark, fans would become drunk and disorderly, they claimed. And, if we let baseball fans drink at the stadium, what would come next—beer at a *hockey game*? Egad.

One pro-beer party took exception to the puritans and chartered a plane to fly above Exhibition Stadium and tow a pointed message for the premier of the province. "Good Luck Jays! Now Give Us Our Beer, Bill," it read.

But their pleas fell on deaf ears, and the stadium patrons had no choice but to sip on non-alcoholic delights such as cola, cream soda, and some flavourless, clear fluid they call "water," for five years.

In the end, the goat became the hero. Davis, still in office in 1982, overturned the ban and allowed booze to flow freely at the Jays' ballpark on July 30, 1982. Paul Godfrey served as bartender for the pouring of the first glass of Labatt, commemorating the bizarre occasion.

There was a bright spot for those long-deprived fans. Draught beer was initially sold at the stadium for $1.75—about 85 percent cheaper than a large draught at the Rogers Centre these days.

28 The Emergence of Joey Bats

Three players named Jose Bautista and four others named Jose *Batista* toiled in the minor leagues without ever getting the call up to the show. There's Jose (Arias) Bautista, who pitched for five different teams in nine years in the majors, producing a 32–42 record. And then there's Joey Bats—Toronto's version of Jose Bautista—the man who overshadows them all.

At one point, it seemed he was destined to join the mix as just another ordinary Jose. Drafted in the 20th round of the 2000

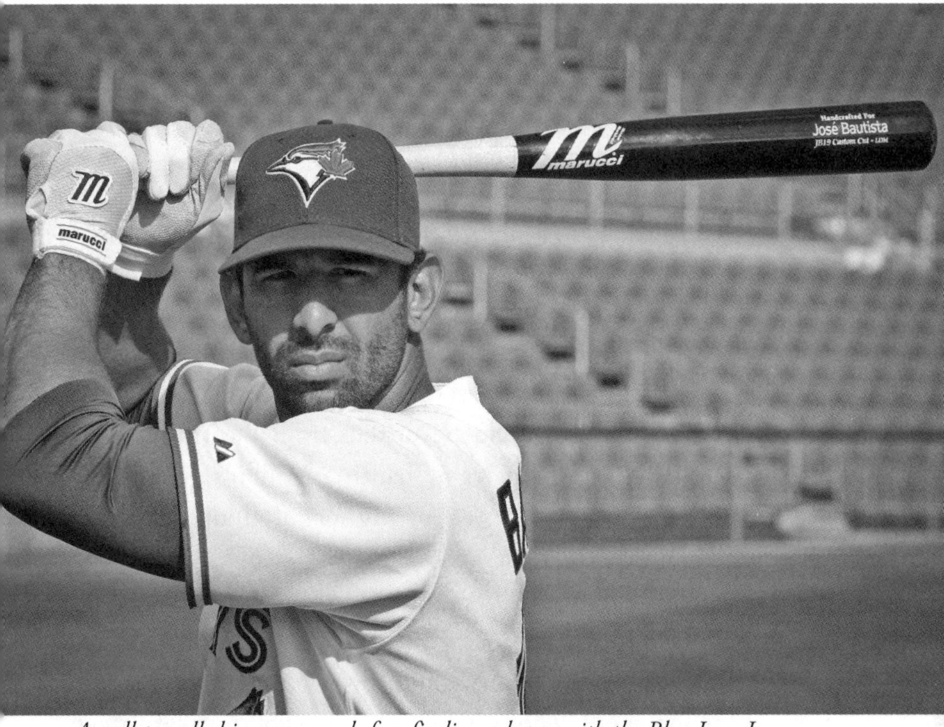

A well-travelled journeyman before finding a home with the Blue Jays, Jose Bautista has developed into one of the game's best power hitters.

Draft by the Pittsburgh Pirates, this Bautista produced respectable numbers and began to advance in their minor league system. By late 2003 Bautista had progressed to the Pirates High A affiliate in Lynchburg, Virginia, where he collected 20 extra-base hits in 195 plate appearances and began to flash some power. But his strikeout totals in the low levels of the minors were troubling to the Pirates, who left him unprotected for the Rule 5 draft.

Then came chaos.

The Baltimore Orioles picked up Joey Bats in the Rule 5 draft on December 15, 2003, but didn't find much playing time for him in 2004. When the Orioles placed Bautista on waivers that June, the Tampa Bay Rays snapped up his rights. Twenty-five days later the Kansas City Royals purchased the rights to Bautista. Just more than a month after that, the Royals traded him to the New York Mets for Justin Huber. The Mets then almost immediately traded him back to the Pirates.

Bautista thought that was where the wild ride would come to an end. If they had gone to the efforts of bringing him back, the Pirates must have wanted to give him regular playing time. "I figured, 'This team is losing anyway. They're like 40 games out,'" Bautista said. "It was the organization that originally drafted me, and they gave up something to get me back. I thought they'd give me a chance." Nothing could be further from the truth. Even for a perennially struggling team, Bautista couldn't get regular at-bats. He simply couldn't get into any sort of groove if he was spending so much time on the bench and enduring frequent demotions.

Frustrated, Bautista approached Pirates management. "I asked what my situation was," Bautista said, "and they said they didn't view me as somebody who was going to contribute toward their future." Knowing he wasn't a part of Pittsburgh's plans, he requested a trade. J.P. Ricciardi, who was looking for a utility-type for his Blue Jays team, offered onetime prospect Robinzon Diaz.

The rest was history.

Arriving in Toronto, Bautista worked with Blue Jays hitting coach Dwayne Murphy and manager Cito Gaston, who was once considered one of the game's top hitting coaches himself. They studied his swing and made a few relatively minor adjustments. The results, though, were major. During the final month of the 2009 season, Bautista earned the nickname "Joey Bats" by hammering 10 home runs. He followed it up with a Blue Jays record of 54 home runs in 2010 and hit 43 bombs in just 513 at-bats in 2011.

During that 2011 season, Bautista produced a Ruthian OPS (on-base plus slugging percentage) of 1.056 to go along with a league-leading .608 slugging percentage. Simply put, he's one of the top power hitters in baseball. Bautista said he might have produced the same numbers for any of the other teams he played for—if only they had enough faith in him to give him a chance.

29 The EdWing

It was yet another hitless game. Mired in a 1-for-28 slump, Edwin Encarnacion took an ugly 0-for-4 vs Roy Oswalt and the Houston Astros on April 27th, 2009. Exacerbating the situation was the fact that in the five games leading up to this contest, Encarnacion committed twice as many errors as he had base hits.

The defensive blunders were nothing new, but it seemed that something just wasn't right with the lumbering Dominican slugger. Tests the next day indeed revealed a chipped bone in his right wrist. The Cincinnati Reds placed their exasperating young third baseman on the disabled list. It was just the latest in a long series of frustrating occurrences involving the man Reds fans nicknamed "EdE." Wild throws and fielding errors had been par for the course since Day One, and now after a 26-home run season a year prior, his bat had also gone cold.

Encarnacion missed the months of May and June with the ailment but returned to the club prior to the trade deadline—just in time to rebuild a bit of his damaged market value. He put together a solid July with a .276/.375/.526 slash line and four dingers. Heck, he didn't even make a single error in the 21 games leading up to the deadline. But in the eyes of Reds general manager Walt Jocketty, Encarnacion wasn't the long-term third-base solution for Cincy. In place of EdE's inconsistency, the executive sought the stability of a veteran replacement and he found what seemed to be an ideal trading partner in the Blue Jays' GM J.P. Ricciardi.

Ricciardi was anxious to talk trade, but Encarnacion was the last guy he had in mind. The Jays GM had developed somewhat of a man-crush on Reds minor leaguer Zach Stewart and looked at Josh Roenicke as a possible late-inning solution for Toronto. The teams negotiated, agreeing to the general parameters of a deal. Jocketty was willing to let go of the two pitchers Ricciardi desired in a package centered around veteran Scott Rolen. But to make the deal work, Ricciardi was told he must accept Encarnacion as part of the deal. Signed to a two-year extension prior to the 2009 season and with a price tag that was on the rise, EdE simply had to be included in the deal to make the finances work. The trade was consummated soon after.

If there was any doubt how unaware he was of the fortune that had been foisted upon him, note that Ricciardi didn't even mention Encarnacion during the post-trade conference call. J.P. simply had no idea what had fallen into his lap.

After arriving midseason in Toronto, Encarnacion's performance was decidedly mediocre. He made seven errors in 42 games, and some of them were rather ugly. His bat showed a glimmer of potential, as it occasionally had in Cincy, producing a .240 average, .442 slugging percentage with eight homers and 23 RBIs.

Encarnacion's 2010 season brought more questions than answers about his ability to be a full-time player in the majors. At the height of his struggles, he was designated for assignment and demoted to Triple A—a relegation that might crush the ego of a lesser man. Instead, the move to the minor league team in Las Vegas motivated him to double down on his efforts to improve. "The reports we got back from the staff in Las Vegas were unbelievable," Anthopoulos said. "They said Edwin was going out every day for early work. He went down there and he hit .400, but his attitude was unreal. And it's rare. He could've sat there and said,

'Woe is me' and put his head down, but he kept fighting...That was a telling sign for me, as a general manager, of what the makeup was like."

This display of tenacity gave Toronto fans perhaps their first real glimpse into the bigger-than-life personality encased in the 27-year-old. On the aggregate he slugged 21 bombs in 367 MLB plate appearances that year. But his defense was still just so *gawd awful*, and he even lived up to his E5 moniker with 18 errors in 95 games that season.

No one would doubt his offensive potential, but the overall package was seen as far from indispensable. He was designated for assignment, following the conclusion of the 2010 season. News hit that the Oakland Athletics claimed Encarnacion on waivers on November 12th. But barely a month later, the Jays re-signed Encarnacion to a one-year contract for $2.5 million with a club option for $3.5 million in 2012. In announcing the move, the Jays made a point of indicating that he would now be listed as a first baseman/designated hitter on their roster.

With the burden of defending the hot corner mostly in the rearview mirror, he began his transition from a disposable asset to one of baseball's most feared sluggers. Slowly, he learned the art of manning first base defensively. Steadily, he built a hitting resume that would be the envy of most other players in the major leagues. It was Encarnacion's performance in the 2012 season that caused the baseball world to lean back and react with a collective "Holy shit, this guy's good."

Encarnacion nearly doubled his walk total from the year before and slashed a .280/.384/.557. He crushed 42 home runs and even stole 13 bases. This was a guy who transformed himself from a waiver wire dweller to a bona fide MVP candidate. The Baseball Writers' Association of America (BBWAA) unanimously selected him as the Blue Jays' Player of the Year. It was quite a year. And it was during this amazing 2012 season that a key component of Encarnacion's public persona was born—the EdWing.

In an interview on MLB Network's *Intentional Talk*, Jose Bautista told hosts Chris Rose and Kevin Millar that it all started April 28th of that season in a game versus Seattle Mariners starting pitcher Hisashi Iwakuma. Wobbling as he rounded first base, Edwin raised his right elbow to kind of stabilize himself as he watched his bases-loaded liner clear the fence. "He was just kind of leaning and kind of just stayed that way," Bautista said. "And everybody was like, 'that looked cool, you need to do that again.'"

Encarnacion elaborated to The Canadian Press. "When I hit the grand slam, I got excited and rounded the bases from the side, turning like an airplane," he said. "My teammates liked it and said I should keep doing it, so I've kept doing it."

But, where did the term, "Walking the Parrot" originate? Followers of Blue Jays bloggers Andrew Stoeten and Drew Fairservice credit them with popularizing the phrase online. If they didn't invent the term itself, they certainly played a massive role in making it known to fans around the world. Their site held the first known GIF of the parrot riding Edwin's arm around the bases, an endlessly entertaining creation from Archi Zuber and Scott Johnson. The unusual home-run trot became fodder for water cooler talk across Canada. Kids tied stuffed parrot dolls to their arms as Halloween costumes. Teammate Ezequiel Carrera brought one such parrot into the Jays dugout, showing it off for cameras following Encarnacion's blasts.

Between 2012 and 2016, Encarnacion took his parrot for an awful lot of rides. Over that stretch the slugger bashed 193 dingers in the regular season and four in the postseason. He was rewarded with three All-Star appearances along the way, twice finishing in the top 10 WAR in the American League. His 11th inning walk-off blast in the 2016 American League wild-card game versus the

Baltimore Orioles will live in the annals of Blue Jays history as one of the team's most memorable moments.

30 The Rocket's Red Glare

Roger Clemens is a true Texan, inside and out. Built like a rock and tough as nails, he's not the kind of guy who suffers fools. So you just knew he wouldn't walk away from an insult hurled at him by a dumpy middle-aged baseball executive.

The superstar flamethrower shocked the baseball world by signing with the Toronto Blue Jays prior to the 1997 season. Earlier that offseason, Boston media reports suggested that the Rocket would only consider re-signing with Boston or heading to his home state to play for the Houston Astros or Texas Rangers.

During the '96 season, Clemens hinted that his days in Boston might soon come to a close. "I've got to know where my family is going to be in four years," Clemens said. "I'm gonna play four more years and try to win a championship. [General manager Dan] Duquette is big on one-year contracts. I know what I can do. There's no reason to even discuss that." Red Sox CEO John Harrington also acknowledged that he might not be able to hang onto the second-winningest pitcher in his team's history. "This is going to be a complicated situation," Harrington said. "We can't give away the franchise, as some people want us to do simply to give Roger what he wants."

If their rival Sox wouldn't do it, the Blue Jays knew they could step in to give Roger what he wanted. President and CEO Paul Beeston quarterbacked the negotiations, making an impassioned presentation at the hurler's home. Clemens liked what he heard and

10 Questions with "Rocket" Roger Clemens

You joined the Blue Jays after a successful career in Boston. How did it feel to wear a new uniform for the first time?
It was a solid transition—from the Jays' front office to the guys in the clubhouse, and the fans, and the city. My family and I really enjoyed our time there.

Before you came to Toronto, who was your toughest out in the Blue Jays lineup?
Paul Molitor.

Money aside, what was the biggest motivator that drove you to sign in Toronto?
Paul Beeston was the deciding factor for me. A great man, fun to visit with, and had a passion to get the Blue Jays back on top.

Describe your state of mind when you returned to Fenway Park for the first time.
A great deal of fun. My teammates commented on how they felt it was like a playoff atmosphere.

Who was the toughest Red Sox batter you faced?
Mo Vaughn

Who was your favourite teammate while you played in Toronto?
All the guys. Very talented players on those two teams. Everyone played a solid role in doing their jobs. Over the years I had some fantastic catchers, and Charlie O'Brien and Darrin Fletcher are right there on that list.

What's your fondest memory of life in Toronto?
The fans. How clean the city of Toronto was...and also some fantastic golf courses in and around the city!

What's it like to watch your son, Koby, work on a career of his own in the Toronto system?
Koby likes the Toronto club. He met new people and coaches. He loves the game and puts his heart into it. He's looking for his chance...that one opportunity.

What's your favourite aspect of retired life?
I need to un-retire to retire! Staying busy with the four boys, our foundation, and working with other players at every level. Busy. Busy. It keeps you young!"

Will we see you play again in the big leagues?
Nothing yet...mind says, "Yes, you can"...body says, "No, you can't." Doing some fun things for the local hometown teams.

signed a three-year deal, $24.75 million deal with Toronto, which included a $9.75 million signing bonus and a fourth-year option. At his introductory press conference, Clemens repeatedly stated how excited he was to sign in Toronto and how pleased he was to be treated so well by the Jays.

The Red Sox brass stood their ground, stating that they offered Clemens as big a financial commitment as they could justify. After all, they couldn't go over the top with a ridiculous offer to a player who was, as Duquette famously said, entering "the twilight of his career." Those comments seemed to fuel Clemens' ire as he tore through American League hitters throughout 1997. He carried a sub-2.00 ERA into mid-July and was well on his way to a Cy Young Award.

But the biggest moment of his season came on July 12, 1997, when he stood on that familiar Fenway Park mound—this time in the uniform of an opponent.

The crowd greeted him with a mix of applause and boos, but nearly all of them began to cheer him on as he sliced through Boston's offence like a hot knife through butter. He struck out 16 Red Sox and gave up just four hits along the way. By the end of the eighth inning, Clemens had much of the sold-out crowd of 33,000 on their feet, chanting "Roger, Roger, Roger."

In fact, the loudest boos of the day were showered down upon Jays manager Cito Gaston for pulling the Rocket after the eighth inning. In appreciation of the impressive performance—not to mention 13 years as the ace of the Boston rotation—the fans cheered enthusiastically for their former hero. As he walked off the field, Clemens directed his eyes toward the owner's box in Fenway Park, which was occupied by Harrington and Duquette.

This wasn't just a glance. It was a Texas-sized glare.

Clemens went on to prove the pair was dead wrong in saying his best days were behind him. The Rocket's tenure in Toronto may have been brief, but the results were spectacular. He won the 1997 and 1998 AL Cy Young Awards during his only two seasons with the team.

31 Toronto's Own Tom and Jerry

For a couple guys who never played a single game in the big leagues, Tom Cheek and Jerry Howarth sure made an impression on the game of baseball. They went together like milk and cookies, providing fans of the Blue Jays with silky smooth broadcasts in their contrasting tones. Cheek was the bass; Howarth was the treble. Cheek was cool as a cucumber; Howarth was excitable.

That mixture of styles and tones became *the* soundtrack for Blue Jays fans. They were with us while we were cruising in our car, relaxing on our back patio, working in the garage, or mowing the lawn. Their voices could be heard through the pillows of some crafty 12-year-olds (the author of this book, for example) who hid their radios to hear one more inning before going to sleep.

When the Blue Jays hit their first home run, Cheek was behind the microphone. When the team won its first American League pennant, Cheek was the man making the call. When the Jays won their first World Series, Cheek said the legendary words Toronto fans will always savour, "Timlin to Carter…and the Blue Jays win it! The Blue Jays win it!"

The next season, his words became even more memorable. His call on Joe Carter's World Series winning walk-off home run likely will remain as famous as the blast itself: "A swing and a BELT… left field…way back…BLUE JAYS WIN IT! The Blue Jays are World Series Champions, as Joe Carter hits a three-run home run in the ninth inning, and the Blue Jays have repeated as World Series Champions...Touch 'em all, Joe! You'll NEVER hit a bigger home run in your life!" Those words struck a chord across Blue Jay nation. Fans could hardly be blamed if they welled up upon hearing Cheek's famous call. When combined with the homer itself, it is likely the team's signature moment.

Cheek got his start in the big leagues with the Montreal Expos, filling in as a guest announcer during the course of several seasons. When Toronto landed an expansion franchise, he was the man chosen to partner up with Early Wynn for the team's radio broadcasts.

He wouldn't miss a single game from April 7, 1977 to June 3, 2004. Only the death of his father would cause him to end an incredible streak of 4,306 consecutive games. Unfortunately, Cheek himself was diagnosed with a malignant brain tumour and passed away at the age of 66 on October 9, 2005.

He has been nominated seven consecutive years for baseball broadcasting's highest honour—the Ford C. Frick Award, which is awarded by the Baseball Hall of Fame and may yet be granted to Cheek.

Although Jerry Howarth wasn't around until 1981, he's as much a part of the Blue Jays history as any other broadcaster involved with the team, including Cheek. Jays fans have heard Howarth's cheerful voice leading off the vast majority of radio broadcasts of the team's games, saying, "Yes sir, it's time for Blue Jays baseball!"

It's Howarth who greets the Blue Jays' first run of any given game with his trademark call, "And the Blue Jays are in flight!" When one of the hometown heroes hits a dinger, we hear him say, "Up! Up! Up! And there she goes!"

Raised in San Francisco, Howarth got his start in broadcasting in 1974 after being hired as a play-by-play man for the Triple A Tacoma (Washington) Twins. For a brief period, Howarth dipped his toes into a sports management career, working as the assistant general manager for the Salt Lake City Prospectors of the Western Basketball Association. He returned primarily to broadcasting, working as a sports talk show host before landing the gig in Toronto.

Howarth currently lives in Etobicoke, Ontario, where, in addition to his broadcasting career, he coaches the Etobicoke Collegiate Institute junior varsity basketball team. He's now partnered up on broadcasts with Joe Siddall and Mike Wilner.

32 The Blunders of J.P. Ricciardi

In November 2001, Toronto warmly welcomed its new general manager, J.P. Ricciardi. By all accounts, the former New York Mets minor league infielder seemed like exactly the right man for the job. The bean counters at Rogers Communications loved that he had earned a reputation for helping a team achieve maximum results on a minimal budget. After all, he'd worked alongside Oakland A's GM Billy Beane to establish the strategies we now famously know as "Moneyball." Fans were excited, too, figuring Beane's protégé would be the perfect man to return Toronto to its winning ways.

But time would prove that not only was Ricciardi unable to bring a glorious revival to the Blue Jays, he instead brought forth some of the darker days in team history. Shortly after joining the Jays, Ricciardi dismissed the team's entire scouting staff, replacing them with a skeleton crew of his own choosing. Scouting with the Blue Jays was done via spreadsheet—and the few players the team actually saw were judged based on small sample sizes. Ricciardi's legacy quickly devolved into a stark contrast to the winning ways of Pat Gillick and the warm, player-friendly days of Gord Ash.

Ricciardi authored some of the most unfortunate contracts in baseball history, the worst of which was likely the notorious Vernon Wells deal. At the end of the 2006 season, despite considerable evidence to suggest such an investment might be unwise, Ricciardi signed Wells to a seven-year, $126 million contract.

Other recipients of his questionable pacts included B.J. Ryan, Alex Rios, Frank Thomas, Corey Koskie, Gregg Zaun, and Kerry Lightenberg. Noted sportswriter Joe Posnanski even suggested Ricciardi should be enshrined in the Bad Contracts Hall of Fame.

Bad investments aside, more serious issues began to arise. Some of the more alarming allegations surfaced when Geoff Baker, then of the *Toronto Star*, wrote an article detailing Ricciardi's aversion to African American players.

Ricciardi's tactical skills were again being called into question as he let Carlos Delgado, one of the greatest players in Toronto history, leave town without offering salary arbitration. In doing so, he forfeited the opportunity to acquire a high draft pick as compensation for Delgado's departure. One of the greatest Blue Jays of all time slipped away with nothing move than a wave good-bye. Another egregious error in judgement occurred when Ricciardi released starting pitcher Chris Carpenter in 2003 as he was recovering from injury. The Blue Jays had traditionally stood by their wounded warriors, but Ricciardi instead opted to cut ties with one of baseball's emerging stars. The St. Louis Cardinals were certainly happy he did, and he has anchored their pitching staff since 2004, even winning the Cy Young Award in 2005.

Rejecting the advice of his entire scouting staff, including noted prospect guru Keith Law, Ricciardi selected pitcher Ricky Romero ahead of Troy Tulowitzki in the 2005 Draft. The shortstop quickly turned into a perennial All-Star, while Romero has been inconsistent at best and is now with the San Francisco Giants. Jeff Blair of

Sportsnet 590 The Fan noted that, "the Blue Jays went through 16 shortstops—16—while Ricciardi was GM."

Ricciardi's draft mantra was to focus almost exclusively on college seniors. This strategy proved to be a major factor in his undoing, as it left the minor league system bereft of high-upside talent. He also principally abandoned the Blue Jays' commitment to Latin American scouting, a move that damaged long-standing relationships in those regions. Toronto's aggressiveness in pursuing Latin American players had previously propelled their playoff teams of the 1980s to success.

Callers to local sports talk radio skewered Ricciardi, urging ownership to cut ties. Ricciardi battled with callers on talk shows, even going so far as to turn one fan's call into an unprovoked attack on Adam Dunn—a player on a different team. It seemed Ricciardi, though, did have one team's best interests at heart—the Boston Red Sox. He openly flirted with the idea of taking the Red Sox GM position, though it was eventually filled by Theo Epstein. In the midst of the 2006 season, Ricciardi sold the rights to Eric Hinske, who had hit 12 home runs in 197 at-bats, assisting the Blue Jays' division rivals with their pennant chase.

He angered the media, even admitting that he misled reporters about Ryan's season-ending elbow injury, which he suffered in spring training. Ricciardi's abrasive personality again caused problems for the Jays when Triple A affiliates were being shifted. Because of its close proximity to Toronto and the connection that exists between the cities with the NFL's Buffalo Bills, the Blue Jays had long considered Buffalo as an ideal place to locate its top-level minor league squad. Instead the New York Mets landed the Buffalo team, and the Jays moved their Triple A team to Las Vegas. "[The] Jays were in the finals," wrote Richard Griffin in a chat on Thestar.com, "but the Jays' then-GM was socially inept in dealing with affiliates, and word got around." (After Ricciardi's departure from the team, the Blue Jays moved their affiliate from Las Vegas to Buffalo for the 2013 season.)

Under Ricciardi's "reign of error," the team further angered fans by changing the blue-and-red colour scheme to a black hat and uniform. Traditions were cast aside in favour of a logo which featured an absurd cartoon befitting the Angry Birds video game.

As fans and media became more and more alienated by Ricciardi's regime, less people went to the park. From 2008 (2.399 million) to 2009 (1.876 million), Blue Jays game attendance fell by more than 20 percent. Some reports surfaced suggesting Ricciardi was less than committed to his job, insinuating that he spent more time at his home in West Boylston, Massachusetts, than in Toronto.

In the end, Blue Jays brass decided it was time for Ricciardi to spend even more time in the Boston area. He was fired with two games remaining in the 2009 season and replaced by one of his assistants, Alex Anthopoulos. Ricciardi's legacy will be remembered as a reversal of nearly everything that the Jays had established during their successful years in the '80s and '90s. Relationships with scouts, media, agents, players, and connections in Latin America needed to be patched. A farm system needed to be restocked. What it meant to be a Blue Jay needed to be rediscovered.

33 Find Babe Ruth's First Professional Home Run Ball

In 1998 the baseball hit by Mark McGwire to set a record of 70 home runs in a single season was sold at auction for $3,005,000. Canadian bazillionaire Todd McFarlane was the buyer, making the ball the most expensive piece of sports memorabilia ever sold.

Imagine the price he or another well-heeled collector might pay for the very first home run ball hit by baseball's most legendary figure, Babe Ruth.

Historians say the only minor league home run ball Ruth ever hit is still located in Toronto. This treasure of epic significance is likely just a short distance from the shadow of the Rogers Centre. But no one can buy Babe Ruth's first professional home run ball, because it's never been found.

Heritage Toronto erected a plaque to commemorate this significant baseball moment, which reads:

> Near this site, in Maple Leaf Park on September 5, 1914, the now legendary baseball player Babe Ruth hit his first home run as a professional. It was to be the only home run he ever hit in the minor leagues.
>
> As a 19-year-old rookie, playing for the Providence Grays in the International League, he connected with a pitch from Ellis Johnson of the Toronto Maple Leafs, sending the ball over the fence in right field and scoring three runs. Pitching for the Grays, Ruth allowed only one hit, earning the title "southside phenom" from the Toronto Daily Star. The final score was Providence Grays 9, Toronto Maple Leafs 0.
>
> Babe Ruth quickly moved up to the major leagues, and played his way to a phenomenal career. The Toronto team went on to win a total of eleven pennants before folding in 1967.

Ruth, still in this teens, swatted Johnson's pitch so deep, it apparently landed in Lake Ontario, just offshore. Dozens have tried to find the ball, but none have unearthed the treasure. While it's quite easy to believe the ball may have disintegrated in the water and sludge of Hanlan's Point, the possibility exists that it may still remain undiscovered in some form.

Before grabbing your snorkel and fins in an attempt to find the collectible, you may want to give it a second thought. Like some stories of Ruth's exploits, the ball might be better to remain a grand, romantic mystique, rather than something baldly tangible.

34 Redhead Redemption

A handsome young redhead, he had all the makings of a champion: raw athleticism, lean muscle, and an imposing stature. But, despite possessing a truckload of natural gifts, the young foal Secretariat would not become a horse worthy of facing serious competition until undergoing intensive training to reshape his psyche.

He had to be broken.

Roy Halladay was also born a thoroughbred, and the redhead would eventually carve out his own niche in sports history. He would win 148 games during his time with the Blue Jays, and establish himself as one of the game's elite pitchers. But, like Secretariat, he hit a few potholes on the road to success.

Halladay moved quickly through the Jays' farm system, debuting with the major league club in 1998 at the tender age of 21. He stayed in the show for the duration of 1999 and held his own, winning eight games and producing an ERA of 3.92. He walked too many batters—79 versus just 82 strikeouts—but he wasn't the first young pitcher to experience control issues. All signs pointed to improvement in the new millennium, and the 6'6" righty took his spot in the Jays' rotation. But instead of getting better, what followed was epic failure.

Five of his first six starts in 2000 went miserably. He won the first, but coughed up six, five, seven, nine, and six runs during the next five April outings. Halladay was pounded twice more, leaving the Jays with little choice but to option their young pitcher to Triple A.

He was recalled later in the season but not much changed. He continued to walk batters and gave up more hits than the team's batting practice chucker. *Sports Illustrated*'s Joe Sheehan called Doc's 2000 season "the worst in history for any pitcher with at least 50 innings pitched." Halladay finished with a dreadful ERA of 10.64, to go along with a WHIP (walks plus hits per inning pitch of 2.20. Using the sabermetric measurement RAA (runs better than average), Doc finished with a -44. In other words, he gave up 44 more runs than an average pitcher would have in his place. Opposing hitters batted a staggering .357 against Halladay that season.

The offseason arrived, and simmering frustrations amongst Toronto's brain trust boiled over. The team was more than disenchanted with the performance of their former first-round draft pick. It was time for a wake-up call.

The Blue Jays demoted Halladay to Single A Dunedin, Florida, prior to the 2001 season—a humbling move. General manager Gord Ash called player development guru Mel Queen to discuss Halladay's struggles. "You've got to fix him," Ash told him.

The notoriously grouchy Queen agreed to the assignment and asked that Halladay be promoted to Double A Knoxville, Tennessee, and placed on the disabled list. *Sports Illustrated*'s Tom Verducci detailed how Queen broke his new stallion.

Halladay was called to Queen's office in Knoxville and received the verbal beatdown of a lifetime. "Look at you! You're stupid! You're an idiot with no baseball intelligence and no guts! You're a pussy!" Queen hollered. Halladay sat silently and took the abuse. "Now, you can walk out of here if you want. You have a guaranteed contract worth millions. You can walk right out of here and you're not going to pitch in the big leagues ever again. But if you want to pitch in the big leagues again, you will do everything I tell you without question."

"Okay," Halladay said. "I'm ready."

"Good. Let's start. How are you doing, Doc?"

"I'm good."

"What?! That's why you're so stupid! You're in Dunedin with a 10 ERA and you're telling me you're good? No! You're not good!"

Queen paused. "Okay, *now* we're going to start."

Looking back on the incident, Queen recalled being pretty harsh with the youngster. "I don't think I ever talked to anybody I hated worse than I talked to him, and I liked him," Queen said. "It was unbelievable how bad it was. He should have knocked my head off and walked out."

Instead, Halladay worked with Queen on his arm slot and release point, changes which produced almost instant results. But the changes to Roy Halladay were also mental. The anguish of the demotion to Single A and the brutal boot camp served to ignite a spark within Halladay. "After being sent to the minors," Halladay said, "I vowed that if I was going to be out of baseball I would be able to look back and say I did everything to the best of my ability."

No longer the passive kid from Denver, Doc became one of the most feared pitchers in Blue Jays history. He won the Cy Young Award in 2003 and went 148–76 during his 12 years with the team.

35 El Cabeza

One glance at a photo of a young Tony Fernandez, and there's little doubt why his childhood nickname was "el Cabeza" or "the Head." His noggin looked a little large and disproportionate, primarily due to the fact the rest of him was so dang skinny. Fernandez came from a poor Dominican Republic family, where his parents worked long hours for miniscule pay in sugar mills. With 11 children and a combined income of just a few dollars per week, food was scarce in the Fernandez household.

They lived in a tin-roofed shack just beyond the outfield fence of Tetelo Vargas Stadium in San Pedro de Macoris. El Cabeza was known to make his way over to the ballpark during game action and dangle from a tree branch positioned along the foul line, waiting for an opportunity to catch a foul ball. On those rare occasions he snared one, he rejoiced that he had an actual baseball with which to play—instead of a dried up fruit or whatever other spherical object he and his pals could find.

Over the course of his childhood, he developed a friendship with renowned scout Epy Guerrero. Whether invited or not, he would climb over the outfield fence from his home and make his way to shortstop to show off his skills for Guerrero at every opportunity.

"When I was a kid, all I ever wanted to be was a baseball player," Fernandez told Buck Martinez in the former catcher's book, *The Last Out*. "We idolized the winter ball players in my hometown. I liked that, and I wanted to be idolized. We listened to every word those players said." Fernandez recalled the kindness of some of the big leaguers who came through his town, "I remember Ray Knight. He came to winter ball in my hometown, and I used to borrow his glove to field ground balls in the infield. I remember Rico Carty. He always brought back supplies and equipment every year for the young kids and clothes for their parents." Little did he know one player who helped him out would someday become his teammate. "I saw Cliff Johnson when I was just a kid, as well," he said. "Cliff would always give me some change to buy oranges from an old lady who had a stand outside the park."

Fernandez rarely strayed from the stadium as a youngster, studying the game with a rabid passion. "I knew most of the players playing winter ball. I'd watch them, listen to them, imitate them." His intense study of the players paid off. Fernandez began to make a name for himself with the Blue Jays, not long after being brought to the team by Guerrero.

Oddly enough, locals from San Pedro de Macoris showered Fernandez with catcalls when he returned for winter ball, angered that the youngster was pushing local legend Alfredo Griffin out of a job. But in time they came to realize they could celebrate the accomplishments of both. "It's safe to say in the Dominican Republic, Tony Fernandez is absolutely respected as a pioneer," said ESPN's Jorge Arangure Jr., an expert on Latin American baseball.

Arangure said Fernandez's ascent in the game came at a time when Latino players received very little support transitioning to life in the United States. "We see the struggles players face now to try to make it to the majors, the cultural differences, coming to a country where you don't speak the language," he said. "These players are astounded when they think back to what Tony Fernandez must have gone through. There weren't any aides when he came up. Now, guys have English classes. The Dominican academies are much more structured. The instruction is much more sophisticated. Dominican players realize exactly what Tony Fernandez needed to do to become a great player."

And a great player he was. Although he was a skilled hitter, memories of Fernandez almost always hearken back to his highlight-reel defensive plays at shortstop. "I get more satisfaction out of a nice fielding play than from a hit or home run," Fernandez said. "I feel that ground balls are my trademark."

Fernandez collected four Gold Glove Awards for his slick fielding. He inspired another generation of young Dominicans, who wanted nothing more than to play like el Cabeza. "He's an icon," Arangure said. Miguel Tejada and Erick Aybar are just a couple of the shortstops who have said they idolized the Toronto superstar.

Announcer Tom Cheek once observed that Fernandez's career was intertwined with the history of the Blue Jays. Fernandez was around to enjoy the successes of the 1980s but left in the team's biggest move—a blockbuster trade, which brought Roberto Alomar and Joe Carter to town. He returned to Toronto for its World Series season of 1993 and was back again in 1998–99. He came and went four separate times, moves which said as much about Fernandez's loyalty to Toronto as the desire of other teams to acquire him. No team could take Fernandez away for long. In a fitting end to his career, the great shortstop returned to Toronto in 2001—one last time—to finish his career playing in the town that embraced him as its own.

Fernandez is now an ordained minister and operates a nonprofit organization with offices in Canada, the United States, and Dominican Republic, which raises funds to assist those in need. "I'm happy in the game and I'm happy out of the game. My faith is a very strong force in my life right now and will continue to be a strong force even after I have left the game of baseball," he said.

36 The Vernon Wells Trade

Samuel Taylor Coleridge famously wrote about the albatross in his poem, *The Rime of the Ancient Mariner*. Seen as a symbol of good luck, the beaked creature leads the ship's trail out of the Antarctic. The Ancient Mariner (insert your own Jamie Moyer joke here) uses his crossbow to kill the bird and is then subjected to a series of unfortunate events. Like with that great story, the legend of Vernon Wells started off rather well.

Selected by Gord Ash with the fifth overall pick in the 1997 Draft, Wells performed admirably, both defensively and offensively. In 2003, he crushed it to the tune of a .317 average, 33 homers, 117 RBIs, and 118 runs, while earning a reputation for stellar glove work.

But, his production with the bat over the next couple of seasons was a bit more pedestrian by comparison.

2004: 536 at-bats, .272 average, 23 home runs, 82 runs, 67 RBIs.
2005: 620 at-bats, .269 average, 28 home runs, 78 runs, 97 RBIs.

A performance trend emerged over those 1,156 at-bats (hardly a small sample size), and it seemed that the real Vernon Wells had stood up. He wasn't Willie Mays. He was—maybe—Jermaine Dye.

But, in a bit of a surprise, Wells bounced back in 2006 with a .303 average and 32 home runs. Who was the real Vernon Wells? The situation was confusing, to say the least.

Baseball Prospectus chimed in on the subject after the season in their annual guide. His profile page reads, "He has had two great seasons in his past four years along with two merely good ones. There's no reason to reject the Occam's razor conclusion that the truth is somewhere in between."

The Other Vernon Wells

Unlikely as it may sound, a 70-year-old Australian actor of some repute shares the name with the ex-Blue Jay. This particular Vernon Wells has been featured in dozens of films, particularly action flicks, starting in the early 1980s. His filmography includes *Commando*, *Mad Max 2*, and *Power Rangers: Time Force*. Most, however, will remember Wells as the terrifying biker (Lord General) who scares the bejesus out of the pimple-faced lead actors in the John Hughes classic, *Weird Science*. Equally impressive as his slice of movie history are his numerous television cameos in shows like *MacGyver*, *Knight Rider*, *The Fall Guy*, and *Hunter*. Sadly, like his baseball-playing namesake, Wells failed to sustain his peak-level production and was reduced to accepting a role in the short-lived television series *The Amazing Live Sea Monkeys*.

But J.P. Ricciardi and others in senior management and ownership seemed convinced they had one of baseball's biggest stars capable of maintaining superstar-level production. Their negotiations were, perhaps, buoyed by Ricciardi's apparent philosophy that Toronto must overpay to retain or acquire talent (because heaven knows talented baseball players wouldn't possibly sign for fair market value to play in one of the world's greatest cities).

Quicker than baseball experts and sabermetricians could say, "They signed him for *how much*?" Wells was inked to a massive $126 million contract spanning seven seasons. The contract was the sixth largest in baseball history and was made all the more imposing by a no-trade clause.

Before the ink on his contract had dried, the former fan favourite began to barrel down the lonely highway from stardom to notoriety. Within months of the deal, Wells' production reverted to levels more consistent with 2004 and 2005. Fans booed mightily.

Wells was a thoughtful guy, generous in community service, and quick to sign an autograph for a young fan…but he just wasn't good enough at the game of baseball to justify the massive sums of money flowing to him. Ricciardi was skewered in the media for the extension. Former *Sports Illustrated* writer Joe Posnanski called it the worst contract in the game of baseball. "[Wells] never got on base much, and he was inconsistent, and…then the Blue Jays gave him this hysterical contract," he said. "This deal, to be honest, is not the sort of thing that leads to a general manager getting fired. It's the sort of thing that leads to entire villages getting pillaged. I mean, this contract alone should be enough to put [Ricciardi] in the Bad Contract Hall of Fame. But when you look over the whole body of work… he IS the Bad Contract Hall of Fame. In fact, really, we should just start referring to bad baseball contracts as 'Ricciardis.'"

So, just as that dead albatross hung from the neck of the Ancient Mariner, the Wells deal became a lingering burden for Ricciardi. The weight of the contract swung from the GM's neck until Paul Beeston dismissed him on October 3, 2009. His firing wasn't just due to one bad contract. It came in response to the team's performance, embarrassing controversies, poor drafts, and a bevy of questionable signings.

Unfortunately, baseball teams can't just fire their centre fielder and walk away from the contract. Incoming general manager Alex Anthopoulos inherited this albatross named Vernon, and there was little hope that he'd be able to rid the team of this crippling contract.

Somehow, some way, Anthopoulos successfully negotiated a deal with Tony Reagins, GM of the Los Angeles Angels of Anaheim, to ship Wells and his horrendous financial commitment to Southern California. In return, the Angels sent Mike Napoli and Juan Rivera to Toronto.

Dumping Wells was a major addition by subtraction for Toronto. How significant a relief was it? This wasn't Rolaids relief. This was burying the dead hobo you've been storing in your trunk for the last couple of years relief. The stench was gone…even if we'll kind of miss having him around.

The dead albatross—the symbol of bad luck—now hung from the neck of Reagins. Compounding his misfortune was the next move, which shipped Napoli to the Angels' division rival, the Rangers, strengthening them as an AL West power.

Soon after, the Angels fired Reagins, and Wells walked away from his playing days in Major League Baseball.

37 Celebrate Jays Legends in Cooperstown

Because of the simple and conservative way it celebrates the game, Cooperstown, New York, is a must-visit for any baseball fan. The village tucked amongst the lush foothills of the Catskill Mountains remains remarkably unexploited. Cooperstown is a pleasant surprise, serving as a stark contrast to some of the less quaint U.S. cities bordering Ontario. (Buffalo and Detroit come to mind.)

Visitors would be remiss if they didn't wander over to Doubleday Field—built upon the grounds where the game is said to have been born. Although historians have debated the origins of baseball, it's safe to say the stadium serves as a powerful monument to the history of the sport. The Blue Jays twice played at the tiny ballpark during the Hall of Fame Game, most recently in 2007.

If you can schedule your visit to include the annual Hall of Fame Weekend, you'll find yourself in the presence of many of the game's greatest living legends, who assemble to honour the newest inductees. Don't be surprised to see former Jays like Paul Molitor or Phil Niekro strolling through town, or notice Dave Winfield enjoying lunch at Nicoletta's Italian Café.

Regardless of when you visit, any fan would enjoy the opportunity to view artifacts which tell the history of baseball. The Baseball

The Blue Jays' Imprint on Cooperstown

Notable Blue Jays Artifacts

- Jersey worn by Frank Thomas when he hit his 500th home run on June 28, 2007
- Jersey worn by first baseman Carlos Delgado during the 2004 season
- Bat used by Carlos Delgado when he hit four home runs in one game on September 25, 2003
- Cap worn by Tony Batista against the Texas Rangers on Opening Day of 2001, Major League Baseball's first Opening Day game in Puerto Rico
- Bat used by Cliff Johnson to set a major league record for most career pinch hit home runs (19)
- Cap worn by Roger Clemens when he recorded his 3,000th strikeout on July 5, 1998
- Ticket from All-Canadian interleague play game between the Montreal Expos and Blue Jays on June 30, 1997
- Ball from Roger Clemens' 200th career win, against the New York Yankees on May 21, 1997
- Bat used by Joe Carter to hit the game-winning home run in Game 6 of the 1993 World Series
- Cap and shoes along with an autographed ball from Dave Stieb's no-hitter on September 2, 1990
- Ball used for first pitch of first game at Toronto SkyDome on June 5, 1989
- A 3-by-3 foot piece of turf from the Toronto SkyDome

Blue Jays in the Hall of Fame

With the election of Roberto Alomar and Pat Gillick in 2011, manager Bobby Cox in 2014, and Frank Thomas in 2016, a total of seven former players and one executive in the Hall of Fame spent some of their professional careers with the Toronto Blue Jays.

Alomar spent five seasons (1991–95) with the Blue Jays and is the first player to enter the Hall of Fame wearing a Blue Jays cap. Pat Gillick joined the team's front office in 1978 and left the team in 1994. They join Rickey Henderson (1993), Paul Molitor (1993–95), Phil Niekro (1987), and Dave Winfield (1992).

Hall of Fame and Museum stands elegantly at 25 Main Street, a short walk from nearly everything else in town. Within the Hall's imposing brick walls are a remarkable collection of memorabilia and tributes to baseball, showcasing the game's evolution.

Toronto-area residents can drive to Cooperstown in about five hours. To celebrate the growing list of baseball legends who've played for the Blue Jays, the journey is well worth it.

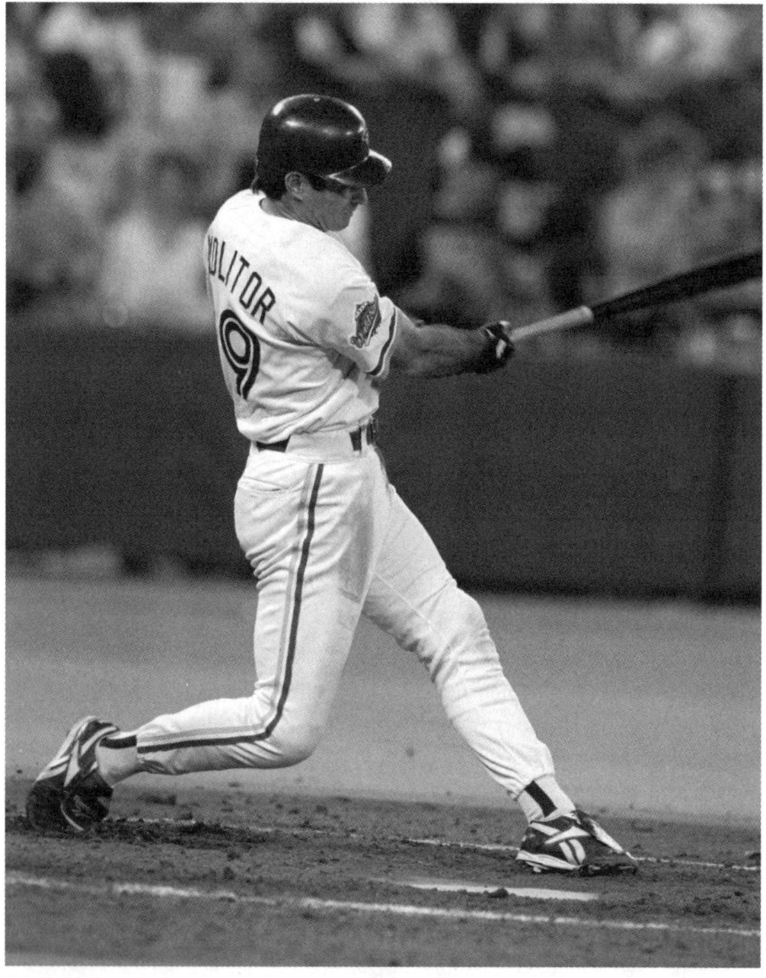

Paul Molitor, who played for Toronto from 1993 to 1995, is one of the seven Blue Jays players in Cooperstown, New York's Hall of Fame.

38 Three Outfielders Born 15 Days Apart

How infinitesimal are the chances that all members of one of the best starting outfields of the 1980s would be born within 15 days of each other?

Three talented teammates, born in a span of a little more than two weeks, rose through the Blue Jays' minor league system to emerge as high-calibre major leaguers. The Jays' outfield trio of Jesse Barfield in right field, Lloyd Moseby in centre, and George Bell in left truly defied the craziest odds to emerge as the linchpins to the team's success in the '80s.

The first to the party was George Antonio Bell Mathey, born on October 21, 1959. Growing up in the city of San Pedro de Macoris, Dominican Republic, Bell was discovered as a teenager by legendary Dominican scout Epy Guerrero.

Guerrero helped Bell land with the Philadelphia Phillies as an amateur free agent in 1978. Left unprotected in the 1980 Rule 5 Draft, Bell was snapped up by Pat Gillick and brought into the fray as a Toronto Blue Jay. After establishing himself as a regular in 1984, he never looked back.

Over the course of his 12-year major league career—nine seasons of which were spent in Toronto—Bell walloped 265 home runs and drove in 1,002 RBIs. Fans who only saw him during the twilight of his career, when he bulked up (translation: got fat), might be surprised to discover that Bell was once a 20–20 player, stealing 21 bases to complement 28 homers in 1985. Bell remains a beloved fixture in Blue Jays history and is treated like a national hero in the Dominican Republic. "Whenever George Bell shows up at a winter league game, it's always a big deal," ESPN's Jorge Arangure Jr. said. "He's an iconic name in the D.R.—one of their first big home run hitters."

Just eight days after Bell's birth, his counterpart in right field, Jesse Lee Barfield, was born in Joliet, Illinois. After playing high school baseball at Joliet Central High School, Barfield was selected by the Jays in the ninth round of the 1977 Amateur Draft and 233rd overall.

His peak season at the plate came in 1986, when the slugger crushed a major league-leading 40 home runs—a feat made more impressive by the fact that it seemingly predates baseball's so-called steroid era. He hit .289 that season with 108 RBIs and 107 runs, collecting a Silver Slugger Award for his efforts.

But Barfield was far more than just an offensive force. The Jays' right fielder gunned down a staggering 162 base runners during his 12-year career. Heaven only knows how many more runs were saved when timid runners retreated to the nearest base rather than test Barfield's laser of an arm.

The third component of the star-studded triumvirate was "Shaker Mo," Lloyd Moseby. Born on November 5, 1959 in the poor southern town of Portland, Arkansas, Moseby might not have had the star power of the other two but was no less valuable to Toronto baseball.

As blogger Andrew Clayman wrote on TheClevelandFan.com, "If you don't remember Lloyd Moseby, you likely don't remember *ALF*, *Real Genius*, or *Tecmo Bowl*, either." He might have been a .257 career hitter, opined Clayman, "but he could steal you 30 bases and hit you 20 bombs."

All told, the Shaker hit 169 major league home runs while stealing 280 bags. He scored 869 runs and collected 737 RBIs. His defensive prowess was equally balanced, as he demonstrated tremendous range and a solid arm. Fans recall that Moseby had a lot of work to do to compensate for Bell's defensive issues in left, and he did so admirably.

And that word, 'balanced,' probably describes Moseby better than any other. He had above-average power, speed, defence, and baseball intelligence, though those skills didn't quite elevate him to the stardom of his outfield mates, Bell and Barfield.

Three stud outfielders, born thousands of miles from each other within 15 days. The chance they would unite to form a truly superb outfield in Toronto is nearly unfathomable.

Suffice it to say, the days from October 21 to November 5 of 1959 were significant ones for the Blue Jays franchise.

39 Dave Stieb's Agonizing Pursuit of a No-No

So what if Dave Stieb couldn't get a no-hitter? He, like nearly every other pitcher to take the mound, might just have to accept the fact that he couldn't dominate an opposing lineup, start to finish, top to bottom, in one sitting. He was a hell of a pitcher, and maybe that was good enough.

Almost from the moment Stieb arrived, he took the league by storm with an aggressive assault on American League hitters. He'd brush them back with high inside heat, then make them look foolish with one of the game's nastiest sliders.

In the 1980s Dave Stieb wasn't just the owner of a devastating repertoire. He was also tough as nails. He pitched an astounding 242 innings for Toronto in just his second season in the big leagues, and later stretched his season high to an even more impressive 288 innings. Those two elements—great stuff and durability—might just be the key ingredients in the recipe for a no-hitter.

And he came awfully close on a number of occasions. He threw a pair of two-hitters between '81 and '82. In five separate games between '82 and '83, he gave up just three hits while pitching complete games. He added three more three-hitters by the end of '85.

Dave Stieb, one of the best pitchers in the majors during the 1980s and the Blue Jays' first ace, went through many close calls before finally notching a no-hitter in September of 1990.

Then came 1988.

Roughly two months into the 1988 season on May 31, Stieb toed the rubber against the Milwaukee Brewers. The Brewers were shut down in order by Stieb until the fourth inning, when B.J. Surhoff collected a single off the Jays ace. Surhoff would prove to be the Brewers' first and only baserunner of the day. With that, Stieb collected his first career one-hitter, and nearly achieved the rare distinction of throwing a perfect game. Nearly.

Five months after his close encounter with perfection, Stieb again flirted with immortality. Facing the Indians in Cleveland, he mowed batters down with relative ease, and despite giving up a pair of walks, appeared destined to slam the door on his first career no-hitter. With two outs in the bottom of the ninth inning, Julio Franco dribbled a grounder to Manny Lee at second base. For a brief moment it seemed a given that Stieb would slay the dreaded no-hitter dragon and earn a spot in baseball history. Instead, baseball history played him. On its way to right field, the ball took a ridiculous bounce over Lee's head, giving the Indians' their only hit that night.

Just six days later, in his very next start, Stieb took on the Baltimore Orioles at Exhibition Stadium in Toronto, he sat the Orioles down in order, with the exception of a hit batsman and a walk. Once again he found himself toeing the pitching rubber with two outs in the ninth inning. He was one ground ball or pop-up away from immortality.

But the baseball gods intervened yet again, allowing pinch-hitter Jim Traber to loop a lazy single over Fred McGriff for the Orioles' only hit.

Now, achieving a no-hitter had seemingly become personal, both for Stieb and for Toronto baseball fans. Maybe he would never fully finish what he started. Maybe Stieb was destined to be just another All-Star pitcher without a no-hitter, like Steve Carlton, Lefty Grove, (and later Greg Maddux, and Roger Clemens).

Maybe it was too monumental a quest. From 1950 until 1988 season, only 96 no-hitters were thrown. Heck, the New York Mets *franchise* didn't even notch a no-hitter until the 2012 season, their 51st year of existence.

The 1989 season brought similar results, fuelling speculation that the star-crossed Stieb might never be able to close the deal. He had a few close calls in '89—two at the expense of the New York Yankees and one versus the Brewers.

The first, and less painful of the two, involved an early-season Yankee Stadium matchup on April 10 versus Andy Hawkins and the Yankees. The only hit he gave up that day was a single to Jamie Quirk in the fifth inning.

The second was perhaps Stieb's most frustrating close encounter, as he carried a perfect game into the ninth inning against the Yankees at the SkyDome on August 4. New York's Roberto Kelly crushed Stieb's hope for perfection with two outs in the ninth, doubling off the ace. Kelly scored on a Steve Sax single, further obliterating the pitcher's nearly spotless performance.

Three weeks later, the one-hitter monster reared its ugly head again, as Stieb one-hit Milwaukee for the second time in as many years. At least the pain was more merciful this time. The solitary hit came in the sixth inning off the bat of the great Robin Yount.

On September 2, 1990, Dave Stieb finally accomplished what seemed utterly impossible. Taking on the Cleveland Indians, he defied detractors who said he couldn't "seal the deal." Stieb tossed his first and only no-hitter that night, striking out nine along the way.

Junior Felix caught Jerry Browne's fly ball for the final out of the game. It was enough to make even the most stoic Jays fans get a bit misty eyed—or at least start growing out Stieb-like moustaches in his honour.

40 Visit the Steam Whistle Brewery

There aren't a heck of a lot of things in life better than heading to a Blue Jays game on a hot summer night in downtown Toronto. As fans stream down Front Street and Queen's Quay, the anticipation of the upcoming game fills the air. It won't be too long before the boys in blue charge out to their positions in the field. Will Aaron Sanchez throw a no-hitter tonight? Will Josh Donaldson launch one into the upper deck?

No matter what might happen, there's something special about the game. It's a steamy night in one of the best cities in the world, and the odds are pretty good that excitement and applause will soon overflow the open Rogers Centre and spill out into the downtown core.

But the game hasn't started yet, and as the crowd walks in lockstep toward the stadium, reality kicks in. It's really freakin' hot. And beers are upwards of $12 at Rogers Centre.

Thankfully, refreshing ways to cool down stand in your midst. You could hit any of the dozens of bars lining Front or maybe hit a wing joint tucked behind the stadium zone. One of the coolest options, literally and figuratively, is the Steam Whistle Brewery, just a five-minute walk from the Rogers Centre.

Fans of local beer dare not cross the stadium turnstiles before enjoying all there is to see and do at the old John Street Roundhouse. Known for its tasty signature pilsners, the brewery is a cool oasis on a balmy baseball night.

Founders Greg Taylor, Cam Heaps, and Greg Cromwell opened the brewery in 2000 with the goal of producing a first-rate pilsner. After formulating their contribution to the world of beer, they set up shop in an impressive old railway building in Toronto's core. Almost equidistant to Rogers Centre and the Air Canada Centre, it's both convenient and a must-see for those attending sporting events and concerts.

After 11:00 AM you can tour the brick-walled brewery, learn how their beer is made, and see how Steam Whistle's facility became designated one of Toronto's green buildings.

Oh—and you'll get to drink some beer, too.

Visitors are shown how Steam Whistle beers are naturally carbonated, and how this process will make Blue Jays fans less bloated when they later head to the game…and perhaps a bit less hungover the next day.

The tour costs around $10, but would be a bargain at twice the price. Cool, fresh pilsner flows, as full-size samples are doled out generously. Considering the cost of a pint in a downtown pub—let alone those Rogers Centre beers—the tour is a downright deal.

Josh Hillinger, retail manager for Steam Whistle, noted the brewery has become a staple of Toronto's gameday experience. "Coming to Steam Whistle prior to a Jays game is a tradition to a lot of people, and not just locals, but also people coming from New York, Detroit, and other U.S. cities," Hillinger said. "On Blue Jays Saturdays, the whistle blows at 11:00 AM to announce that we're opening. We typically have a crowd of 50 to 80 people rushing the front door, dressed in their Jays gear, coming in to get their complimentary sample.

"It's a chance to have a great beer that's brewed in Toronto. We take pride in making sure our staff are always smiling, happy, and welcoming. They love their jobs. We love the fact we're right across the way from the Blue Jays and we'll continue our Blue Jays Saturdays as long as the fans keep coming out."

Heck—tell your better half you went there for a cultural experience. As you walk through the industrial-chic building, pull out your phone and snap a few pics of the unique art and creative design to justify your claim.

Your loved one will be impressed with your worldly tales of culture and history, while you savour fond memories of frosty mugs of local deliciousness.

41 The Jays Promote Anthopoulos

The cream tends to rise to the top, and Alex Anthopoulos was no exception. The Blue Jays' former leader didn't just walk into the role of general manager. He earned it by paying his dues. He got his start in baseball in one of the lowest positions around—so low that he wasn't even paid for it.

After cold-calling Montreal Expos GM Jim Beattie and offering to do any job available just to get into professional baseball, he was offered a volunteer position sorting fan mail. Ever the overachiever, Anthopoulos diligently sifted through autograph requests for the Expos players. And once the mail was properly distributed, he focused on his true love—baseball. "[I] spent my evenings attending Expos games, sitting in the scout seats, and trying to learn more about my passion—scouting and evaluating players," Anthopoulos told BattersBox.ca.

His extracurricular activity began to pay off when the team promoted him into a paid (albeit $7 per hour) internship in media relations and later a scouting-related role. Aware that Montreal's team would soon be heading south, Anthopoulos attended the Major League Baseball Scout School, a forum he used to enhance his knowledge of the game, while also doing as much networking as he could. Along the way, he befriended Jon Lalonde, the Blue Jays' scouting coordinator. In 2003 Anthopoulos landed a scouting position with the Blue Jays, thanks in large part to Lalonde's assistance. "The first time I met him, I thought, 'Where did we get him?'" said Blue Jays president Paul Beeston. "He was different. He was more...worldly. He thought outside the box. He was street smart and intelligent. And he never stopped asking questions. I thought, 'This is the package.'"

His big break came when J.P. Ricciardi was fired, ending the GM's acrimonious and fruitless run at the helm of the Blue Jays. Although Anthopoulos had worked closely with the dismissed Ricciardi, he was clearly his own man and held a completely different view of roster construction.

At the ripe age of 32, Anthopoulos was introduced as the team's new general manager during a press conference. Beeston spoke with reporters about the hiring. "Alex comes with six years working with the Blue Jays and working with J.P," Beeston said at the time. "He knows the organization, he knows the players, he knows the farm system, he knows the scouts, and we're very, very pleased he's accepted the role."

Almost immediately, Anthopoulos took action, shaking up the front office. He relieved player development coordinator Dick Scott, scout Rob Ducey, and Triple A manager Mike Basso of their duties while promoting Tony LaCava, Andrew Tinnish, and Lalonde. "[The] foundation of this organization is going to be scouting and player development," Anthopoulos told reporters. "Scouting and development is very important to me. It's going to be the pillar of what we do here."

In keeping with his philosophies, Anthopoulos added 39 scouts to the Jays' staff—a drastic departure from the methodology of his predecessor, Ricciardi. "If we can't sign CC Sabathia, then we have to find him and develop him," Anthopoulos said. "We have to find as many high-ceiling guys as we can find. We have to look harder, then hit it and hit it hard."

The results were exceptional. Anthopoulos and his staff transformed a system bereft of talent into one of baseball's best. In addition to stocking the minor leagues with high-upside bats, "there's not another team in baseball that has amassed as much really exciting young pitching talent as the Blue Jays," said Kevin Goldstein, former prospect guru at ESPN and Baseball Prospectus. "There's no question about it. It's really impressive."

42 Ricciardi Passes on Tulo

"It's a textbook example of a managerial failure," said Keith Law, ESPN's lead baseball analyst and former special assistant to Blue Jays general manager J.P. Ricciardi.

"The consensus of the people who were hired to evaluate players was to take [Troy] Tulowitzki over [Ricky] Romero," Law told EastWindupChronicle.com. "It wasn't unanimous, but it was the majority opinion."

Blue Jays scouts studied the star shortstop, Tulowitzki, during his impressive college career at Long Beach State, which included selection to the U.S. national team. They saw a guy with incredible range, a power bat, and the ability to take a walk. This guy was the real deal, a sure thing. Picking him was a no-brainer. But without regard to the pleas of others, Ricciardi took his own path in the draft. "The GM substituted his own evaluations based on one observation for each player—and a flawed one at that for Tulowitzki, who was just coming off of a wrist injury," Law said. "Several of us made the case for Tulowitzki over Romero, myself included, but Ricciardi is not one to change his mind. I always thought he rather enjoyed digging in his heels when anyone questioned a decision."

Ricciardi's advisors were taken back by this rash unilateral decision. "There had to be a million dollars in salaries sitting in that draft room, and the GM overruled them. If you're going to hire talented people and pay them all that money, let them do their jobs," said Law, never one to mince words. "If the Jays had Tulowitzki at short, they'd probably be one of the top four teams in the AL."

Ricciardi later said that his decision to choose the left-hander Romero was based on his faith in Russ Adams to develop into a force at shortstop. Adams was Ricciardi's first draft pick in 2002, and the GM wanted to give the youngster every opportunity to succeed. Unfortunately for all parties involved, Adams was a butcher in the field, with 26 errors in 2005, and failed to develop much power or speed.

Romero brought some level of redemption to Ricciardi, contributing three solid seasons to the Jays. But Tulowitzki has been widely considered one of baseball's best shortstops for much of his career. The connection between Tulo and Toronto would take a twist long after Ricciardi was given his walking papers and many years after Tulowitzki trimmed his prodigious early-career mullet. Ricciardi's protégé, Alex Anthopoulos, obtained the Gold Glove shortstop from the Colorado Rockies in a 2015 deadline deal involving Jeff Hoffman and Jose Reyes. Since being acquired, Tulowitzki has grown into a fan favourite for his savant-like defense and has become a respected voice in the Toronto clubhouse.

43 Leading the League in Mormons Since 1977

In the 1800s xenophobes would occasionally use the derogatory term "Blue Jay" to refer to those of the Mormon faith. Although the specific origin of this term is unclear, it has been tracked back to regional lore and folk songs. This little historical fact becomes all the more noteworthy when you consider that the Toronto Blue Jays have featured more notable players of Mormon faith than any other team in baseball history.

Yes, it's quirky and probably nothing more than an odd coincidence, but the Jays have fielded a steady diet of Mormon players, including some of the biggest names in sports. Considering that just 1.4 percent of Americans identify themselves as Mormon, it's fascinating to see how many of the Jays stars of the past come from this religious group.

A parade of Mormon athletes started in 1977, as the Jays acquired their first catcher, Alan Ashby, then followed that move by selecting Danny Ainge in the 15th round of the amateur draft. Louie Gomez was then acquired, and another Mormon member, Jerry Garvin, stepped to the rubber to win 10 games in '77. Garth Iorg worked his way into the lineup the following year, sparking his solid big league career.

At one point, 20 percent of the Jays' roster were Mormons—roughly 10 times the average for the American population.

Ainge would later become the best known of that Mormon quintet, earning notoriety for the legal battle between the Jays and basketball's Boston Celtics. But his best achievements came on an entirely different type of court, as he enjoyed a string of successful seasons as an aggressive—some say dirty—NBA guard. Following his retirement, Ainge moved to the front office and currently serves as the Celtics general manager.

Even as Ainge flirted with his NBA dreams, the Jays steadfastly continued to stockpile Mormon talent, adding the recently baptized Barry Bonnell to their squad. Aware that they had accumulated an unusually large collection of Mormon players, the Blue Jays scheduled "Mormon Night" at Exhibition Stadium during the '81 season to honour them. But the event never occurred because of the players' strike.

Jim Gott was the next to join the group, making his big league debut with the Jays in 1982. Besides building a 14-year career in the bigs, he's also known for coaching Dennis Quaid on the intricacies of pitching to prepare the actor for his lead role in the movie, *The Rookie.*

In later years, Cory Snyder brought his Mormon talents to Toronto followed by reliever Brandon Lyon. A talented pair of Mormons would become crucial to the Blue Jays teams of the 1990s. Jack Morris arrived in Toronto for the 1992 season and won 21 games for Toronto, boosting the team to its first ever World Series championship. That same team included a stud pitcher, David Cone, who was acquired in exchange for a talented Mormon by the name of Jeff Kent. Cone's contributions were nearly as vital to the '92 victory as those of Morris, while Kent went on to stardom elsewhere.

But the biggest Mormon star who would ever suit up for the Jays made his first appearance roughly six years after the Jays' first World Series. Known now throughout the baseball world by just a single-syllable word—Doc—Roy Halladay embarked on a career in 1998 which would net Cy Young Awards in both the American and National Leagues.

Catcher John Buck is the most recent Mormon to suit up for the Blue Jays. Maybe, someday, the most famous current Mormon player, Bryce Harper, will find his way to the Blue Jays.

44 Sit in the Jose Canseco Home Run Section

Joe Carter's 1993 World Series home run remains the most memorable blast in the history of the SkyDome/Rogers Centre. But Jose Canseco's upper deck shot on October 7, 1989 may be the most jaw-dropping home run the building has ever seen.

Long before the 1998 season, in which Canseco joined the Blue Jays and hit 46 home runs, he left a mark on the SkyDome that won't soon be forgotten.

In the fifth game of the American League Championship Series, Canseco of the Oakland A's stepped to the plate against the Blue Jays' Mike Flanagan. The behemoth crushed an inside fastball into the stadium's upper deck—an epic blast which was the first ball to reach the fifth level of the park.

The ball's landing place? Roughly halfway up section 539 and seven seats away from the foul pole. To get a greater appreciation for how far the slugger crushed this pitch, pull up a chair in the section and look toward home plate.

The final measurement of the home run was 484 feet. Rickey Henderson, an A's player who would later win another World Series title with the Jays, calculated it differently. He told reporters the ball travelled *at least* 600 feet. The clout, he said, was "unbelievable." Billy Beane, then a teammate of Canseco on the A's, agreed. "That wasn't just a home run," he said. "It was a home run of biblical proportion."

Canseco, with all his usual bravado, fell short of humility in discussing the moonshot. "I've probably hit 10 or 15 longer ones in Oakland alone," Canseco said. "I hit one there in September of '85, when I first came up, that carried over the seats behind the centre-field fence and hit the back wall. That was at night and at least 500 feet. If I were to hit it that hard here, it might go through the roof."

The instant the ball launched off Canseco's bat, the crowd at the Blue Jays' packed stadium fell silent. It was almost as if the jaws of each patron in attendance fell in unison, and you could hear a pin drop. "[There are] 50,000 people here, and I've heard libraries louder," announcer Bob Costas said.

The crowd, though, quickly recovered from the shock, showering the archenemy Bash Brothers (Canseco and Mark McGwire) with jeers. And anyone who believes Bud Selig's claim that the game of baseball wasn't aware of the use of performance-enhancing drugs until the 2000s clearly wasn't in attendance that afternoon. The crowd keenly observed—in October 1989—that Canseco and others might be getting a bit of assistance with their power strokes. "STEROIDS, STEROIDS!" they chanted before Canseco's at-bats.

It took commissioner Bud Selig another 16 years to make the same observation. Ironically, it was Canseco himself who exposed baseball's dirty little PED secret in his autobiography, *Juiced: Wild Times, Rampant 'Roids, Smash Hits, and How Baseball Got Big.*

45 The 1976 Expansion Draft

Where did it all start? The Seattle Mariners and Toronto Blue Jays met in New York City on November 5, 1976 to participate in the Major League Baseball expansion draft. For the paltry investment of $175,000 per player, the teams acquired the rights to unwanted/unprotected players from other major league rosters.

The Mariners entered the draft with a jovial tone, allowing cornball comedian and part-owner Danny Kaye to announce their first selection and deliver a few cheesy punch lines along the way. Asked to state the age of the Mariners' first pick, Ruppert Jones, Kaye said "21—and isn't that a shame?" in a joke only our parents' parents might appreciate.

The Jays, on the other hand, took on a dry tone, assigning general manager Peter Bavasi to conduct their draft and announce the team's first pick.

From a strategic standpoint, the teams differed, as well. While the Mariners sought more established talent, the Jays came into the draft targeting high-upside youth. Toronto grabbed a super-utility player, Bob Bailor, with its first selection with the intention of starting him at short. "He was the best shortstop available," Bavasi said. "We've said all along we'll concentrate on building strength up the middle."

After grabbing Bailor, the Jays used three of their other first round selections to grab 20-year-old pitchers Jerry Garvin, Jim Clancy, and Claude "Butch" Edge. "We decided to bite the bullet," Bavasi said. "We thought they were the best young arms available, so we took them."

In a move which appeared to contradict its tactical plan, the Blue Jays selected Rico Carty, an established big league veteran coming off a .310, 83-RBIs season with the Cleveland Indians. But Bavasi grabbed him as a trade chip, and sure enough, the designated hitter was soon dealt back to the Indians for Rick Cerone and John Lowenstein.

Bavasi observed quite early that his expansion rivals, the Mariners, were headed in a different direction, strategically. "Seattle is going for older players than we are," he said. After grabbing the youthful Jones first overall (as noted by Mr. Kaye), they picked up Gary Wheelock (24), Bill Stein (29), Dick Pole (26), Dan Meyer (24), and Grant Jackson (34). Lou Gorman, the Mariners chief of baseball operations, was somewhat defensive when it was implied his club's strategy as less sound than Toronto's. "I don't think

1976 Major League Baseball Expansion Draft

Toronto's Selections

Pick	Player	Position	Former Team
2	Bob Bailor	OF-SS	Baltimore Orioles
4	Jerry Garvin	P	Minnesota Twins
6	Jim Clancy	P	Texas Rangers
8	Gary Woods	OF	Oakland Athletics
10	Rico Carty	DH	Cleveland Indians
12	Butch Edge	P	Milwaukee Brewers
13	Al Fitzmorris	P	Kansas City Royals
15	Al Woods	OF	Minnesota Twins
17	Mike Darr	P	Baltimore Orioles
19	Pete Vuckovich	P	Chicago White Sox
21	Jeff Byrd	P	Texas Rangers
23	Steve Bowling	OF	Milwaukee Brewers
26	Dennis DeBarr	P	Detroit Tigers
28	Bill Singer	P	Minnesota Twins
30	Jim Mason	SS	New York Yankees
32	Doug Ault	1B	Texas Rangers
34	Ernie Whitt	C	Boston Red Sox
36	Mike Weathers	IF	Oakland Athletics
37	Steve Staggs	2B	Kansas City Royals
39	Steve Hargan	P	Texas Rangers
41	Garth Iorg	3B	New York Yankees
43	Dave Lemanczyk	P	Detroit Tigers
45	Larry Anderson	P	Milwaukee Brewers
47	Jesse Jefferson	P	Chicago White Sox
49	Dave McKay	2B-3B	Minnesota Twins
51	Tom Bruno	P	Kansas City Royals
53	Otto Velez	OF	New York Yankees
55	Mike Willis	P	Baltimore Orioles
57	Sam Ewing	OF	Chicago White Sox
59	Leon Hooten	P	Oakland Athletics

Seattle's Selections

Pick	Player	Position	Former Team
1	Ruppert Jones	OF	Kansas City Royals
3	Gary Wheelock	P	California Angels
5	Bill Stein	3B	Chicago White Sox
7	Dick Pole	P	Boston Red Sox
9	Dan Meyer	1B	Detroit Tigers
11	Grant Jackson	P	New York Yankees
14	Dave Collins	OF	California Angels
16	Frank MacCormack	P	Detroit Tigers
18	Stan Thomas	P	Cleveland Indians
20	Juan Bernhardt	OF	New York Yankees
22	Rick Jones	P	Boston Red Sox
24	Glenn Abbott	P	Oakland A's
25	Bob Stinson	C	Kansas City Royals
27	Carlos Lopez	OF	California Angels
29	Dave Pagan	P	Baltimore Orioles
31	Roy Thomas	P	Chicago White Sox
33	Tom McMillan	SS	Cleveland Indians
35	Pete Broberg	P	Milwaukee Brewers
38	Steve Braun	OF	Minnesota Twins
40	Leroy Stanton	OF	California Angels
42	Bob Galasso	P	Baltimore Orioles
44	Steve Burke	P	Boston Red Sox
46	Joe Lis	1B	Cleveland Indians
48	Alan Griffin	P	Oakland A's
50	Bill Laxton	P	Detroit Tigers
52	Julio Cruz	2B	California Angels
54	Steve Barr	P	Texas Rangers
56	Puchy Delgado	OF	Boston Red Sox
58	Tommy Smith	OF	Cleveland Indians
60	Greg Erardi	P	Milwaukee Brewers

Toronto has done better," he said. "I would not swap our list for their list. They took some real young pitching arms who may be heard from later."

Bavasi, on the other hand, glowed about his selections. "We have youth and speed," he said. "We are strong up the middle. We have a strong foundation." As part of his quest to strengthen the team up the middle, Bavasi flipped pitcher Al Fitzmorris to the Indians for catcher Alan Ashby and first baseman Doug Howard just moments after the final round of the draft.

Bavasi admitted that the team began to experience a serious case of self-doubt as they watched the Mariners grab more established players. "We came close to changing direction and going for age about halfway through," Bavasi said. "Maybe we were influenced by what the other team was doing, but our scouts advised us to stay with the policy we had established."

When all was said and done, the 1976 MLB Expansion Draft took seven hours, with each team selecting 30 players to fill their new rosters. The Jays grabbed 16 pitchers, one catcher, seven infielders, five outfielders, and one designated hitter.

It took a few years for the talent to blossom, but the ultimate returns strongly favoured the Jays. Their selections helped them achieve 11 consecutive seasons above .500, a string which started in 1983. The Mariners, on the other hand, struggled mightily and failed to post a winning season until 1991, their 15th season in the league.

The Mariners' biggest prizes out of the draft were Dan Meyer, who played five solid, if unspectacular, seasons with them, and Jones, who played three years in a Mariners uniform before being traded to the Yankees. Their only other notable selections were Puchy Delgado and Dick Pole—who might have been drafted just to provide Kaye with some new material.

The Blue Jays walked away from the draft with a number of talented players, some of whom would be crucial to their success in the 1980s. Jim Clancy became a workhorse in the Jays rotation, while Ernie Whitt was a future All-Star. Garth Iorg, Otto Velez, and several other draftees went on to varying levels of success in Toronto.

Years later, Bavasi was asked to describe the expansion draft process. Despite the relative success his Blue Jays team experienced in 1976, he was still brutally honest about the calibre of talent coming out of the draft these days. "If you understand the other owners just want to take your money and make you lousy, you'll have a better time," he said. "You're going to get has-beens, never-weres, and used-to-bes."

Another general manager who went through the expansion process was equally sceptical of the talent level of the available players. Former Houston Astros GM Tal Smith suggested the Blue Jays had carried out a clever expansion draft strategy, succeeding where others had failed. "The best example I can give is with Toronto in 1976," Smith said. "They picked a 21-year-old guy named Jim Clancy who few people had ever heard of, no previous experience, and he's had a very solid career, obviously."

46 A.A. Reshapes the Jays

Engaged in a bidding war with the Chicago Cubs and Los Angeles Dodgers, Alex Anthopoulos spoke with the catcher's agent. "Just so you know, I'm signing the player," he said.

Never before had he given a free agent more than a three-year contract—and never for more than $16 million. But opportunities like this one don't come around often. The Blue Jays ponied up and got their man.

Russell Martin, All-Star receiver and pitch framer extraordinaire, signed with Toronto for five years and $82 million. There was a buzz around the league, as other teams took notice of the Jays' bold contract and the fact they beat out the Cubs and Dodgers for the prized commodity. "Definitely the hardest I've ever worked on pursuing a free agent," said Anthopoulos in describing the signing as the "key" to the team's offseason.

Martin's addition not only upgraded the catcher position from an offensive perspective, but it also provided the benefits that come with his Gold Glove-caliber presence behind the plate. It also provided the intangible benefit of adding an established veteran with a winning track record. Oh, and he's also Canadian, which is always a bonus. The signing wasn't the first November transaction completed by A.A. Two smaller deals brought fly ball pitcher Marco Estrada to Toronto for Adam Lind and Triple A second baseman Devon Travis for Anthony Gose.

With those three pieces in place, A.A. continued to work the phones. About two weeks later, he traded for Josh Donaldson. While the Martin signing was viewed as a foundational move, the addition of Donaldson was downright franchise-altering. The multi-talented Donaldson was under an affordable contract with four years of control remaining. "In acquiring Donaldson, the Jays get a player who by all rights should never even have been available," Blue Jays broadcaster Mike Wilner told Sportsnet. "Guys like this almost never get moved in trades, but the Blue Jays used their surplus of young starting pitching and dangled the carrot of the super-toolsy and fantastically talented Barreto in addition to the super-toolsy and fantastically talented Lawrie and wound up picking up what may not wind up being the biggest name to be moved this winter, but who will certainly be the most productive player to be moved."

Both Martin and Donaldson lived up to the hype, diving into the stands and jumping into dugouts, providing superlative

Russell Martin: Video Game Cover Model

In quite an honour, Russell Martin was selected to grace the cover of the Canadian edition of MLB 15: The Show. Martin said that many of his childhood evenings were spent with a controller in his hand. "I'd spend the whole day out playing baseball with friends and my dad and then later at night instead of watching TV, I'd play video games. Whatever way I could find to compete, I'd compete," he said. "R.B.I. Baseball, Blades of Steel, I logged a lot of hours playing those types of games back in the day."

The Jays clubhouse is home to a bit of gaming as well with players like Martin, Brett Cecil, and Dioner Navaro playing FIFA and Mortal Kombat.

Always thinking strategy, Martin gave his thoughts on how one might hope to strike out teammate Jose Bautista when facing him in the midst of a game. "Jose's very aggressive, so I know he's probably going to be looking for early contact and he definitely wants to swing the bat," Martin said. "So I would just throw a lot of pitches outside the strike zone, try to get him to chase and I think he'd get a little tired, a little impatient. That's how I'd beat him."

offensive production, and bringing veteran leadership to a team that had been known to have at least a modicum of clubhouse issues. The Jays headed toward the trade deadline hovering around .500. Just when it seemed the roster was cemented, another stunner came across the wire. The Blue Jays had acquired the immensely talented Troy Tulowitzki and veteran reliever LaTroy Hawkins. "After dealing for Donaldson, signing Russell Martin, and now adding one of the game's best-known stars in Tulowitzki," wrote Jeff Todd of MLB Trade Rumors, "Anthopoulos and his club are fully committed to win now in a manner not previously seen."

News of the Blue Jays' acquisition of Tulo seemed to come completely out of left field for many observers, as most speculation had the Jays working to bolster their struggling rotation. Hawkins would fill a void in the pen, but this was still an incomplete roster.

If the Jays wanted to win now, why add to an already powerful offense when the team so badly needed a starting pitcher? Like a late night informercial host darting out from the corner of your TV screen, Alex Anthopoulos said, "But wait...there's more!"

As in, frontline starter David Price.

The Blue Jays capped off this massive rebuild with the additions of reliever Mark Lowe, speedy Ben Revere, and the multi-positional Swiss Army knife known as Cliff Pennington. "He kept pushing and identified if we're going to get over the top here this year we're in a good position," manager John Gibbons said. "But we need to do something else. He went out and made the big trades and we took off."

Acquisitions of this sort come at a cost—sometimes hefty (cough-cough Noah Syndergaard). Gone were highly regarded pitchers Jeff Hoffman, Miguel Castro, Jesus Tinoco, and clubhouse favorite Jose Reyes in the Tulo deal. Top pitching prospect Daniel Norris was sent to the Detroit Tigers, along with Matt Boyd and Jairo Labourt. Wild-cards Alberto Tirado, Jimmy Cordero, Jake Brentz, Nick Wells, and Rob Rasmussen also left in the trading flurry.

Some of those names may eventually come back to haunt the team to a degree. But the 2015 Blue Jays were *all in*, and Anthopoulos had pulled off one of the most remarkable midseason remodeling jobs in MLB history.

47 Listen to the *Birds All Day* Podcast and Visit the Tao of Stieb

If there is a voice of reason for rabid Blue Jays fans, it comes in the form of a podcast known as *Birds All Day*. Guiding fans through the various and sundry happenings of the team, hosts Andrew Stoeten and Drew Fairservice provide perspective in times that need it most. When the bungling son of Ted Rogers makes infuriating decisions, the podcast is there. When the team's performance wavers between thrilling and putrid, the podcast is there to provide perspective and share our angst. When the team fails to tender an offer to someone like, say, David Price, Stoeten and Fairservice are there to tell you they didn't have a hope in hell of re-signing him anyhow. Clubhouse controversies, on-field issues, questionable transactions…nothing is off-limits for the semi-regular recordings, which have become the gold standard of Toronto sports podcasting.

Why does it work so well? Stoeten and Fairservice speak bluntly and from the heart. The result is a pragmatic, thoughtful account of everything Blue Jays, often serving as the most honest assessment of the realities surrounding the team. It's also highly entertaining, as the sardonic hosts pull no punches in their commentary.

It should also be noted that the pair of hosts have their own separate blogs, which are also some of the most insightful Jays-related writing on the interwebs. Stoeten's work, and the work of others like Cam Lewis, can be found at BlueJaysNation.com. The site is a daily must-read for anyone looking for thoughtful opinion and commentary pertaining to the Jays.

The site JaysFromTheCouch.com has emerged as a source of high-quality content for fans of Toronto's team. Led by founder and senior editor, Shaun Doyle, the site is packed with analysis, rumours, and great writing by folks like William Wilson and Roy-Z.

The Tao of Stieb blog, now affiliated with Rogers Sportsnet, is an equally insightful look at the team. Written by an anonymous blogger, the site's writing is insightful and cutting. The man behind the blog explained the site's name to a source at Sportnet. "The blog title is a tribute most obviously to the man with the greatest slider-moustache combination in baseball history," he said, "as well as to one of my all-time favourite movies, *The Tao of Steve.*"

The Blue Jay Hunter is a blog which hankers for the golden era of Blue Jays baseball. An equally secretive writer, Ian, covers the Blue Jays with particular consideration to the players of years gone by. His writings serve to document moments—big and small—in Blue Jays history, which helped shape the team into whatever it is today and will be in future years.

Bluebird Banter, a member of SB Nation, serves as a high-calibre forum for Jays bloggers and fans to vent their innermost feelings about the team. The content is as compelling as the sites run by more seasoned writers and often has an edgier tone. Radio host Mike Wilner and Ben Ennis's "Blue Jays this Week" landing page on the Sportsnet.ca offers a recap of postgame call-in shows, and Blue Jays Rundown, also on the site, provides ongoing team coverage.

JaysProspects.com offers a bevy of high-calibre coverage of the team's minor league system. It's the ideal place for fans to follow the development of the next wave of Jays talent with in-depth player profiles, interviews, and columns. Kevin Gray's blog, Gray Matter, is another prospect-related blog but comes from the perspective of a reporter covering the New Hampshire Fisher Cats. BattersBox.ca is the Vancouver Canadians' equivalent.

Some of baseball's most clever bloggers cover the Blue Jays. They are sometimes raunchy, often scathing, but always devoted to their one true love—the Blue Jays.

48 Little White Lies

A jay's gifts, and instincts, and feelings, and interests, cover the whole ground. A jay hasn't got any more principle than a congressman. A jay will lie, a jay will steal, a jay will deceive, a jay will betray; and four times out of five, a jay will go back on his solemnest promise. The sacredness of an obligation is a thing which you can't cram into no bluejay's head.—Mark Twain, "What Stumped the Bluejays"

Many employers offer an Employee Assistance Progam (EAP) as part of their compensation package. The subsidized programs typically allow staff to talk about their issues with a professional—often a psychiatrist or psychologist. When Tim Johnson, manager of the Toronto Blue Jays, called the team EAP, he wasn't looking for help dealing with a family matter, or stress pertaining to the team's on-field performance. The Jays, in fact, had finished with an 88–74 record in 1998, his first season as a big league manager. It was a decent finish in the tough American League East and perhaps a harbinger of good things to come.

But Johnson contacted the EAP to set up a meeting with Tim Hewes, the program director. He had something kind of big he needed to get off his chest—something about his service in the Marines.

Time and time again throughout his playing and coaching careers, Johnson told elaborate tales of his service in Vietnam. He shared such stories with teammates in the Milwaukee Brewers organization and Toronto and later—as a scout, coach, and manager—he used the brutal details to motivate players. He spun his epic yarns throughout the minor league systems of the Los Angeles Dodgers, Montreal Expos, Chicago Cubs, and Boston Red Sox.

In one clubhouse sermon, Johnson spoke of shooting a young Vietnamese girl during his service, emoting all the pain and agony of the experience, to push his team to work harder on the field. During a key series versus Boston in 1998, Johnson chose to pitch Roger Clemens in the final game of the series, bumping Pat Hentgen from his normal slot in the rotation. When Hentgen complained, Johnson told him he didn't know the first thing about how to handle tough scenarios, telling his pitcher, "Pressure is Vietnam."

The stories were gory, and they were gruesome. They were inspirational, and they were motivating. But above all else, Johnson's stories were 100 percent, Grade-A bullshit.

Johnson hadn't spent even a moment of service time on Vietnamese soil. The truth of the matter was that he was a member of the Marine reserve and had been involved in training recruits on the use of mortars at Camp Pendleton near San Diego. While brave Marines headed to Vietnam to put themselves in harm's way, wading through swamps and wondering if they'd see another sunrise, Tim Johnson woke up to warm California mornings and headed to the Dodgers' minor league stadium for batting practice.

The Jays coaching staff, including pitching coach Mel Queen and first base coach Jack Hubbard, suspected that Johnson might not have been entirely truthful early in the '98 season. They'd heard rumblings that their manager was a bit of a fibber from within the Red Sox organization, for whom Johnson had worked prior to accepting the gig with the Jays.

But it wasn't until players in the organization spoke with Geoff Baker, then of the *Toronto Star*, that the crap really hit the fan. Baker heard those same rumblings and began to dig deep with several Blue Jays players and coaches in an attempt to unearth the extent of Johnson's lies. He compiled the accounts, both on and off-the-record, and went public to lambaste Johnson with a detailed exposé. Baker's story appeared on the front page of the *Star* sports section during October. *The Boston Globe* columnist

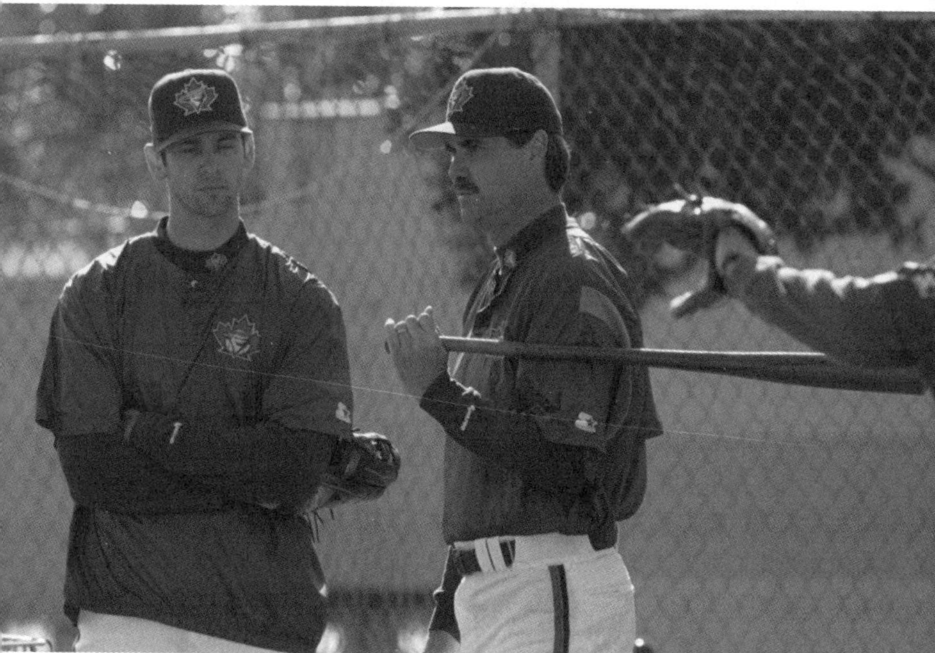

During spring training, Shawn Green (left) talks with manager Tim Johnson, whose lies about his Vietnam War experience led to his dismissal.

Will McDonough corroborated the story by confirming Johnson "used to enthrall players and management alike with tales of his adventures in Vietnam with the U.S. Marines."

The reports by Baker and McDonough spread like wildfire and quickly became the lead story on Canada's TSN sports program. Johnson's world was crumbling around him. Remorseful, he sat down with EAP director Hewes. "This has been something that's been bothering me for 28 years," Johnson said. "It's been a guilt for a long time that I've had. There's been this big weight on me."

Following a team meeting, Johnson spoke with local and national reporters to confront his shame. "Friends of mine were going to Vietnam when I was going to spring training," he said. "While they were off fighting and getting killed, I was playing baseball. I've dealt with the guilt for 30 years."

Farrell Leaves for His "Dream Job"

He came, he saw, but he didn't do a whole hell of a lot of conquering. John Farrell served as Blue Jays manager for two years, winning just 154 games during that span, while losing 170.

Arriving in Toronto as a sought-after managerial prospect, Farrell produced a .500 record in his first season at the Jays' helm. His second year, however, had more than its share of acrimony, as injuries and an apparent lack of accountability created strife in the clubhouse. Was Farrell distracted?

The *Toronto Sun* said, "The man was just putting in time before his 'dream job' opened up." Farrell classified the Boston Red Sox job as such during his introductory press conference, an unfortunate choice of words which implied the Toronto position was of lesser value.

Technically, Toronto traded Farrell to the Red Sox (for shortstop Mike Aviles), but the move was a foregone conclusion the moment he approached Toronto brass to request permission to leave. "Boston is, in my mind…is the epicenter of the game," Farrell said. "The passion of this region, the energy that is in this ballpark every single night, I think, to a certain extent that energy and what people expect, holds our players accountable with the effort that they put out every single night."

In fleeing Toronto for pastures he perceived to be greener, Farrell joins an extensive group of sports personalities on the city's list of "persona non grata." Most recently, J.P. Ricciardi was the most reviled subject of scorn, and before him, Vince Carter (the former Toronto Raptors wing) was booed vigorously every time he touched the ball, in response to his snub of the T-Dot. Since the move to Boston, Farrell has been mercilessly jeered by the Toronto faithful whenever he steps on the Rogers Centre field.

The move was also significant because of the unconventional major league player for manager swap. It was the first in the majors since the Tampa Bay Devil Rays snagged Lou Piniella from the Seattle Mariners in exchange for Randy Winn in 2002. Ozzie Guillen was also acquired by the Miami Marlins from the Chicago White Sox before the 2012 season, but he was traded for minor league prospects—infielder Ozzie Martinez and reliever Jhan Marinez.

Ultimately, Aviles and utility player Yan Gomes were traded to the Cleveland Indians for reliever Esmil Rogers. And in a fitting conclusion to the Farrell saga, the Blue Jays received a significant injection of talent (Josh Johnson, Mark Buerhle, Jose Reyes, and others) just weeks after shipping Farrell to Boston. On the other hand, Farrell inherited a troubled Boston squad which won just 69 games in 2012.

Farrell's replacement was John Gibbons, who managed the Jays from 2004–2008 to a .500 record (305–305) and spent the 2011 season managing the San Diego Padres' Double A affiliate, San Antonio Missions. Gibbons was all smiles when introduced as the new leader of the massively-improved Blue Jays and for good reason.

He admitted the stories of Vietnam were total fabrications. Oh, and that line in his biography in the Blue Jays media guide, saying he was a high school basketball All-American who turned down a scholarship at UCLA? Yeah, that was utter bullshit, too, he would later admit.

General manager Gord Ash stood by his manager, believing that he deserved a chance to redeem himself. Johnson made peace with Coach Queen about the issues and prepared for a fresh start in 1999.

But as the Jays carried out their first spring training following the exposé and confessions, former Blue Jay Ed Sprague brought the story back to the headlines by sharing his disgust for Johnson. He referred to his former manager as a "backstabber" and a "liar." Hentgen's displeasure with his field boss was also well-known.

When the team sputtered to a 3–12 start in spring training of '99, Ash had seen enough. He dismissed Johnson. "The unsettledness and the distractions had become the issue," Ash said. "It had become apparent it wasn't going to work."

After filling various managerial roles for clubs in the Mexican League and independent baseball, Johnson is currently unemployed.

49 Visit the Jays' Minor League Affiliates

There might not be a better way for Blue Jays fans to enhance their appreciation for the franchise than to visit each of its minor league components. Although recent trades have sent away some captivating minor league talent, a plethora of exciting arms and big bats await at every stop.

A tour of the Jays' affiliates should start with a visit to the Dominican Summer League, the most junior affiliate of the big club. The season typically runs from the end of May until the third week of August and has recently featured players like pitchers Henderson Alvarez, traded to the Miami Marlins during the 2012 offseason, and Nestor Molina. A visit to this rookie level team is made even more compelling by the fact the team plays in San Pedro de Macoris, the birthplace of George Bell, Tony Fernandez, and Manuel Lee—key components of the great Blue Jays teams of the 1980s.

Not far from the Dominican Republic is another rookie level affiliate of the Blue Jays. The Gulf Coast League Blue Jays play their games at the Bobby Mattick Training Center at Englebert Complex in Dunedin, Florida. Not to be confused with the Dunedin Blue Jays, who also play at the complex, the GCL Jays play an abbreviated season in the low minors.

Besides being the longtime spring training home of the Jays, the Englebert Complex offers fans a relaxing atmosphere to watch some of the freshest talent in the organization. The team features a number of recent draft picks and international signees, but visitors will find no shortage of available seats, as the games are typically only watched by scouts and a handful of bored retirees looking for a bit of entertainment.

If you're looking to check out the Blue Jays' top prospect, Vladimir Guerrero Jr., head to Bluefield, West Virginia, home of another rookie league affiliate. The Bluefield Blue Jays play their home games at the recently renovated Bowen Field, the park where Cal Ripken Jr. and Eddie Murray began their baseball careers. Head downtown after the game and you might even get a free beverage. For almost 75 years, the local chamber of commerce has distributed free lemonade whenever the temperature exceeds 90 degrees Fahrenheit (32 Celsius).

Vancouver, British Columbia, is home to Canada's only remaining team in the minor leagues. The Single A Vancouver Canadians play at Scotiabank Field at Nat Bailey Stadium and have a long history of star talent flowing through their roster. Rickey Henderson, Jose Canseco, and Sammy Sosa are just a few of the players who have sat in Vancouver's dugout. In 2012 the Blue Jays sent first-round pick Marcus Stroman to the Canadians to introduce him to professional ball and Canadian culture.

The Class A Lansing Lugnuts take the field in the Michigan state capital, just a five hour drive from Toronto. There may never be a better time to make the drive than right now, as the team is absolutely loaded with high-ceiling talent about to move up the organizational ladder. Right-hander Justin Maese is one to watch, as is fellow righty T.J. Zeuch. Cavan Biggio, son of Hall of Famer Craig, mans second base for the squad.

The Dunedin Blue Jays (Class A Advanced) are the senior of the two teams playing at the Bobby Mattick Training Center. Typically, pitchers assigned to the squad are sent there to work on their command and control, while batters are working on their swing and defensive inconsistencies. Tickets are typically just $6, even when major league superstars like Jose Bautista play there on rehab assignments, as he did in 2012.

To check out Double A action, head to Manchester, New Hampshire, home of Northeast Delta Dental Stadium. With a friendly ballpark atmosphere, the New Hampshire Fisher Cats have earned a reputation as one of the best-run minor league teams in baseball.

For a sneak preview of some of the Blue Jays of tomorrow, fans from the Toronto and southwest Ontario region can make the short drive to Buffalo, New York, to watch the Triple A Bisons. With just 160 kilometres (99 miles) separating the Rogers Centre from Buffalo's Coca-Cola Field, Blue Jays fans can easily cross the U.S./Canada border, attend a game, and return to their Ontario homes in time to catch the middle innings of games on the West Coast. But, if you're looking for some local flavour after the game, head over to the Anchor Bar, home of the original Buffalo-style chicken wings.

The Blue Jays had hoped to place their Triple A team in Buffalo years ago, but former general manager J.P. Ricciardi botched the deal, and the team put its affiliate in Las Vegas instead. On September 18, 2012, the Blue Jays organization announced it had moved its squad to Buffalo, while the New York Mets have moved theirs to Las Vegas. Ironically, J.P. works for the Mets now. Coincidence?

For fans of the Blue Jays, there might never be a better time to take a tour of the team's affiliates.

50 The Football Star and the Beauty Queen

He was called "Xanthos," which means "blond male" in Greek. According to Greek mythology, Achilles used an immortal blond-haired horse of the same name during battle. So, when a young, blond stallion named Kelly Gruber arrived in Toronto, the media assigned him an apt nickname. His flowing locks were unquestionably a product of his genes. The fire that burned in the belly of Gruber, however, was likely fuelled by external sources.

Gruber's biological father was an athlete in his own right, football standout Claude King. By all accounts, King treated Kelly well, but he was devoted to his career as a running back with the Chicago Bears, New England Patriots, and Houston Oilers. He left Kelly and his mother, Gloria, to focus on that football career, which would ultimately end with the Saskatchewan Roughriders.

Gloria, a former Miss Texas, was forced to go back to work following the split, leaving Kelly to be raised by his grandparents. Not long after, she remarried a man named David Gruber, who adopted Kelly as his own. The return to a nuclear family fell short of normalizing his life. David beat Kelly for perceived indiscretions and childish behaviour. The elder Gruber was a control freak, which caused Kelly to rebel even more against his new father. Later in life, David apologized for his actions. "Unfortunately, I was only twenty-six or twenty-seven at the time," he said, "and I didn't know how to handle a strong-willed child."

David and Gloria eventually agreed upon a better disciplinary strategy for their child. "Instead of whipping him so much, I'd get him to run whenever he acted up," David said. "He'd burn off energy, release his frustrations, and improve his speed." The move paid off. Kelly Gruber excelled at sports, and the Jays took an interest in the kid from Westlake High School in Austin, Texas. "Gruber just stood out," Jays scout Al LaMacchia said. "You knew you were dealing with a tremendous athlete. The way he fielded. Nice soft hands. The arm. The way he hit. His stroke. It was all there, and he was just a kid. First swing he took, I made a mental note to come and see him next year."

But the Jays didn't draft Gruber. The Cleveland Indians selected him 10th overall, while the Jays grabbed the immortal Garry Harris with their pick. Gruber failed to live up to his draft slot in four minor league seasons. Unimpressed, the Indians left him exposed for the Rule 5 draft. The Blue Jays, who excelled at scouring Rule 5 players, snapped up Gruber's rights from Cleveland.

Gruber showed marked improvement in the Jays system, hitting .269 with 21 home runs and 55 RBIs in 97 games. He travelled back and forth between Triple A Syracuse, New York, and the big leagues for months, which became years. But his big break came in 1987, when Garth Iorg was cut loose by the Jays. Gruber was called up to platoon with Rance Mulliniks. He earned his big league stripes the following season, hitting .278 with 16 home runs and 81 RBIs. Gruber started 156 games at third in 1988, and he was everything the team hoped. He hit .278 with 16 home runs, 23 stolen bases, and 81 RBIs, establishing himself as one of the best third basemen in the game. He topped it off in 1990, crushing 31 HR and collecting 118 RBIs. The offensive outburst earned him a Silver Slugger Award, while his stellar defence at third landed him a Gold Glove. He finished fourth in the American League MVP voting and made his second All-Star team.

It seemed nothing could stop the rise of the 28-year-old third-base dynamo…until the injury bug bit him. Gruber missed 49 games in 1991 with various ailments, most serious of which was a torn ligament in his hand. But in 1992 things went from bad to worse when Gruber felt a popping sensation in his neck while swinging the bat in a game against the Kansas City Royals. "I had a bone spur embedded in my spinal cord. If the positioning was just right and I took the right jolt, that would sever my cord," he told the *National Post.* "My motor skills were starting to become affected, because the bone spur that was growing into my spinal cord would actually pinch and crimp my cord every time I bent a certain way. And that bruise on the spinal cord was like a gel." Pain or no pain, there was nothing stopping Xanthos from making an appearance in the 1992 World Series, the Blue Jays' first ever appearance in the Fall Classic.

He didn't hit much—just 2-for-19—but Gruber still worked his way into the headlines. In Game 2 of the World Series, the third baseman caught the final out and mocked the Braves' Tomahawk

Chop in front of the Atlanta fans as he ran off the field. The incident remains etched in the minds of fans on both sides of the border.

During the next game of the series, Gruber found himself at the centre of one of the more controversial calls in World Series history. Devon (formerly White) Whyte made a spectacular catch near the centre-field fence and threw the ball to second base. Jays second baseman Roberto Alomar tossed the ball to John Olerud at first to get the Braves Terry Pendleton, and Olerud returned the ball to Gruber.

Perhaps this is where Claude King's genes came into play. Gruber chased Deion Sanders—the multi-sport star and one of the fastest players in NFL history—and caught him, tagging him on the foot. This was the second triple play in World Series history… or was it? Gruber knew he tagged Sanders. The umpire saw it differently. "He told me 'Kelly, you might have [tagged him], but I saw daylight,'" Gruber said.

Battered body and all, Gruber hit a home run in the eighth inning. But things were really never the same for Gruber after that game. In 1993 the Blue Jays traded him to the California Angels for Luis Sojo. Gruber played just 18 more games, ending a career which fell just as quickly as it rose.

Gruber is long retired from baseball but remains a beloved figure in Blue Jays history. He stays involved in the game, recently coaching his son Kody's baseball team, the Austin Black Wings, to a national championship. Kelly also stays in touch with the Jays by making appearances at the Rogers Centre and on team caravans and participating in events for the Jays Care Foundation.

As for David Gruber, he just wishes he had another chance to assist in Kelly's upbringing. "I would have disciplined him a lot less," he said. "There would have been a lot less anger and afterward a lot of love."

51 Toronto's All-Star Game

Baseball sure was the toast of the town in Toronto circa 1991. The Blue Jays were nearing the pinnacle of their success, drawing enthusiastic fans in droves to their gleaming new SkyDome—the Eighth Wonder of the World. The team was the topic of watercooler conversations throughout Canada, and kids actually considered it (gasp) cool to wear the team's logo in public.

Recognizing the Jays' success, Major League Baseball awarded the baseball-crazy region its first All-Star Game, the 62nd such event of its kind. Baseball mania reached a fever pitch as the July 9th Midsummer Classic approached.

With gametime just hours away, stadium staff worked feverishly to ensure every last detail was covered. Team buses warmed their engines at the Harbour Castle Westin, and, as the hotel doors opened, a stream of baseball legends filed by and climbed the steps of the bus. Chock-full-o-stars, the chartered coaches made the short trek to the SkyDome.

Of the 30 players elected into baseball's Hall of Fame through 2016 by baseball writers, an incredible 17 of them sat in those All-Star team buses, gliding through the throng of cheering fans on the Toronto streets, surrounding the stadium. In one window you could see the face of the man who broke Lou Gehrig's consecutive-games-played streak. In another, was the greatest base stealer of all time. On board were a Wizard, a Hawk, a Rocket, a Kid, Steady Eddie, Puck, and Captain Video.

As with most All-Star Games, the 1991 classic would be remembered more for the spectacle than the on-field action. Cal Ripken did most of the damage on offence, hitting a three-run

Hall of Famers from the 1991 All-Star Game

American League—Roberto Alomar, Cal Ripken Jr., Wade Boggs, Ken Griffey Jr., Rickey Henderson, Dennis Eckersley, Carlton Fisk, Kirby Puckett, and Paul Molitor. (Roger Clemens, Tony La Russa, and Jack Morris remain eligible for election.)

National League—Craig Biggio, Tom Glavine, Ryne Sandberg, Ozzie Smith, Tony Gwynn, Andre Dawson, Eddie Murray, and Barry Larkin.

bomb to centre field in the third inning to bring home Rickey Henderson and Wade Boggs. The National League stumbled in an attempt to come back in the sixth, and the American League seized their fourth consecutive All-Star Game victory against the NL.

At the ripe age of 43 years, seven months, and 13 days, Carlton Fisk hit a bit of a milestone that day, becoming the oldest player to collect a hit in All-Star Game history. The game also marked one of a handful of times brothers would play in the same All-Star Game, as Roberto, a key player on Toronto's World Series championship teams, and Sandy Alomar teamed up for the AL.

In another notable twist, pitchers for both of Canada's teams were involved in the decision. The Blue Jays' Jimmy Key was credited with the 4–2 victory, while the Montreal Expos' Dennis Martinez took the loss.

More so than the game-play itself, the night's events served as a sort of validation for the city of Toronto. It not only strengthened Toronto's image as a world-class destination, but also cemented its legacy as a baseball town. For a brief moment, the city stood at the forefront of the baseball world.

52 The Collapse of 1987

Roy Johnson of *The New York Times* described the American League East race in 1987, "It will either be remembered as one of baseball's most inspired comebacks or one of its most embarrassing collapses." The Tigers weren't even expected to even contend for the AL East title, while the Jays were nearly consensus favourites to win the division. But the Blue Jays endured an epic breakdown, which is remembered as one of the more painful stretches in team history.

With just seven games remaining in the season, four of which were head-to-head against the second-place Detroit Tigers, the Blue Jays seemed to have a stranglehold on the division. Their lead was three and a half games, a seemingly comfortable margin. That is, until the Jays went out and lost…and lost…and lost.

They didn't just keep losing games. They also started losing players. On September 25, shortstop Tony Fernandez suffered a broken elbow after a brutal hit by Bill Madlock. Detroit's Madlock had gone out of the base path to knock the slender Fernandez to the ground, where his elbow struck a board holding a seam of the Exhibition Stadium turf. "A bone at the tip of the elbow, the olecranon, was fractured," said team spokesman Howard Starkman. The injury dealt a crippling blow to Toronto's club, as it lost a key force. Exacerbating the problem was the fact his replacement, Manuel Lee, was hardly the second coming of Honus Wagner. Then on September 30 after breaking up a double play at second base, catcher Ernie Whitt cracked two ribs on his left side and missed the final week of the season.

And it wasn't just injuries that were killing the Jays. Their other big bats were practically silenced over the final week. George Bell went just two for his final 26 and laid a 1–11 egg in the Tigers series. Jesse Barfield was almost as bad, with just three hits in his last 24 at-bats. Juan Beniquez finished zero for his last 15.

Talk about Killer B's.

Each of the final games played between the Tigers and Blue Jays was decided by a single run. Just a few timely hits stood between the Blue Jays and their second division championship, but their sluggers couldn't come through. The collapse became etched in history when Frank Tanana pitched a six-hitter to defeat Jimmy Key and the rest of the Jays 1–0, clinching the AL East crown for the Tigers. "They slumped at a bad time and ran up against a pretty good ballclub," Tanana said.

The only run scored was aided by strong October winds, which carried a Larry Herndon poke over the left-field wall at old Tiger Stadium. The homer was only one of three hits surrendered by Key on the day. The Blue Jays threatened early, but the Tigers' pitcher summarily stymied any semblance of a rally in the early going. They were unable to put forth a serious challenge to Tanana at any other point in the game. The final nail in the Blue Jays' coffin was a Garth Iorg dribbler to Tanana, who flipped it to Tigers first baseman Darrell Evans. Fans erupted with excitement in the stadium, and carried their party to the streets of Detroit.

Tigers manager Sparky Anderson was amazed at the turn of events that led his team to a division title. "I don't ever have to do one other thing in my career," he said. "I've done it all." As champagne flowed throughout the Tigers' clubhouse, second baseman Lou Whitaker reflected on the season and particularly the final few days. "This series put a real strain on our hearts, our bodies, and our minds," Whitaker said. "It took us time to catch on this season, but once we got through that, we put it all together. Any time we needed something, somebody in this room provided it."

Though understandably dejected after the loss, Blue Jays manager Jimy Williams defended his team. "We played well. We just didn't hit," he said. "It wasn't for a lack of effort. Things just didn't work out."

53 Weird Injuries

Strange injuries are as much a part of baseball as hot dogs and Cracker Jacks. While playing for the St. Louis Cardinals, Vince Coleman missed the 1985 World Series after suffering a knee injury as a result of getting trapped under the roll-away tarp. Colorado Rockies shortstop Clint Barmes hurt himself carrying raw deer meat up a flight of stairs. Carlos Zambrano, then pitching for the Chicago Cubs, went on the disabled list with carpal tunnel syndrome from spending five hours a day on the Internet. Cleveland Indians pitcher Trevor Bauer famously and idiotically cut open the pinky on his pitching hand repairing a radio-controlled toy drone before a crucial American League Championship Series start against Toronto in 2016.

The Blue Jays have had their share of peculiar injuries as well. In September of 2011, Toronto pitcher Brett Cecil sliced open his hand while cleaning a blender. Perhaps with tongue in cheek, Cecil blamed the kitchen implement for the incident. "It had two blades that were sticking straight up and then two out to the side, and I hit one of the ones that were sticking straight up," Cecil said. "I'm scared of a butter knife right now." It wasn't the first time Cecil had suffered a kitchen-related wound. He missed part of 2010 spring training, nursing an injury he earned "chopping up chickens."

Strangely enough, Cecil was the third pitcher that season to miss time after cutting himself with a household gadget. Chris Narveson of the Milwaukee Brewers sliced his thumb while using a pair of scissors, and Giants reliever Jeremy Affeldt lacerated his hand while attempting to separate frozen hamburgers patties with a sharp knife.

In recent years both Kevin Pillar and Ricky Romero suffered abdominal strains while sneezing. Joaquin Benoit was lost for the 2016 postseason when he injured himself charging in from the bullpen to engage in a brawl with the New York Yankees. Paul Quantrill broke his leg in a snowmobiling accident.

But Glenallen Hill, a former top prospect with the Jays, may own the weirdest and oddest disabled list story of all. Drifting off to la-la land, Hill began to dream about spiders, some of his least favourite critters. As he tried to run away from the arachnids in his dream, Hill hopped out of bed and began to climb his apartment stairs on his hands and knees. What was left were bloodstains on the carpet, and a pair of scraped his knees and elbows to match. "When I woke up, I was on a couch, and my wife, Mika, was screaming, 'Honey, wake up,'" Hill said. The injuries forced the arachnophobe onto crutches, and onto the DL.

While Hill acknowledges that spiders were present in his nightmare, he believes the odd sleep-crawling was a product of a bigger issue. "I'm uneasy with spiders, but I don't think it's spiders that caused that nightmare. It might've been diet, might've been stress...more of a sleeping disorder. Spiders just happened to be what I dreamt about that night. It could've been about a car that kept running over me. It could've been about...you know, caterpillars."

Even visiting players run the risk of a weird injury when they set foot in Toronto. When the Boston Red Sox were in town for a series against the Jays, third baseman Wade Boggs injured the muscles in his back while pulling off his cowboy boots at a Toronto hotel. Fortunately Boggs recovered from this strange strain and returned to the lineup shortly thereafter. The Jays also came back from their bizarre ailments. Cecil still pitches for the Jays, and Hill manages the Albuquerque Isotopes in the Colorado Rockies minor league system.

The latter also earned an appropriate nickname—Spiderman.

54 Up in Smoke: Damaso Garcia

When it came to baseball, Damaso Garcia was an amazing soccer player. That's not to say he wasn't a capable hitter and fielder, but Garcia, once the captain of the Dominican national soccer team, had a prima donna personality befitting a European footballer.

On the baseball field, Garcia was unquestionably talented, earning two All-Star selections and collecting the 1982 Silver Slugger Award. But those who saw the passionate second baseman play for the Jays could envision him emotionally pleading with a referee after receiving a yellow card.

Superscout Epy Guerrero, the man who discovered Garcia, said he had to go through a colossal struggle to pull the young man away from the game of soccer and toward baseball. "[Garcia] was the toughest sign I've ever had," Guerrero told *Sports Illustrated*. "There was big trouble with the soccer federation. He was the best player on the team, and they were really mad. The president of the federation called me to his office and said very upset, 'How can you take my best player?'" But Garcia would soon find himself hitting balls, not kicking them, when he signed with the New York Yankees as an 18-year-old in 1975. He made his major league debut just three years later, and played primarily as a backup until being traded to the Blue Jays after the 1979 season. That's when his career took off.

As a Blue Jay, the man with the (rather unimaginative) nickname "Damo" compiled a .288 batting average, 194 stolen bases, and 453 runs scored during seven seasons. Long before Billy Beane would be credited with pioneering advanced statistical analysis, Garcia was a player who made a living through contact hitting, while keeping his strikeout totals low. His WAR (wins above replacement) of 4.3 in 1982 was borderline Alomar-esque.

On the other hand, Garcia would have likely given Beane fits with his petulant aversion to bases on balls. He told coaches he didn't like to take walks and hated to bunt. On numerous occasions, he also tried to dictate to coaches where he would hit in the batting order, which was never well received.

Garcia was tempestuous, volatile, and a bit of a whiner...perfect qualities for a soccer player, not so perfect for a Major League Baseball player. His antics weren't always appreciated by his teammates. Catcher Ernie Whitt wrote that Garcia wasn't just complaining and being difficult. In his autobiography, *Catch*, Whitt suggests that Garcia was dogging it. "[T]here were days when Damo simply didn't want to play," he said. "There's no excuse for not giving it all you've got for the three hours you're out on the field. There were times when Damo wouldn't do that. He'd just go through the motions."

Frustrations grew after the Blue Jays got off to a 12–18 start in 1986. After losing to the lowly Seattle Mariners, tensions peaked in the clubhouse. Buck Martinez described a dramatic confrontation in his book, *The Last Out*. Both Whitt and Jesse Barfield took exception to Garcia engaging in clubhouse tomfoolery with George Bell, while the team was mired in a streak of poor performance. The players shouted back and forth, with Barfield saying the team needed to work harder, and Garcia telling him to mind his own business.

"I've had it with you!" Whitt shouted. "We're sitting around in here, losing, getting our butts kicked regularly, and nobody seems to care."

"You shut up!" Garcia yelled. "We do care. We care out on the field. That is where we do our talking. Don't you tell me what to do off the field!"

Further shouting erupted in the clubhouse, though fists never flew. Before it got to that, pitcher Jim Acker stepped in as the voice of reason, and his words managed to calm down the agitated players. But that confrontation was a drop in the bucket when compared to the bizarre events, which occurred a few days later on May 14th.

Garcia, still fuming over the dispute between him and Whitt and Barfield, entered the game against the Oakland A's as a "firecracker waiting to explode," according to Martinez. When he misplayed a grounder in the seventh inning, leading to five runs for Oakland, the fuse was lit. Garcia stormed into the clubhouse and headed into the bathroom.

Unaware of what was going on, Martinez completed his radio show and headed back to the clubhouse. He noticed a nasty stench as he sat down at his locker next to Whitt. He asked the catcher: "What the heck is that smell?"

"Damo just burnt his uniform," Whitt said. "He took it into the bathroom, piled it up, and set it afire."

"Some guys break bats, break up clubhouses," Garcia explained to reporters. "I just decided to go a little crazy and burn my uniform."

Blue Jays management was less than amused by the act. At first, they dealt with the issue internally. They quietly reprimanded Garcia for his behaviour and the constant demands he placed upon the team. But, in the offseason, they decided they'd had enough. They traded him to the Atlanta Braves, ending his reign at the Blue Jays' powder keg. He would play just 101 more games in the big leagues.

A year after he retired, Garcia was diagnosed with a malignant brain tumour and told he had just six months to live. Fortunately, however, he made an unexpected recovery. While Garcia suffered lasting neurological damage from the disease, his cancer is reportedly in full remission. He's since dedicated himself to working in the Dominican Republic with children suffering from traumatic injuries.

55 J.P. Ricciardi Feuds with Adam Dunn

Say what you want about general manager J.P. Ricciardi, but he wasn't shy about sharing his thoughts with local media. In fact, he was much more open than most Jays team executives had ever been. His media relations lacked the polish and warmth of his predecessors, Pat Gillick and Gord Ash. He pushed buttons in the local media by leaking false injury reports and possessed an air of negativity and condescension, but he made himself very available, a quality appreciated by the local radio hosts, newspaper writers, and television reporters.

Suffice it to say he made himself just a bit too available to Sportsnet 590 The Fan on June 18, 2008. A caller, Kevin from Halifax, to be precise, asked Ricciardi on the Wednesday night talk show whether Cincinnati slugger Adam Dunn, a premier power-hitting outfielder on the trade block, might be a fit for the Jays' anaemic offence. "He's a lifetime .230, .240 hitter that strikes out a ton and hits home runs," Ricciardi said.

"Yes," retorted the Haligonian, "he hits home runs, which none of the Toronto Blue Jays are doing!"

Ricciardi unloaded. "Do you know the guy doesn't really like baseball that much?" he asked the caller. "Do you know the guy doesn't have a passion to play the game that much? How much do you know about the player? There's a reason why you're attracted to some players and there's a reason why you're not attracted to some players. I don't think you'd be very happy if we brought Adam Dunn here. We've done our homework on guys like Adam Dunn, and there's a reason why we don't want Adam Dunn. I don't want to get into specifics."

Dunn—who got caught in the bizarre crossfire between a big league GM and a dude known simply as Kevin from Halifax—was rightfully pissed. "I don't know the clown," said Dunn referring to Ricciardi—not poor Kevin. "I really don't care what one guy thinks, to be honest with you. If I'm a GM, I don't know that I'd go out of my way to discredit a player…He's obviously won more than me, I guess. Or hasn't. I know nothing about him.

"[He's] just some clown sitting in a front office, pushing paper. I don't play for any other reason than the guys here. I've said it all along, 'It doesn't bother me what people say or think, especially someone outside of the organization who has no idea of anything that goes on here.' He's not even in our country. This guy's in another country, talking shit. He felt like he needed to say it for some reason. I have no idea why and I don't care. He could be in this clubhouse right now. I wouldn't know. I couldn't tell you his name, what he looks like. He's got a big mouth. That's all I know about him.

"I don't know who he is. It pisses me off, to be honest with you. He doesn't even know me. If he knew me, fine. Say what you want. But this guy doesn't know anything about me, other than what he sees on whatever *SportsCenter* they have on up there. That's it."

Silly Adam. Of course, Canada has *SportCentre*. We just spell it kind of strangely, and pack it 99.9 percent full of hockey and curling highlights to torture fans of any other sport. "I don't care about the perception people have of me," Dunn said, concluding his rant. "It looks like I ain't going to Toronto. I can eliminate one team. I'm not converting my dollars into loonies just yet."

Ricciardi's integrity was called into question when he told reporters he spoke with Dunn, who accepted his apology for the comments. Speaking with MLB.com, Dunn vehemently denied ever talking with the Jays GM. "If he said he talked to me, it is a lie," he said.

Claiming perhaps he'd been pranked, Ricciardi told sceptical reporters he couldn't prove making the call, since he'd deleted the phone number and call log from his phone. As for Dunn, he hit 38 home runs during each of the next two seasons with batting averages in the .260s.

56 Josh Donaldson's MVP Season

The trade went down on the night of November 28th, 2014. Six-year-old Amelia Lyttle's parents had no choice but to sit her down on the couch to share with her the most disheartening of news. Brett Lawrie, her idol, had been sent packing by the Jays and traded across the continent to Oakland for some stranger named Josh Donaldson.

Inconsolable, Amelia sobbed, imploring the baseball gods to return Lawrie to his rightful place in Toronto, all of which was captured on video by her father, Alex. In an age where the most intimate moments of daily life are smeared across the Internet for the world to see, her dad did what anyone would do with such juicy footage. He promptly uploaded her admittedly cute emotional outburst to YouTube, and it became an Internet sensation.

Meanwhile, the breaking details of the trade elicited a much more joyful reaction from others in the Toronto Twittersphere. "I was crying too," posted an ecstatic Jays fan known as cloudpartner. "I was like 'Ohmigawd I can't believe we just got Josh Donaldson' * cries *."

The Bringer of Rain himself—perhaps the top third baseman in the major leagues—had just become a Blue Jay. Like Amelia, Oakland fans were roundly devastated. While tears of Bay Area residents soaked now obsolete shirseys, Donaldson would soon prove why A's general manager Billy Beane had been reluctant to move him and why Anthopoulos pursued a deal for him relentlessly. With an aggressive leg-lift batting approach modeled after Jose Bautista's, the new Blue Jay dazzled teammates and fans from the moment he donned a Toronto uniform.

As with any player transitioning to a new team, Donaldson didn't immediately settle in with the boys in blue. The first moment he really felt at home with Toronto occurred during a 10th inning walk-off blast against the Atlanta Braves in April. "You want to be able to go and show these guys the type of player you are in the regular season," Donaldson said. "After that first walk-off against Atlanta, that was when I felt a part of the team."

That bomb was the first of three walk-off homers Donaldson would hit in 2015. On the year the Bringer of Rain hit .353/.440/.618 with runners in scoring position and .351/.426/ .713 in high-leverage situations. Of the 41 total regular-season home runs he hit in 2015, almost three quarters of them either tied the game or gave Toronto the lead. More than any other singular play by Donaldson in 2015, the one that will be remembered most vividly is the incredible diving catch he made to keep starter Marco Estrada's perfect game alive on June 24th.

Now an iconic moment in Blue Jays history, the stunning play came as the hard-nosed third bagger risked life and limb to dive headlong into the stands in Tampa in pursuit of a foul ball. "I know I'm going into the stands," he said, describing the play. "As soon as I leave my feet, I know I'm going in there. At that point of the game, as far as the score and then as far as what Marco was doing, I was willing to lay it on the line and take a couple of bruises to hopefully get him another out."

He caught the ball with his body in mid-air, his arm fully extended, and his glove twisted sideways. Donaldson narrowly

Donaldson Goes with the Flow

Josh Donaldson is known throughout the baseball world for his flow (aka hairstyle for those of you who are over the age of 30 or unhip like me). In fact, his unorthodox lid helped him land a cameo appearance on the History Channel's *Vikings*.

The concept of a different kind of flow was featured on an MLB Network interview with Donaldson in January of 2016, as he demonstrated his unique hitting style to former player Mark DeRosa. Focusing the "pre-load flow" that he borrowed from Jose Bautista, Donaldson showed how he establishes tempo in the batter's box and said: "I have my weight in my back heel, which is going to allow me to stay balanced into my back hip...Once I get into my back hip, my weight's going to be able to transfer from my back knee."

But the word "flow" has become an even bigger theme in Josh's life of late. Donaldson's agent contacted entrepreneur Nicholas Reichenbach as part of an effort to endorse his packaged water brand with eco-friendly packaging called Flow. Reichenbach was excited by the notion but had no idea who the heck Josh Donaldson was. Researching the third baseman, Reichenbach quickly realized the value of this endorsement. "Josh tried the product at the clubhouse and wanted to see if he could work with us to build more awareness in Canada as well as in the U.S.," Reichenbach told the Financial Post. "As luck would have it, he ended up playing an amazing season and winning the MVP award."

The water brand is now available in thousands of stores across North America.

avoided a substantial dental bill thanks to a Toronto fan whose chest stopped his face from smashing into the seats.

His defensive prowess not only raised his profile among award voters, but it also escalated his WAR (wins above replacement) to 8.8—second only to Mike Trout. In May and June, Rogers Centre patrons began to make Donaldson's MVP case in earnest, chanting "MVP! MVP!" at every opportunity. The chants grew more and more ear-punishing as the accomplishments and memorable performances accumulated. Donaldson said he enjoyed the support but made a conscious effort of staying within himself to avoid letting the crowd noise translate into added pressure. "I stayed focused on the task at hand, which was winning games and I was able to accomplish that," he said.

Anthopoulos himself didn't fully realize how truly special a player he had acquired until the 2015 season had fully played out. "I didn't know how smart he was and how much of a student of the game he was," A.A. said. "And I didn't know how much of a leader he was and how driven he was to succeed and how driven he was to win."

When Donald Trump suggested that NAFTA was the worst trade deal in American history during his presidential campaign, @50_MissionCap wrote on Twitter: "Actually, America's worst trade deal was Josh Donaldson for Brett Lawrie, Kendall Graveman, Sean Nolin, and Franklin Barreto." When the baseball votes were tallied, Donaldson had won the American League MVP award, a Silver Slugger, and the Hank Aaron Award.

And Amelia Lyttle's admiration for a certain helmet-slamming Red Bull-guzzler took a nice turn as well. After months of mourning, an unsuspecting Amelia was led to a Boston Pizza restaurant in her area where her hero, Brett Lawrie, surprised her with an in-person visit and a bag of gifts.

57 Three Strange Days

Manager Tony La Russa is remembered for his habit of tinkering with his lineups at seemingly any opportunity. He came by his esteemed reputation honestly. He studied stats and scouting reports tirelessly and used the information gleaned to make as many in-game adjustments as any manager in recent memory. While some consider this micromanagement, his moves often worked out the way he planned.

Jimy Williams' legacy is a bit different. Although he's also remembered for voluminous lineup changes, much of his reputation is based on the peculiarity of many of his decisions. His substitutions and defensive switches were often quite unconventional, and every once in awhile, they worked in his team's favour. More often, though, these odd decisions left the Blue Jays in unenviable situations.

Take, for example, the May 9, 1987 game when Williams' chess moves led to the nightmarish scenario of having stud closer Tom Henke bat cleanup. Or consider other games, when star pitchers Jimmy Key and Dave Stieb subbed in as pinch runners, even while other hitters (and seemingly more capable runners) sat on Williams' bench.

But his reputation for bizarre in-game management went to an entirely different level during an odd three-game road trip to Seattle in early 1988. The weirdness was spawned when second baseman Nelson Liriano was optioned to Syracuse, New York, of the International League on May 2. The light-hitting Dominican earned his demotion by batting just .203 through his first 59 at-bats of the season, producing just four RBIs. In a corresponding move, third baseman Rance Mulliniks was activated from the 15-day disabled list, leaving a bit of gap at second. This gap widened to a chasm when Liriano's backup, Manuel Lee, complained to Williams that his bruised shoulder was causing too much pain for him to play.

Mulliniks, himself, was hardly a picture of health at this point, and even though the team activated him from the DL, his knee strain hadn't fully healed and necessitated a further stay on the bench. Veteran infielder Juan Beniquez was normally first in line to cover third base for Mulliniks, but he too pulled himself out after experiencing sharp arm pain during warm-ups.

While the situation was far from perfect, Williams' tactical moves made it much more fascinating. Rather than follow conventional wisdom by assigning second base duties to one of the players on his bench, some of whom had infield experience, Williams concocted a platoon for the history books. The weirdness did not show up in the lineup card he handed to home-plate umpire Jim McKean, but the unusual events would soon confound the dedicated few who tracked the game on their scorecards.

Officially, Williams had placed Cecil Fielder at third base to start the game, with Kelly Gruber at second. But before the first pitch was thrown, the players traded positions. Gruber remained at third for next few outs and Fielder at second. The second inning began with left-handed-hitting Alvin Davis stepping up to bat, and Williams shifted Gruber over to second base. Fielder was sent to handle third base—his original assignment. After Davis flied out, right-handed-hitting Jim Presley took his turn in the batter's box, prompting Gruber and Fielder to retreat to third and second base, respectively.

Again and again, throughout the game, the two switched positions to place Gruber in the position Jays Manager Williams believed the ball would be hit. When all was said and done, Gruber and Fielder had traded spots a stunning 19 times. The official scorecard showed something unprecedented:

> Kelly Gruber—2B-3B-2B-3B-2B-3B-2B-3B-2B-3B-2B-3B-2B-3B-2B-3B-2B-3B-2B
>
> Cecil Fielder—3B-2B-3B-2B-3B-2B-3B-2B-3B-2B-3B-2B-3B-2B-3B-2B-3B-2B-3B

Throw in all the other switches, pinch-hitters, and miscellaneous tinkering enacted by Williams, and the Blue Jays played 13 players at a total of 50 different positions—which remains a record for positional changes.

Manager Jimy Williams (left) seated next to his hitting coach, Cito Gaston, is remembered by Blue Jays fans for his bizarre and overly aggressive substitution patterns.

The next day the insanity continued. Catcher Pat Borders filled Fielder's role, perhaps giving the big man a rest from the exhausting defensive switches. Borders shifted between second and third, as matchups dictated, alternating with Gruber. Each was charged with an error in the game, but ultimately it didn't matter as the Jays crushed the Mariners 9–2.

On May 5, Lee declared himself fully recovered from that bout with shoulder pain, and Jimy Williams' defensive experiment seemed destined to draw to a close. The Jays faced the Oakland A's with Lee at second that day, and everything seemed back to normal...until the seventh inning. Like Carrie's hand darting out of the grave in the classic horror flick, Williams' scheme reared its nasty head one last time.

Fielder pinch hit for Rick Leach, and Pat Borders came in to bat for Ernie Whitt. When the substitutions fell into place, Fielder and Gruber found themselves alternating positions yet again. They shifted back and forth, and forth and back, throughout the seventh and eighth innings, as lefties and righties came to bat.

Williams' last-ditch attempt at defensive creativity drew to a close, after the A's feasted on his alignment. Mike Gallego reached on an infield single, and Jose Canseco topped it off with an infield double. The A's, managed by La Russa, scored three runs, mostly involving balls hit no farther than the infield grass. They went on to win by the same margin. Williams' experiment was over. He was let go by the Jays the following May, and Cito Gaston took over.

Williams would later manage the Boston Red Sox and then the Houston Astros, frequently raising the ire of fans in both cities with his puzzling strategic decisions. Despite the criticism hurled at Williams, it's hard to question his career win-loss record of 910–790.

58 Watch a Game From the CN Tower EdgeWalk

If you're incredibly ~~idiotic~~ brave, you could become part of an elite group who has watched Blue Jays game action from 1,100 feet above the playing field. Since 2011 the tallest free-standing structure in the western hemisphere has allowed its visitors the privilege of dangling in open air over Toronto's downtown core for the mere investment of $195.

The terrifying, hands-free tour takes place on a 1.5-metre-wide ledge, encircling the top of the Tower's main pod 116 stories above the ground and almost directly over the Rogers Centre playing field. Visitors walk in groups of six and are attached to an overhead safety rail via a trolley and harness system. On the world's highest full circle, hands-free walk, EdgeWalkers will hang like drying laundry off the side of the tower for 20 to 30 intense minutes. While some might argue that the influence of drugs and alcohol would be the only reasonable explanation for the desire to do the EdgeWalk, all participants are screened for narcotics and booze to ensure they are clean and sober.

When the roof is open, many of the fans in the Rogers Centre can watch the tour from their seats. Blue Jays announcers Pat Tabler and Buck Martinez of Sportsnet agreed to take the daring walk for the Jays Care charitable foundation during the 2012 season. "My partner opened up his big mouth and he goes, 'Hey, we need to do that!' And I'm like going, 'You need to do that, so let's make a day of this kind of thing and see how much money we can raise,'" Tabler told Toronto's 680News. While Tabler appeared less than thrilled with the event, Buck Martinez called the EdgeWalk "maybe the best thing I've ever done in my life."

Other EdgeWalkers have come from all corners of the earth—many from Europe, Asia, Africa, and various parts of the Americas. "I'm pretty sure I saw Jose Bautista hit, but for all I know, it could have been Colby Rasmus," said Craig Schmidt, a tourist who watched game action from 1,100-plus feet. His life partner, Tom, swore it was Bautista but acknowledges the players appeared no bigger than ants from their vantage point.

These daring—or perhaps crazy—EdgeWalkers are known to draw the attention of in-stadium cameras and have become a novel, though infrequent, sideshow during Blue Jays broadcasts.

59 The Pearson Cup

Unlike most teams, the Blue Jays didn't play their first midseason interleague games in 1997. They were 20 years ahead of the crowd.

From 1978 until 1986, the Jays took on their fellow Canadian-based counterparts, the Montreal Expos, in a one-game, midseason exhibition called the Pearson Cup, which did not count in the Major League Baseball standings. The two teams met up every year when the schedule permitted, flipping back and forth between Olympic Stadium in Montreal and Exhibition Stadium in Toronto.

The exhibition series was named after former Canadian prime minister Lester B. Pearson, the country's 14th leader. Pearson was an avid baseball fan and would often interrupt parliamentary meetings to check baseball scores. During his 20s, he was also a pretty decent ballplayer himself, playing third base for the Guelph Maple Leafs of the Intercounty League. But the Oxford graduate admitted he probably wasn't big league calibre. "I think the term, 'good-field, no-hit' was first used to describe me," Pearson said during a 1970 interview, "and the only way I can add anything to that is to say I was on the verge of respectability."

Instead of chasing big league dreams, Pearson was left to do more mundane things such as win a Nobel Prize, encourage peacekeeping throughout the world, and bring universal healthcare to Canada.

Roughly six years after his death, the series began, and proceeds of the event were distributed to amateur baseball organizations throughout the country.

Season	Location	Result
1978	Montreal	Expos 5, Blue Jays 4
1979	Toronto	Tied 4–4
1980	Montreal	Expos 3, Blue Jays 1
1981	Toronto	Cancelled due to strike
1982	Toronto	Expos 7, Blue Jays 3
1983	Montreal	Blue Jays 7, Expos 5
1984	Toronto	Blue Jays 2, Expos 1
1985	Montreal	Tied 2–2
1986	Toronto	Blue Jays 5, Expos 2

The most notable games are probably the two that ended in ties. In both cases, the games were abandoned due to time constraints. (Commissioner Bud Selig would have no doubt approved.) It's not a huge surprise that the Expos took the first three decisions from the Jays and their flimsy expansion team roster. But the tide turned in 1983, and the Expos never again took home the gold cup.

When baseball introduced league-wide regular season interleague play in 1997, the Expos and Jays played meaningful head-to-head games, but the Cup wasn't awarded. It was, however, brought back to life for a fleeting moment. For the 2003 and 2004 interleague games, it was determined that the winner of the season series between the Expos and Blue Jays would win the cup. But each team won three of the six games during both 2003 and 2004, so a winner could not be determined.

Oh...and then the Expos moved to Washington, so that kind of further wrecked things.

Now displayed at the Canadian Baseball Hall of Fame in St. Marys, Ontario, the Pearson Cup remains a unique piece of the country's baseball heritage.

60 Buck Martinez's Broken-Legged Double Play

One of the most jarring—and bizarre—baseball plays occurred on July 9, 1985 as the Blue Jays took on their expansion cousins, the Seattle Mariners in the Kingdome. With Tom Filer on the mound for the Jays, Phil Bradley led off the third inning with a grounder up the middle for a base hit. After a routine out by Alvin Davis, Filer was called for a balk, which pushed Bradley to second.

That's when things got interesting.

Slugger Gorman Thomas stepped into the batter's box for Seattle and launched a liner into right field. Realizing the ball would be a base hit, the speedy Bradley took off from second base looking to score on the play. What he did not count on—but should have—was a laser-beam throw from outfielder Jesse Barfield, who had one of the game's best arms. The throw to home had Bradley beat. Knowing he was destined to be dead on arrival, the Mariner lowered his shoulder to barrel into Toronto's catcher, Martinez. A train wreck ensued. Martinez's right leg was broken and his right ankle dislocated. But Buck held onto the ball, and Bradley was called out.

The Jays catcher was on his back in obvious agony. But the play was still alive. Unaware of the extent of his injuries, Martinez's teammates shouted at him to throw the ball to third to gun down Thomas. Buck mustered up the wherewithal to heave the ball toward third, but it flailed toward foul ground. Jays left fielder George Bell, known to be a less-than-stellar defensive player, was covering third and was positioned to field the wild throw.

Still wincing in pain at the plate, Martinez came to the stunning realization that Bell was about to try nail Thomas at the plate. Didn't he understand that his catcher was incapacitated? "I said to myself, 'My God, it looks like he's going to throw it,'" said Martinez. In a surprising moment of fielding skill, Bell managed to throw a perfect strike to Martinez.

Thomas was out at the plate, and Martinez was out, too—on a stretcher.

The play was officially scored 9–2–7–2, likely one of the first and last double plays of the sort.

Unfortunately, Buck Martinez was never the same. He attempted a comeback in 1986 but struggled through a .181 average with just a pair of homers and 12 RBIs in 160 at-bats. As the 1986 season came to a close, the Blue Jays were faced with the tough task of cutting ties with a man who played all out for the team and risked life and limb (or at least limb) to help the team win its first pennant.

The trio of Pat Gillick, Paul Beeston, and Jimy Williams called Martinez in for a meeting. Gillick, the general manager, was emotional. "It was harder on Pat than me," Martinez said. "He fumbled with the words, and I said, 'Pat, we knew it was coming.'"

Martinez retired shortly thereafter, but it wasn't the last the city of Toronto would hear of Buck. In 1987 he was hired to serve as colour analyst for Blue Jays games. Soon after, he transitioned to TSN (Canada's equivalent of ESPN) as the colour analyst for the team's television broadcasts. He was so good that ESPN invited Buck to provide colour commentary on a number of its gameday telecasts.

Then, heading into the 2001 season, Martinez was hired to manage the Blue Jays, replacing the dismissed Jim Fregosi. He led the team to an 80–82 finish, finishing third in the competitive American League East. The following year, however, the team got off to a rough 20–33 start, and the Jays again cut Martinez loose, making his managerial gig appear to be his last hurrah in Canada.

Toronto baseball was left without one of its early heroes over the next several seasons. He drifted away to enemy territory, broadcasting games for MASN in Baltimore, then Atlanta's TBS, and even serving a brief stint at NESN for the—gasp—Boston Red Sox. But all was not lost. The Blue Jays made right with Martinez in 2010, bringing him back to do play-by-play for Rogers Sportsnet alongside another former Jay, Pat Tabler. In this role Martinez continues to earn acclaim as one of the finest announcers in baseball, offering keen insight and intelligent commentary.

And although he was badly hurt that day in Seattle—on a play that essentially ended his career—Martinez still believes taking a hit is just part of the catcher's job and part of baseball. When Buster Posey of the San Francisco Giants suffered a similar injury in 2011, Martinez flat-out rejected the suggestion that the league should implement a ban on home-plate collisions. "It's part of the position," he said. "There is no way you can legislate no contact behind the plate, because then you take it away from the catcher, too."

61 Attend a Dominican Winter League Game

"The intensity is unbelievable. People are banging on drums, playing horns, and the crowd has a tonne of energy."

No, ESPN's Jorge Arangure Jr. isn't talking about the atmosphere at Rogers Centre during a scintillating midweek match with the Minnesota Twins. He's attempting to describe the indescribable—the smorgasbord for the senses that is a Dominican Winter League ballgame.

The aroma of *arepas* and *pasteles en hojas* (popular Dominican street foods) fills the air around the stadium, while the crowd buzzes with a festive mood throughout the game. Dancers shimmy atop the dugouts. *Cervezas* (beers) for $1.50 and cups full of Mama Juana (a potent booze mixture) keep things cool on a hot Dominican night.

It's baseball night in the D.R., and Arangure, a respected authority on Latin-American sports and an accomplished sportswriter, said Blue Jays fans would be remiss if they didn't check out the experience. "It's lively, and it's an atmosphere, where the fans are completely into it. It's really a unique experience," Arangure said. "No one's sitting on their hands. There are no quiet moments like you tend to see in the major leagues."

Lively? Fans are into it? No quiet moments? Sounds just like, ahem, the good ol' Rogers Centre during the early part of the 21st century.

Arangure said that Blue Jays fans heading south to watch a game should keep an eye out for legend George Bell, who's known to make the occasional appearance at winter league games. The crowd takes notice when the man, whose Ontario license plate once humbly read "GB MVP," enters the building. "Whenever George Bell shows up at a winter league game, it's always a big deal. He's an icon in the D.R., and was one of their first big home run hitters," Arangure said. "Fans cheer wildly for Bell in recognition of what he meant to their country. He was so important to a transitional period in Dominican Republic baseball history and helped usher in a whole new era."

Travellers from Canada usually can find accommodations near winter league stadiums and cheap flights easily. Some might prefer to stay in town and soak in the local culture, while others might prefer the luxury of one of Punta Cana's famous all-inclusive resorts. The beaches of the Dominican Republic are among the best in the world, and the locals are some of the warmest, kindest people one could ever encounter. Plan your vacation for a visit between October and January, while Winter League baseball is in action at stadiums in Santo Domingo, Santiago, San Pedro de Macoris, and La Romana.

62 John Olerud Makes a Run at .400

The John Olerud story almost ended before it could start. *Baseball America*'s 1988 College Player of the Year collapsed and nearly died during preseason warm-ups.

Olerud fell ill while jogging to prepare for one of Washington State coach Bobo Brayton's conditioning exercises. "I can honestly say Bobo just about killed me with that timed mile," Olerud joked. Although doctors cleared Olerud to return to practice, his father, a medical doctor and faculty member at the University of Washington School of Medicine, recommended further testing. Frustrated and anxious to get back on the field, the younger Olerud reluctantly complied.

The tests showed a significant brain aneurysm. "I remember the doctor putting the slide up and I could point out the aneurysm," Olerud said. "It turned out it wasn't a bad decision at all." He underwent surgery three days later and recovered quickly enough to return to the Cougars in just two months.

Although the Blue Jays knew Olerud intended to stay another year at WSU, they "decided to take a flyer and draft John and see if he would be at least be open to signing," Pat Gillick said. The team wasn't concerned with Olerud's near-death encounter. They knew the kid could hit.

"The Blue Jays started talking to me a couple of weeks before school started," Olerud said. "One of their big attractions was they would bring me up as a September call-up when they expanded the rosters." In addition to the call-up, he wanted to play in the playoffs—a rare opportunity for any ballplayer. "I remember my dad saying there have been a lot of good players who never got to experience a pennant race," Olerud said. "And it was an awfully

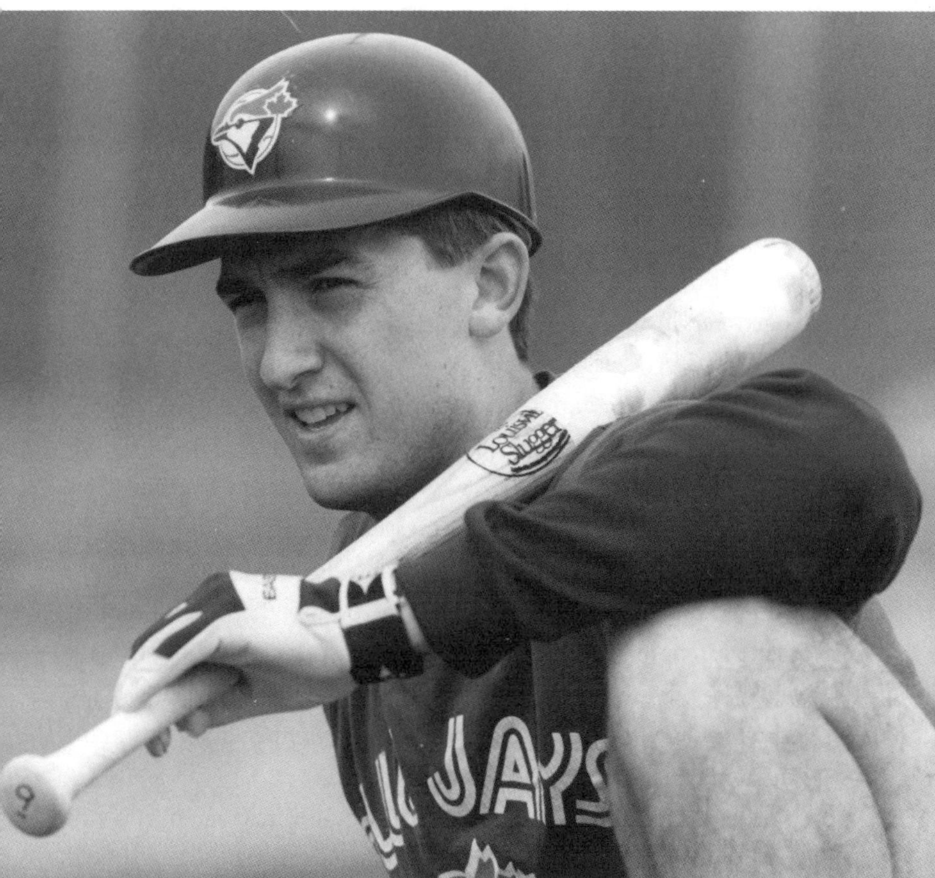

After suffering a brain aneurysm during college, John Olerud wore a batting helmet even when playing in the field at first base.

great offer to sign. I ended up signing and went straight to the big leagues."

With the Blue Jays in 1989, Olerud appeared in just six games, going 3-for-8, resulting in a .375 batting average. Despite the ridiculously small sample size, it wouldn't be the last time Olerud would flirt with .400. Not only did he possess a swing as sweet as Ted Williams', he would soon chase the Splendid Splinter's .406 average from the 1941 season.

During the 1993 season, Olerud hit...and hit...and hit. In fact, since Williams' legendary season, Olerud was one of only two players to maintain a .400 average into August. The other was George Brett, who hit .390 in 117 games while earning the 1980 American League MVP Award. "I don't think I ever thought about it until it got into August," Olerud said. "That was the time I [started] thinking, 'Gosh, I've done it four months, maybe I'll be able to keep it up.'"

When all was said and done, Olerud finished the 1993 season with a .363 average and a stunning 1.072 OPS (on-base plus slugging percentage). His performance earned him an All-Star nod, and he finished third in MVP voting. His on-base percentage was .473—in large part due to an impressive 114 walks, including 33 intentional ones. His season included a 26-game hitting streak, the longest of any major leaguer that season. "I don't know if somebody could hit .400 again. It's hard to say that nobody will ever do it, but it's going to be a very tall order," Olerud told *The (Vancouver, British Columbia) Province* "It's going to very difficult with so many specialty pitchers these days."

How on earth could someone carry a .400 average over a full season? "I think it's going to take a guy who can beat out an infield hit because you're not always going to be able to hit the ball on the nose," Olerud said. "I think it's going to take a guy who can be selective at the plate. I think it's going to take a lot of things. I think it's going to take the right type of player, having a phenomenal year."

63 The Bizarre Departure of Alex Anthopoulos

The ham-handed pursuit of Paul Beeston's successor was a tale of disrespect, tampering, and ignorance by Edward Rogers Jr. and his chum, Roger Rai, who broke all the rules in seeking a new team president. First, they bungled an attempt to land Kenny Williams from the Chicago White Sox (author's note: phew!) Rebuffed, the wondertwits shifted their sights to Baltimore Orioles executive Dan Duquette. Owner Peter Angelos was unamused. They followed this failed attempt with the mind-numbing decision to meet with New York Yankees president Randy Levine to get his suggestions on who the Jays should pursue as Beeston's replacement. It was like a pair of mice meeting with a cat to get his take on appropriate hiding places.

Ultimately, Jays ownership honed in on Cleveland Indians exec Mark Shapiro, and negotiations took place behind the scenes. His hiring was announced in August, but he would not take the helm with the Blue Jays until October 31st. Meanwhile, the Blue Jays became pretty frigging spectacular, having been molded into a murderer's row by general manager Alex Anthopoulos. Stunning acquisition after stunning acquisition put the Jays into position as a World Series contender. The successful 2015 season ended as the Jays fell to the Kansas City Royals in the American League Championship Series. As Matt Gwin wrote for Baseball Prospectus, "Alex Anthopoulos was at the peak of his popularity."

But in recent years the title of team president has transitioned from one in which the titleholder oversees a ballclub's business operations to one in which they oversee virtually every aspect of the ballclub, including decisions related to player personnel. So in hiring Shapiro to the role of team president, Rogers had created a proverbial kitchen with too many cooks.

Shapiro and his crew met with Anthopoulos and his crew in late October in the Rogers Centre offices with the new leadership structure set to begin the following Monday. The meeting didn't go well, to say the least, and Anthopoulos made the decision to leave the Blue Jays. As Shi Davidi reported the news to a stunned Toronto public on the morning of October 29th, 2015, he specified that "the issues leading to the split aren't thought to be financial." Reports surfaced indicating that Shapiro berated Anthopoulos for usurping the team's prospect capital in making a push for the title.

Defenders of Anthopoulos would have no shortage of examples of well-executed transactions to argue his case. Exhibit A would be the deal in which he swapped Brett Lawrie, Sean Nolin, Kendall Graveman, and Franklin Barreto for Josh freaking Donaldson. But the mere fact that his decisions were being questioned was the galling aspect of the confrontation/conversation. Had A.A. not earned the benefit of the doubt? Did he not deserve a heightened level of respect for the work he had done to shape the Jays into the team that came a hair short of making its first World Series in over 20 years?

Reports of a confrontation were later downplayed by both parties, but there's little question that something happened and that Anthopoulos found the situation to be unendurable.

He walked away from the team he had built. He spoke to his scouting team via conference call, keeping his reasons close to his vest and choosing to be the bigger man.

It would be unfair to place judgment on the new regime without considering ownership's role in the debacle. Shapiro and his crew were brought into an impossibly awkward situation, trailing a popular general manager and president who were known for aggressive roster shaping and who were viewed as the architects of the team's first playoff run in 22 years.

Maybe, in time, the Shapiro/Atkins (aka Shatkins) combo will be remembered in a similar way. Maybe they'll be just as clever in unearthing loopholes and acquiring high upside, controllable talent below market rates. The Marco Estrada and J.A. Happ signings prior to the 2016 season gave reason for optimism. More than any other individual, it was A.A. who brought playoff baseball back to Toronto. He really never wanted to leave, but he had no other choice. "My goal, my desire was to remain with the Toronto Blue Jays until the end of my career," he said.

Oh, to have been a fly on the wall of the Anthopoulos residence as he was awarded the MLB Executive of the Year award on the date of his departure from the Toronto franchise.

Anthopoulos ended up accepting a vice president position with the Los Angeles Dodgers on January 12th of 2016. Canadians still hold out hope that—even if he won't come back to the Rogers-owned Jays—he might someday come home to lead a revival of the Montreal Expos. He left a lasting impression of ingenuity, resourcefulness, and relentlessness. Thank you, Alex.

64 A Key Figure

Growing up in Huntsville, Alabama, it's pretty hard not to become a fan of the Atlanta Braves. The cities are separated by just a three-and-a-half hour drive, making the team the obvious favourite for Huntsville residents who chose to watch baseball to fill their football-deprived summer months.

Jimmy Key was no different than any other kid in the area, rooting for players like Phil Niekro and Dale Murphy and the rest of Atlanta's squads of the late 1970s and early 1980s. Although he also admitted an affinity for the New York Yankees, he and his friends followed the Braves closely as kids.

But as the 1992 World Series began, Key found himself taking the mound in a Toronto Blue Jays uniform, battling against the very team he once supported. In Game 4, with the Blue Jays leading the series 2–1, the Jays turned to Key to start against Atlanta. He responded with a brilliant 7⅔-inning performance, giving up just a single run in Toronto's 3–1 victory.

With the series returning to Atlanta for Game 6 and the Jays hanging onto a 3–2 series lead, Toronto again turned to Key. This time the lefty was called in from the bullpen in the 10th inning. He held the fort and left the game with the team up 4–3. Mike Timlin shut the door, and the Blue Jays were world champions for the first time.

All told, Key picked up two of the Jays' four victories in the 1992 series. He would never again throw a pitch for Toronto, signing with the Yankees as a free agent that offseason. Key pitched four years with the Yankees, winning another World Series in 1996 by again helping his team defeat his once-beloved Braves. He even won the clinching game.

Know Your Obscure Blue Jays Facts

Other than simply being the only team in Major League Baseball that plays its home games outside of the United States, the Jays have a number of interesting oddities.

For example, according to a 2011 report, the Blue Jays had the second-most-expensive hot dog in baseball. Along with the Houston Astros, they are one of only two MLB teams without a letter on their baseball cap. They're the only non-Sox (Chicago White Sox and Boston Red Sox) team with a two-word team name.

The Jays have also been home to several star-calibre players whose time in Toronto was relatively meaningless. The list is like a who's who of talented hitters and pitchers, though none made a memorable impact in Toronto: Dave Parker, Phil Niekro, Dave Righetti, Frank Viola, Kevin Millar, Mike Matheny, Lance Parrish, Ruben Sierra, and Omar Vizquel.

Along those forgettable lines, here is a list of the Jays' all-time leaders in some less-than-desirable statistical categories.

Strikeouts by a hitter	Carlos Delgado	1,242
Caught stealing	Tony Fernandez, Damaso Garcia, and Lloyd Moseby	86
Hit by pitch	Carlos Delgado	122
Grounding into double plays	Vernon Wells	146
Hits given up by a pitcher	Dave Stieb	2,545
Runs given up by a pitcher	Dave Stieb	1,208
Home runs given up by a pitcher	Dave Stieb	224
Walks given up by a pitcher	Dave Stieb	1,020
Balks by a pitcher	Dave Stieb	14
Hit batsmen by a pitcher	Dave Stieb	129
Wild pitches by a pitcher	Juan Guzman	88

Key left Toronto with a 116–81 record, to go along with a sparkling 3.42 ERA and 1.196 WHIP (walks plus hits per innings pitched). The four-time All-Star finished second in Cy Young Award voting during 1987 and 1994. During the former season, Key led the American League in ERA with a 2.76 mark and he later led the AL with 17 wins in 1994. His 27.8 WAR (wins above replacement) ranks third all-time among the Blue Jays pitchers, behind greats Dave Stieb and Roy Halladay.

65 "OK Blue Jays"

Canadian baseball fans are a bit weird, eh? Where else but in Toronto would a song about a local baseball team generate 50,000 sales, and become certified gold? "OK Blue Jays," the team's official seventh inning stretch music since 1983, became a smash hit after being performed by Keith Hampshire and The Bat Boys.

The fan anthem quickly became a trademark of attending a ball game in Toronto—like the tradition of singing "Sweet Caroline" in Boston or "New York, New York" at a Yankees game. Accepting the award before a game against the Milwaukee Brewers in June of 1986, Jays manager Jimy Williams likely was the first major league manager to collect a gold record from the recording industry.

Hampshire attempted to repeat his success by compiling an album with this hit song, along with such other memorable musical contributions as "Help Us, Mookie," (to the tune of "Help Me, Rhonda"), "The Blue Jays Rap," and "The Ballad of Tom Henke."

None had the impact of Hampshire's original hit.

"OK Blue Jays" Lyrics

You've got a diamond
You've got nine men
You've got a hat and a bat
And that's not all
You've got the bleachers
Got 'em from spring 'til fall
You got a dog and a drink
And the umpire's call
Waddaya want?
Let's play ball!

Is that a fly ball
Or is it a seagull
Coming in from the lake
Just to catch the game?
It's the last inning
Our guys are winning
Dave's put down a smoker
A strike
And you've got no doubt
(You're out!)
Waddaya want?
Let's play ball!

Okay (okay)
Blue Jays (Blue Jays)
Let's (Let's) Play (Play) Ball!

It's a beautiful evenin', fans
At the ballpark
When the game starts
Warm summer breezes
Sun's goin' down
And it's all dark
At the ballpark
But that's okay…it's a night game

Okay (okay)
Blue Jays (Blue Jays)
Let's (Let's) Play (Play) Ball!

Okay (okay)
Blue Jays (Blue Jays)
Let's (Let's) Play (Play) Ball!

Bring on the White Sox
Bring on the BoSox
Bring on the Brewers
The Rangers and the Yankees, too
We'll beat the Indians
We'll beat the Tigers
We'll beat the A's so bad it'll make
Billy blue
Waddaya want?
Let's play ball!

Okay (okay)
Blue Jays (Blue Jays)
Let's (Let's) Play (Play) Ball!

Okay (okay)
Blue Jays (Blue Jays)
Let's (Let's) Play (Play) Ball!

66 Rick Bosetti—a Whiz in the Outfield

Former Blue Jays outfielder Rick Bosetti has excelled at nearly everything he's done. In 1971 he served as class president at Anderson Union (California) High and was drafted by the Philadelphia Phillies just two years later. He married his high school sweetheart, Patti, and the couple remain happily married while raising four children. He's a Rotarian, a member of the Sons of Italy, a nationally certified USA Swimming official, a former mayor and city councilman…

And he pissed in every outfield in the major leagues.

Was it just for kicks? A youthful indiscretion? Did he have a nervous bladder? Now firmly in the political arena, Bosetti does not discuss the motivations for his…uh…impressive accomplishment.

Bosetti had arrived in Toronto from the St. Louis Cardinals in exchange for Tom Bruno on March 15, 1978. He went on to hit 17 home runs in three and a half years in a Blue Jays uniform, posting a .252 average and stealing 23 bases. His big year was 1979 as Bosetti played each of the team's 162 games. He led all American League outfielders in putouts, assists, and errors…and reportedly started on his whizzing mission.

Bosetti's rights were purchased by Oakland in mid-1981, and his baseball career ended soon after. Not one to let his brief baseball career define him, Bosetti sprung into action in his hometown of Redding, California, where he became involved in local business and politics.

He first served as a member of Redding City Council and later became mayor. He currently manages the Redding Colt 45s in a Northern California summer collegiate league. To date, there are no reports of any outfield urination at Redding's home park.

67 Derek Bell's Jeep and Other Tales of Mischief

The Blue Jays' history is filled with almost as many pranksters as sluggers. For every practical joke the public hears about, there are probably 50 more that remain clubhouse secrets. But some pranks were too large to keep under wraps and made for memorable moments in team history.

With the 1992 American League East pennant safely secured, the final game of the regular season served as a day off for some of the team's veterans. This idle time was just the right opportunity for the vets to come up with a way to prank Derek Bell, their young teammate. Bell drove an ostentatious, boldly coloured, custom-green Jeep. Some of the older players like Joe Carter, Devon (formerly White) Whyte, and Candy Maldonado got ahold of the keys to his pimped-up ride before the game, and they began to execute their devious scheme.

In on the prank, the Blue Jays public address announcer told the crowd that a lucky fan had won Bell's Jeep in a random draw. The crowd cheered, while the pranksters drove the vehicle onto the field. Cameras focused on Bell, who looked shocked, concerned, and stunned, as he sat in the dugout. Carter, laughing, finally came over and slapped him on the back, and Bell realized it was just a ruse. The prank made for a memorable moment in Jays history and served to add to the camaraderie of a World Series-winning club.

But there have also been other fascinating stunts throughout Jays history. While managing the New York Mets in 1999, Bobby Valentine was ejected in the 12th inning of a game against the Blue Jays for arguing an interference call on a catcher. Instead of going to the clubhouse, Valentine returned to the dugout with a fake moustache, sunglasses, and a Mets T-shirt. Though many were amused, Major League Baseball was not. It fined Valentine $5,000 and suspended him three games.

There have been retaliatory pranks. See Vernon Wells, who lit the cleats of teammate Shaun Marcum on fire, a well-known baseball prank called "hot foot." Wells' act was in retribution for an earlier prank. When Wells had tripped and fallen out of the dugout, Marcum made a tape outline of him, like at a murder scene.

There was a musical prank played on a Blue Jays player prior to his arrival in Toronto. Second baseman Kelly Johnson—then of Arizona—came up to bat, only to hear that his walk-up music had been changed to "It's Raining Men." To make fun of a team bromance, Jays pitchers Roy Halladay and A.J. Burnett put their heads together on a stunt. Noticing that young infielders Russ Adams and Aaron Hill were inseparable at spring training, they paid a local pilot to fly over the stadium during warm-ups, dangling a message, which read, "Russ, will you marry me, Aaron." Not satisfied to let a good prank stop there, Halladay and Burnett arranged for the Blue Jays clubhouse to be set up for a wedding reception. As the players headed to their cars afterward, they found both of their vehicles covered in bows and streamers, emblazoned with "Just Married" messages.

The pranks are part of the Blue Jays locker room culture—or the culture of any professional sports team. Put a bunch of 20 to 40-year-old men together over the course of a season, and mischief will ensue.

68 Delgado's Big Day

In the seaside city of Aguidilla, Puerto Rico, nearly everyone knows hometown hero Carlos Delgado. He's arguably the most famous resident in town—and not just due to his exploits as a Toronto

Blue Jay, Florida Marlin, and New York Met. For years, he and his wife, Betzaida Garcia, have made charitable work their joint passion. They are socially conscious and passionate about the betterment of Puerto Rican society, donating generously to schools and paying for medical equipment. He visits local hospitals and doles out gifts to children every year on January 6. This is the day Puerto Ricans celebrate the Epiphany, which is considered more important than Christmas and called "Three Kings Day."

On September 25, 2003, it was the number four that made him a home run king. Delgado became one of just 16 players in baseball history to hit that many home runs in a game.

In the first inning, Delgado hit a three-run homer off Tampa Bay Rays pitcher Jorge Sosa. He tattooed the ball so hard that it caromed off of Windows restaurant, bouncing back onto the field of play. Even as he rounded the bases, Delgado asked the Rays to hang onto the ball. After all, this was the 300th home run of his career, making him the 98th player in baseball history to reach that milestone.

He wasn't anywhere close to being done. In the fourth inning, he crushed a solo shot, giving him two for the day and helping Toronto to a 4–1 lead. His third at-bat led to identical results. Delgado swatted another solo home run off Rays pitcher Joe Kennedy, which tied the game at six.

Three at-bats. Three big flies. Guess what came next…

Delgado tied the all-time record for home runs in a game at four, crushing a deep drive to centre and tying the game at eight. Four home runs in four at-bats. It was an incredible accomplishment, made all the more impressive by the fact Delgado was the only man in the history of baseball to do it in consecutive order.

A paltry sum of 13,408 fans attended the game, but they cheered like they were twice that many, as the ball came off Delgado's bat for the fourth blast. Delgado flipped his bat and headed toward first to begin circling the bases. "I was pretty fired up. I'm not going to lie to you," Delgado said. "As you can tell with the bat flip, I didn't know what I was doing. I was on cloud nine out there and enjoying it." Asked what might have possessed him that night, Delgado had no answer. "I can't think of any other way to explain it. It just kind of happened," he said. "It seems like everything you hit goes into the air and goes out. I wish I could do it more often."

The Blue Jays won 10–8 in large part due to Delgado's long-balls. "It was unbelievable. I'll always remember this," teammate Vernon Wells said. "When he's going good, there is no telling what he'll accomplish. It's something I'll never forget." It even wowed Tampa's legendary manager Lou Piniella, who spent more than 40 years as a player or manager in the major leagues. "It was a Herculean effort," he said. "Delgado is capable of getting into those grooves."

Delgado finished his 17-year major league career with 473 home runs, a .280 average, and a slugging percentage of .546. He won three Silver Slugger Awards in a Toronto uniform and holds the Blue Jays' all-time record of 145 RBIs in a season. He holds the all-time Blue Jays records for home runs (336), RBIs (1,058), walks (827), doubles (343), total bases (2,786), runs scored (889), plate appearances (6,018), career slugging percentage (.556), extra base hits (690), times hit by pitch (122), and intentional walks (128). Heck, he even leads the Jays in career strikeouts (1,242). (Not all stats can be awesome.)

As he announced his retirement roughly five years later, Delgado reflected on his successful life in baseball and his commitment to ongoing charitable work in his home country. "I respected the game and tried to do things the right way," he said. "I've always carried the flag of Puerto Rico in my heart."

An Incredible Inside-the-Park HR

At first glance, former Blue Jay Rance Mulliniks appeared to be more Bill Gates than Bill Terry. He was more Dewey Decimal than Dewey Evans. More Albert Einstein than Albert Pujols. Well you get the idea...

Known for his bristly moustache and Coke bottle-like bifocals, Mulliniks established himself as a valued member of the Blue Jays from 1982 to 1992. Despite his brittle frame, the kid from Tulare, California, defied the odds in carving out a 16-year career in the majors for the California Angels, then the Kansas City Royals, and finally the Jays. He was 5'11", 162 pounds of bespectacled goodness. Let's just say that no one speculated that Mulliniks had taken performance-enhancing drugs, which tarnished other ballplayers of the '80s and '90s. This was a man who punched roughly nine home runs over the fence every year of his big league career. Mulliniks was not a speed merchant either. He averaged less than a single stolen base per year, and never scored more than 55 runs in a season.

But Mulliniks lasted almost two decades in the majors for a reason. He could hit. His batting average reached a high of .324 in 1984. His slugged .500 in 1987. He also would walk about as often as he struck out, an attribute which might make him more appreciated nowadays, considering the emphasis on sabermetrics.

Nevertheless, Rance Mulliniks earned a place in team history by hitting the first inside-the-parker in the SkyDome/Rogers Centre. On July 11, 1991, Mulliniks hit a Kevin Brown fastball on a low line into left field. Kevin Reimer, the Texas Rangers outfielder, lunged to make a shoestring catch, but the ball eluded his grasp. The Blue Jay chugged around first base, hearing the first base coach yell to him that the ball had gotten through. He headed past second and on to third, as the crowd in excess of 50,000 cheered, and finally to home plate. "That was a long run," Mulliniks joked. "I haven't run that far since I won the 1,500 meters in the 1986 Olympics."

69 Ed Barrow: Toronto's Baseball Pioneer

Though his connection with the Blue Jays is a bit more convoluted than some, the historic trail of Major League Baseball Hall of Famer Ed Barrow almost always leads back to Toronto. Hogtown was a strong, knowledgeable baseball market long before the Jays arrived in 1977. Throughout the late 1800s and early 1900s, the Toronto market drew more fans to its minor league games than many of its major league counterparts drew to theirs.

The man behind the box office success was a feisty young business baron, Barrow—perhaps the Alex Anthopolous of his time. In 1900 Barrow was hired to manage the Toronto Maple Leafs baseball club—also known as the Islanders. In addition to his managerial duties, Barrow became a part-owner of the team. Also owned by the Toronto Ferry Company, the Maple Leafs played their home games at Hanlan's Point Stadium on Toronto Island, a spot chosen in an effort to increase ferry traffic.

Barrow succeeded as manager, leading the 1902 Maple Leafs to an International League championship despite enduring a season filled with controversies, ranging from an on-field fistfight with an umpire to the aggressive poaching of his players by the newly formed teams of the rival American League. An entrepreneur first and a baseball man second, Barrow used his powers of persuasion to draw 130,000 fans to Toronto's games that season. The team outdrew two National League teams, and owners in the major leagues took notice. Within months, Barrow would play a formative role in the construction of three of the Blue Jays' biggest rivals.

First, he caught the eye of the Detroit Tigers ownership and fled Toronto to lead both the on-field management and player procurement roles with the Tigers. Barrow improved the team by

13 wins and acquired players who put the team on track for success in the coming years. But, after a series of feuds, controversies, and back-alley boxing matches, Barrow left the team. He headed back to familiar ground—the minor leagues—and resurfaced as Toronto's manager a few years later in 1906.

He would not receive his next big break until 1918, when he again contributed to the formative years of another future Blue Jays foe. The Boston Red Sox hired him as skipper, and he responded by leading the team to a World Series victory. He also earned fame as the man who moved Babe Ruth from the pitching mound to the outfield, an experiment which paid off rather well. Despite Barrow's pleas, Red Sox owner Harry Frazee sold Ruth's rights to the rival New York Yankees to pay down debt. A year later Barrow followed Ruth to New York. There, he made what might be his most lasting impact on the game of baseball. Teams like the Blue Jays indirectly feel the effects of Barrow's contributions to the Yankees to this day. With the Yankees, Barrow was tenacious, pursuing success obsessively. That's why his plaque sits in the team's renowned Monument Park—alongside plaques of Babe Ruth, Joe DiMaggio, and Lou Gehrig, amongst others.

Barrow's plaque reads:

EDWARD GRANT BARROW 1868–1953

Moulder of a tradition of victory under whose guidance the Yankees won fourteen American League pennants and ten World Championships and brought to this field some of the greatest baseball stars of all time. This memorial is a tribute from those who seek to carry on his great works

It's difficult to quantify exactly how crucial Barrow's moves were to the evolution of the Yankees or the Red Sox, but one could easily argue that his role in the growth of each team, during a crucial period in their mutual history, contributed to the fierce rivalry they carry to this day. Is Barrow the man to blame for the long-standing arms race between the American League East rivals? Is he at least indirectly responsible for the Yankees' obscene $200 million-plus payroll, as the team strives to win at all costs?

The magnitude of Barrow's legacy and how it impacts the current Blue Jays would be terrific fodder for debate. But a few of his contributions to baseball are beyond dispute and can be felt at any Blue Jays game. Not only was Barrow a great teambuilder, he was also a relentless innovator. He was the man who put uniform numbers on baseball jerseys and was the first to allow fans to keep foul balls. He was also the man who started the tradition of playing the national anthem at all baseball games.

70 BJ Birdy Gets Tossed

Despite their cuddly exterior, mascots have quite a history of debauchery. Perhaps emboldened by anonymity, many have engaged in acts ranging from the simply stupid to the downright deplorable. Expos mascot Youppi, orphaned by the move of Montreal's team to Washington, was a pioneer of mascot mayhem. The adorable bastard cousin of BJ Birdy became the first mascot to be ejected from a Major League Baseball game in 1989 after thumping noisily on the Dodgers dugout.

The 1990s were a rough decade for these costumed cheerleaders, as they inflicted damage and destruction throughout the sporting (and home decorating) world. Invited to a grand opening of a paint store in 1994, the Philly Phanatic found himself embroiled in controversy after warmly hugging a man by the name of Charles Donoghue. Sadly, the hug was a little *too* warm, and Donoghue sustained significant back injuries from the embrace. He sued the Phanatic and was awarded a $2.5 million judgment.

In August of that year, Dinger the Dinosaur lost his footing at a Rockies game, falling into Colorado broadcaster Jeff Kingery during live action. Kingery shoved the purple beast, cursing him for the interruption. Fans would later vote overwhelmingly in favour of pushing this anthropomorphic purple triceratops into extinction. And to ring in the millennium, Florida Marlins mascot Billy the Marlin knocked an elderly man unconscious with a projectile fired from a T-shirt cannon in 2000. The man attempted to sue but was not awarded damages.

By comparison to the acts of his brethren, BJ Birdy's transgressions seem relatively minor. Brought to life in 1979, BJ Birdy's real (and secret) identity was Kevin Shanahan, a part-time science student at the University of Toronto. Shanahan frolicked atop the Blue Jays dugout and throughout the stadium, providing relief from the slow pace of baseball games and entertaining children and intoxicated fans alike.

He was beloved by almost all in the stands, but developed a tenuous relationship with team management. Underneath that cute, furry exterior, Shanahan had a fiery personality and he was known to stir up trouble with the team. He commented publicly on team issues and criticized the front office both on and off the record. When the *Toronto Star* gave Shanahan the opportunity to create a comic strip for the newspaper, he used it as a forum to air his grievances with the club and its fans. He mocked management and took potshots at fans he perceived to be increasingly abusive. The cartoon was soon cancelled.

But, his most memorable moment came on May 22, 1993, when BJ Birdy became the first Toronto mascot to be ejected from a baseball game. During a matinee match with the Minnesota Twins on this day, Blue Jays second baseman Roberto Alomar laced a line drive toward the outfield. David McCarty moved in to make a play, clearly trapping the ball. Thinking the umpire would call Alomar out, BJ suggested the call stunk by reaching up to plug his nose.

Believing the 6'8" bird's gestures were an attempt to incite the SkyDome crowd, umpire Jim McKean sent him to the showers (or birdbath). Even more embarrassing than the ejection was the fact the umpire actually got the call right—ruling that the ball had not been caught.

Somehow, despite indiscretions like this and his misguided comic strip, BJ Birdy managed to hang around for six more years, until the team cut ties in 1999. "It was bye-bye Birdy before the last homestand," Shanahan told the *Toronto Star*. "I would have liked to have had a fan appreciation day, so I could say good-bye to the fans, but that's the way it goes. It's like throwing out an old pair of socks. Baseball is a cruel sport."

71 The Slugfest

Scientists may never prove for sure if chicks really dig the longball. But we can say, for certain that one particular type of bird loves the art of hitting baseballs out of the yard—the Blue Jay.

Only one team in the history of the major leagues ever hit 10 home runs in a game. It wasn't the 1927 Yankees with Babe Ruth and Lou Gehrig. It wasn't the Big Red Machine with Joe Morgan and Johnny Bench. It was your Toronto Blue Jays, and the date was September 14, 1987.

This Big Blue Machine entered the game with a 85–57 record, duking it out with the Detroit Tigers for first in the American League East. Jim Clancy started for the Jays; Ken Dixon was the man for the Baltimore Orioles. Clancy was crisp from the start—Dixon not so much. Before he was sent to the showers, Dixon coughed up homers to Ernie Whitt, Lloyd Moseby, and Rance Mulliniks. And that was just the start.

After those three homers in the first two innings, the Jays went on to hit two more in the third, one in both fifth and the sixth, two in the seventh, and one each in the fifth and. All told, the Blue Jays hit 10 home runs, breaking the 1939 Yankees' record of eight homers in a game, which had been tied by seven other teams. Whitt was the offensive hero, crushing solo shots in the second and fifth innings and then adding a three-run homer in the seventh. The Blue Jays catcher found himself amidst a home run binge with five dingers in 12 at-bats. "I've never been in a streak like this before," Whitt said. "When I hit home runs, I usually hit two or three a week and then I don't hit any for a month. This is unbelievable."

George Bell added a pair of dingers of his own that day, launching him into the major league lead with 45. Noted powerhouse (read: slap hitter) Mulliniks recorded two home runs, while Rob Ducey, Fred McGriff, and Moseby each put one over the fence. "You're not trying to show anybody up," Mulliniks said. "It's just one of those things. We just happened to hit a lot out of the park."

Ducey's home run was the first of his career. Perhaps unaware that his first longball was part of baseball history, he seemed disheartened that it was lost in the shuffle of an 18–3 blowout. "It wasn't as exciting as I thought it would be, probably because of the game," said Ducey, a Canadian. "But that's all right. I'll take it."

Orioles manager Cal Ripken Sr. was disappointed by his team's effort. "It was an embarrassing baseball game. I'm not the only one embarrassed. Everybody [in the clubhouse] is embarrassed. But this is the game of baseball. You never know what's going to happen."

The night was also historic for another reason. In the midst of the onslaught, ironman Cal Ripken Jr. was benched by his father in the eighth inning, ending an incredible streak of consecutive innings played at 8,243. Although innings-played records were not always kept, baseball pundits generally agreed that Ripken's streak was the longest in history. "We were getting beat very bad in Toronto, and I think Dad, [Cal Sr.—the team's manager] in the weeks coming up to that, thought it was a little bit of a burden that I constantly had to respond…because people started thinking about [my] playing every inning, every game, and there was a certain burden of managing that kind of thing when you came to a new city," Ripken told *Sports Illustrated.*

"When I came to the bench he asked me, 'What do you think of taking an inning off,' and I immediately posed the question, 'What do you think?' He said, 'I think it would be a good thing.' And I said, 'Fine.' And I sat on the bench. Having played in the field so long, naturally, I felt out of place. I didn't know what to do. The irony is that I don't think I missed another inning the rest of the season. I think it was just a point to break it and see if that would help. I trusted my dad's judgment as a father and I trusted my dad's judgment as a baseball person."

Certainly, the game of baseball was sad to see Ripken's inning streak come to a close. Yet, it was a drop in the bucket compared to his eventual consecutive games streak of 2,632, a span which stretched from 1982 until 1998.

The Jays' record of 10 home runs in a game remains intact as well.

72 Capturing the AL East in 2015

History will remember most members of the Blue Jays of '92 and '93 for their smooth athleticism and natural talents. On a roster filled with the likes of Roberto Alomar and John Olerud, the pedigree of that crew was unmistakable. They were slicker than Juan Guzman's Jheri curl.

By stark contrast the core of the '15 Jays was mostly built with players whose careers had taken remarkable twists and turns along the path to stardom. This was a gang of post-apocalyptic marauders...guys who smashed through the low ceilings projected for them earlier in their careers. Many of them were castaways, has-beens, and late bloomers.

Josh Donaldson was a failed catching prospect. Jose Bautista was a former utility player, who had been passed around from organization to organization. Russell Martin didn't even have a regular position on his college team. Edwin Encarnacion was a butcher in the field who was essentially forced upon the Jays in the Scott Rolen trade. This fantastically intriguing gang of dirtballs clubbed and mashed their way to a plus-82 run differential in the first half. But pitching was a trouble spot for the team, resulting in a 45–46 record at the break. Nothing typified this fact more than the final game heading into the All-Star break. Despite scoring 10 runs, the Jays coughed up 11 and lost to the Kansas City Royals.

So what did they do next? They doubled down on their offense, acquiring perennial All-Star Troy Tulowitzki and base runner extraordinaire Ben Revere. The pitching makeover came next, landing David Price, LaTroy Hawkins, and Mark Lowe. The arrival of Price and Tulo added a purebred element to the Toronto squad. Price was a Vanderbilt product and a former first overall pick. Tulowitzki was a high school star in California before excelling at Long Beach State. Many of the fans who had not yet seen much of Tulo were blown away by his savant-like defensive skills. No matter the angle, no matter the scenario, his strong, unorthodox throws were almost always on point and almost always beat out base runners.

Attendance soared, and the victories piled up, ultimately resulting in a 17.6 percent increase in ticket sales. A sea of blue hats and shirts lined Front Street before every home game. If there was a plotline to the 2015 season, other than the surprise moves, it was the incredible fan response to their club. Chants of "MVP", "TUUU-lo", and "Jose, JoseJoseJose" grew louder each and every game. The Rogers Centre atmosphere was electric and earned a reputation as the loudest venue in baseball.

Bolstered by the fan support, the Jays finished with an American League East best 93–69 record. The next closest team, the New York Yankees, finishing six games back. The Boston Red Sox finished dead last, 15 games back of Toronto.

The Jays' AL East clincher will be remembered as somewhat of an awkward event. When a foul tip into the glove of Martin closed out the Baltimore Orioles 15–2, the Jays had officially secured a playoff spot for the first time in 22 years.

But the win came in the first game of a doubleheader, which made for a rather odd celebration. Rather than pile into the dugout and spray each other with champagne, the hooting and hollering was limited to a bouncing group hug around the pitching mound and a stream of high-fives and fist bumps in the clubhouse. The bubbly would have to stay on ice until the Jays and Orioles completed the second game of this doubleheader. The celebration was broken into two parts. The first occurred after the actual clincher, and the second occurred after the completion of the second game of the doubleheader, wherein they were finally allowed to let loose.

Celebration Part I: It was a thrilled but restrained club, as Price filmed teammates with a GoPro camera strapped around a Blue Jays beanie. Marcus Stroman leapt up and down in the clubhouse, visiting lockers throughout. Alex Anthopoulos shook hands with Jays fans as he headed from the stands to join the festivities. While he was interviewed by Sportsnet, Blue Jays fans chanted, "Thank you, Alex."

Celebration Part II: There was nothing reserved this time. With the team finally wrapping up the second game of the doubleheader, the champagne began to fly. As Hazel Mae interviewed Donaldson in the midst of the boozy party, his teammates filled the clubhouse with the same "MVP" chant he had heard all season. Price's voice was raspy from all of the hollering, as microphones surrounded him. Teammates sprayed Mark "Papa" Buehrle across the face as he completed one of the final interviews of his career. The players wore shirts emblazoned with the slogan, "The East is Ours." It was—for the first time since 1993. "It was a big hurdle to get over," manager John Gibbons said of his team ending its 22-year playoff drought. "It's been so damn long."

73 Take a Rust Belt Blue Jays Road Trip

In addition to being an incredible place to live, Toronto occupies a great location—in close proximity to a number of interesting baseball cities. Die-hard Blue Jays fans have an advantage over some of their American counterparts in the sense that (a) they have fairly quick access to a multitude of reasonable baseball road trips, and (b) they likely won't have to fight for prime tickets to see their favourite team on the road. Even with the considerable buzz surrounding the team recently, the Jays remain one of the majors' lowest road draws (ranking 25th out of 30 in road attendance amongst Major League Baseball teams in 2012). Seventeen of MLB's 30 stadiums are within a half-day's drive of Toronto, with several other notable baseball sites in their paths.

Pack your clothes and rest up for an early morning departure. Hop in the Wagon Queen Family Truckster, Griswold-style, and head for the good ol' U.S.A. Whatever you do, don't stock up on expensive Canadian beer before you leave. Like a glowing beacon, a $9.99 case of Natural Ice awaits you the moment you cross the border. (What this beer lacks in flavour, it more than makes up in price-conscious goodness.) Throw them in your cooler with a bag of ice and let the potent mixture marinate as your road trip progresses. You're on your way to an amazing baseball destination, where cheap tickets, great food, and fun times await at every stop.

Cleveland: A visit to this rejuvenated Rust Belt town usually yields affordable tickets, cheap hotels, and tasty restaurants. While the Indians haven't sent many players to baseball's Hall of Fame in recent years, visitors to Cleveland have the opportunity to visit the Rock and Roll Hall of Fame for a non-baseball diversion. While you're there, please boo Andrew Miller for being so damned spectacular in the 2016 playoffs

Pittsburgh: Forget what you've heard. Unless you're completely uptight and insufferable, you'll be impressed with this town's fresh and trendy entertainment district—all within a short walk of the memorable golden bridge to PNC Park. This former Rust Belt city has shaken off the corrosion and is now a mandatory stop on any baseball road trip. If you don't stop in for a world-famous Primanti's sandwich when you visit Pittsburgh, your family and friends will bow their heads in shame at your oversight. Of course, you'll need to hope that the stars align for the Jays to hit Pittsburgh during interleague play. Otherwise, take a break from the bluebirds and watch some National League action.

Cincinnati: The Reds' hometown has all the rust of Cleveland, minus the charm. Cincy's a town in need of a revival, a feeling you'll sense the moment you arrive. Great American Ball Park, though, is like an oasis in the desert. The park is a pretty sweet little modern-style stadium and offers visitors a high probability of seeing dingers cross the Ohio-Kentucky state line. After the game, dig into a bowl of Skyline Chili. It's typically more of a condiment than a meal, but not here, where the chili hits the spot after a long day at the ballpark. It's actually more like spaghetti sauce than chili, but it's an experience that must be had, if only to say you did it.

Detroit: With a beautiful new stadium located in downtown Detroit, you'll hardly realize the city suffered the brunt of the recent U.S. economic downturn. Mike Ilitch—founder of Little Caesars Pizza—has realized that no matter how bad things get, America will still buy endless supplies of Crazy Bread. And he's invested a huge chunk of his greasy fortune into an exciting, high-payroll Tigers squad. Catch a Jays game in Comerica Park and then head to Hockeytown Cafe or Chelly's—two watering holes that might help you forget the economic downturn your wallet experienced paying for parking. If you prefer old school, low-rent charm, be sure to check out the Detroiter Bar, which serves its food and drink generously—with huge plates of appetizers and overflowing jugs of domestic beers.

On the way home, be sure to stop in at the Canadian Baseball Hall of Fame in St. Marys, Ontario. Even if the road trip has left you with a headache and a sore belly, you'll feel much better after celebrating Canada's contribution to the great game of baseball.

74 The Alomar/Hirschbeck Incident

Fans in Toronto would like to remember Roberto Alomar strictly as an incredible baseball player. The second baseman could fill up highlight reels with his memorable plays, both on offence and defence. But there's one particular memorable moment in Alomar's past that Toronto fans would just as soon forget.

On September 27, 1996, Alomar took the field in a Baltimore Orioles uniform. He had signed with the O's prior to the season, leaving the Toronto team, which he helped to a pair of championships. The game marked just the fifth time he'd played in Toronto as a visitor. In the first inning, home plate umpire John Hirschbeck rang up Alomar on a called third strike. Television coverage showed that the pitch was as much as six inches outside. Alomar was incensed at the call. "If Hirschbeck said, 'I missed the call,' I would have done nothing," Alomar said. "But he told me, 'You have to swing at that pitch.' I just reacted."

Hirschbeck ejected Alomar, who continued to holler at him on the way to the dugout. Some say the ump threw a homophobic slur toward the Oriole during the verbal exchange.

"Why did you kick him out?" asked Orioles manager Davey Johnson.

"He's a fucking asshole," replied the confrontational umpire.

And that's when the spit really hit the fan...or the ump. Alomar hurled a loogie directly into Hirschbeck's face. He was then restrained and headed to the showers while the umpire cleaned up and returned to his duties.

But as if that wasn't enough, Alomar found a way to make the situation even worse. Sitting in the SkyDome visitors' clubhouse, he told reporters the umpire's game-calling had gone downhill after

Baltimore Orioles manager Davey Johnson tries in vain to restrain Roberto Alomar, who spit in umpire John Hirschbeck's face. Alomar received a five-game suspension for this incident, which took place at the SkyDome in 1996.

his son, John Drew, died from a rare condition called adrenoleukodystrophy (ALD) or inflammation of the brain. "I used to respect him a lot. He had a problem with his family when his son died. I know that's something real tough in life, but after that he just changed, personality-wise. He just got real bitter."

Hirschbeck had another nine-year-old son who had the same medical condition. When he got word the next day that Alomar had blamed the incident on this incredibly painful aspect of his life, Hirschbeck went ballistic. He charged into the Orioles' clubhouse, looking for blood. Hirschbeck shouted that he wanted to "kill him." Who knows what might have transpired if other umpires hadn't restrained him?

On September 28, the former Blue Jay issued a statement to apologize for the disturbing act, calling his actions "disrespectful" and "indefensible." He apologized to Hirschbeck and his family, admitting that he had "failed the game of baseball," while pledging to make a substantial donation to a charity conducting research into the ailment, which took their young child. To the dismay of the umpires' union, Alomar would ultimately serve just a five-game paid suspension and was even allowed to play in the postseason for Baltimore just a few days later. Hirschbeck accepted Alomar's apology, looking to put an end to the ugly situation.

Remarkably, the ump and the player, whose worlds collided so viciously in Toronto that night in September, actually forged a friendship years later. Alomar helped John Hirschbeck's son, Michael, land a job as batboy for the Cleveland Indians during the player's three years with the team. Alomar and Hirschbeck's donations to the ALD cause have reportedly exceeded $300,000. Hirschbeck has been praised for forgiving the man who did a couple of pretty galling things to him. "If that's the worst thing Robbie ever does in his life, he'll lead a real good life," Hirschbeck said. "People make mistakes. You forgive, you forget, and you move on."

75 The Mysterious Man in White

Alex Anthopoulos is a pretty cool customer. But, when *ESPN The Magazine*'s Amy Nelson accused his team of stealing opponents' signs, the Blue Jays general manager was clearly miffed. "That never happened, will never happen, not even a possibility," he said. "If it did happen, we'd be winning a lot more games at home…I think it's a non-story, because no one ever has picked up the phone and called me about it. It's never been an issue, and I would expect them to do so if it was."

Several anonymous players from opposing teams told ESPN the Jays were stealing signs during the summer of 2010 with the help of a man seated in the outfield stands. Then, the following January, ESPN and Baseball Prospectus columnist Colin Wyers produced a report showing statistical deviations in Toronto's hitting stats that he considered "too great to be random chance."

When New York Yankees manager Joe Girardi suggested to the media that Toronto was stealing signs, he was most concerned that the culprit might be planted in the outfield seats. Girardi was used to opposing teams trying to steal signs on the field, a tradition as old as the game itself. But he didn't want some jerk in a white shirt providing an advantage to the home team. "Obviously, if you feel it's coming from somewhere else besides a player on the field, I do have issues with that," Girardi said. "There's ballparks that you need to protect your signs. I don't really want to get into it because I'm not 100 percent sure about anything, but we need to protect our signs. Signs are coveted. Anywhere you play in the game, you have to protect your signs. Sometimes we have inclinations that things might be happening at certain ballparks and we're aware of it and we try to protect our signs. The last thing you want is the hitter to know what's coming."

Nelson reported that the sign thief raised his arms over his head for curveballs, sliders, and change-ups—anything besides fastballs. Four different players on Jays opponents confirmed the man in white would repeat this routine pitch after pitch.

When Jose Bautista took his position in right field, a member of the visiting bullpen engaged in a verbal exchange with the All-Star. "We know what you're doing," they yelled, referring to the man in white. "If you do it again, I'm going to hit you in the fucking head."

The players even went so far as to do a little detective work of their own. Before pregame warm-ups, they aligned one player in the batter's box and another on the mound. They pinpointed exactly where the man in white was believed to be sitting and determined that he was perfectly positioned to signal the players. "It's premeditated," one of the players told ESPN, "as if the guy was a sniper trying to find the best position to make a shot."

The Blue Jays were flabbergasted by the accusations and quickly brushed them off as foolishness. Anthopoulos called the claims "stupid" and explained that the accusations were flawed. "To do something like this would take a whole lot of work on this organization's part to keep everybody quiet. A lot of work," he said. "I just wish people would look at the common sense component first and say, 'Is this really realistic?' Think of what would have to go into all this stuff."

Bautista was equally perplexed by the logistical and ethical challenges associated with such a stunt. "First of all, I don't even know how you can do that," Bautista said. "And second of all, it's obviously something that's not legal in the game. We do not cheat." J.P. Arencibia was a little more direct with his words, sharing his thoughts through his popular Twitter account: "Teams/pitchers need to accept when we kick their ass in the rogers centre [and] not give excuses." Jays manager John Farrell chimed in: "We play this game to compete and prepare every day and we don't look to any other means than what takes place in between the lines."

The matter was never fully resolved and likely never will be. To prove the man in white existed, someone involved with the purported conspiracy would have to come forward, or the sign-stealer would have to be caught in the act. And if proving he existed was tough, proving he didn't exist was practically impossible. "I think every one of our games is broadcast. There are cameras everywhere," Anthopoulos said. "Why doesn't everyone go through the footage? Spend a month, spend a year, spend your lifetime. Go look for the man in the white shirt. Maybe you'll find someone in a blue shirt or a black shirt. Maybe you'll see a dog. Spend the time. Do a little work."

Bottom line: a man in white probably didn't tip off hitters, but conclusive proof of either side of the story has never surfaced. Like unicorns, ghosts, and (according to former major leaguer Carl Everett) dinosaurs, the man in white seems destined to remain a mythical being.

76 2016 AL East Pennant

While the prior season was a rapturous ride, the 2016 season was more like the Leviathan at Canada's Wonderland. (Google it, non-Torontonians.) Where the previous year's iteration steadily built to a long-awaited crescendo, this year's team put fans through a twisting roller-coaster ride filled with electrifying highs and I-just-threw-up-in-my-mouth lows.

Entering the year, the mood around the team was decidedly different than the one that drove the Jays deep into the 2015 playoffs. The smiling, popcorn-eating face of David Price was gone (to the Boston Red Sox, no less), as were fan favourites Alex Anthopoulos and Paul Beeston, the men considered the main architects of last year's success.

That's not to say that the excitement and expectations weren't still at peak levels, but a different tone had been set. Whereas 2015 felt like a new beginning, the flavour entering the 2016 season was one with a sense of finality. It was the final year of the contracts of Jose Bautista, Edwin Encarnacion, R.A. Dickey, Michael Saunders, Brett Cecil, and others. With an uncertain future, the time was now.

Under the new Mark Shapiro/Ross Atkins leadership team, Price was replaced in the rotation by free agent J.A. Happ, who had been mostly mediocre during his first go-round in Toronto. Marco Estrada was resigned to a two-year deal. The buzz entering spring training was a bit milder than that of the prior year. Bautista aired his salary demands with management (believed to be upwards of $25 million a year over five). A trade involving Jay Bruce and Saunders fell apart over a physical. Estrada and Aaron Loup would start the season on the disabled list. One of the stars of the prior year's run, Chris Colabello, was suspended 80 games after testing positive for performance-enhancing drugs. Cecil became the first relief pitcher since 1913 to lose five games in April. The team finished the opening month 11–14. As if in a post-2015 hangover, the Jays meandered through the first half.

The most notable moment of May's schedule came during a 7–6 loss to the Texas Rangers. After humiliating Rangers pitching with his seventh-inning blast in the 2015 American League Division Series, celebrating with a bat flip, and then crushing a bases-clearing double in that May contest, Bautista was drilled with a pitch from designated goon Matt Bush.

Melvin Upton's Cross-Border Shenanigans

Truth is often stranger than fiction. With the San Diego squad already in Toronto to face the Blue Jays, Padres outfielder Melvin Upton Jr. was swapped to the Jays for minor leaguer Hansel Rodriguez. But he wasn't able to simply walk from one dugout to the other to join his new team because that would have made far too much sense.

Instead, Upton was informed that he had to physically cross back into the United States, obtain a work visa, and then return to Toronto to be eligible to join the Jays. While he had entered Canada on Sunday night as a visitor, he was now under contract with the Blue Jays, and red tape ensued.

Upton headed to the nearest border crossing in Lewiston, New York, by car and jumped through the proverbial hoops needed to make his trade official. "About an hour-and-a-half ride there," Upton said upon his return to the stadium, "sat at border patrol for a little while jumped in the car and came back."

Both benches were warned against retaliatory actions, but an ugly momentum was building. When Justin Smoak hit a routine grounder, Bautista slid hard into second base to prevent a double play. Angered in part by the illegal slide and in part by last year's infamous bat flip, Rougned Odor threw the ball inches from Bautista's head rather than directly to the first baseman. When Bautista stood up from the slide, Odor sucker punched him with a right hook to the jaw. Benches cleared, as the Jays reacted to the petty cheap shots made by a team of sore losers. Odor, Texas' lemur look-alike, was suspended for eight games (reduced to seven on appeal), and Bautista was suspended one game.

In part motivated by these events and in part because their roster was so goddamned loaded, the Jays went 17–12 in May and 15–12 in June. July was the team's best month of the season with a .667 record in 24 games, and the team ran off a seven-game winning streak. Topping it off, five Blue Jays were named to the All Star team: Encarnacion, Estrada, Josh Donaldson, Aaron Sanchez, and Saunders.

Unlike the 2015 season, the July trade deadline this season didn't produce much in the way of headline-grabbing moves. In a sharp contrast to the skull-numbingly spectacular dealings of their predecessor, the moves made by the more conservative duo of Ross Atkins and Mark Shapiro were predictably modest. Rather than go all in with a splashy move that might improve the fanbase's perception of the new regime, the two-headed robot known as Shatkins played it safe in picking up struggling starter Francisco Liriano from the Pittsburgh Pirates, aging reliever Jason Grilli from the Atlanta Braves, and the desiccated carcass of B.J. Upton (now known as Melvin Upton Jr.) from the San Diego Padres. They dumped Jesse Chavez on the Los Angeles Dodgers for Mike Bolsinger and picked up Scott Feldman from the Houston Astros.

But the offense continued to overpower opponents to the tune of a plus-46 run differential in July. August was more of the same, as the Jays won 17 games. Bautista's year was relatively muted in comparison to recent performances, in part due to visits to the disabled list. Encarnacion and Donaldson were predictably amazing. But the unexpected stories of the 2016 regular season were written by Happ, Estrada, Roberto Osuna, and Sanchez.

Happ, rejuvenated and refined by his work under the tutelage of Ray Searage, was a new man. Looking like a completely changed man, Happ delivered a 20–4 record, a 3.18 ERA, and a 1.17 WHIP. Estrada delivered 18 quality starts, finishing with a 9–9 record that shortchanged his actual net impact. Osuna, barely old enough to legally enjoy postgame refreshments, delivered everything Toronto could have expected and more in 2016. Finishing the season with 36 saves, he emerged as one of baseball's most reliable relief aces.

But certainly one of the biggest stories of the 2016 season was the rise of Sanchez to the upper echelons of star pitchers in the major leagues. The pride of Barstow High School took himself out of the discussion as a late-inning reliever and into the Cy Young discussion as one of the American League's best. With a 15–2 record, an AL-best

3.00 ERA, and 161 strikeouts in 192 regular season innings, Sanchez took a leap forward most would consider the best case scenario.

Encarnacion was the Blue Jays' undisputed offensive star, leading the team with 42 dingers and 127 RBIs. He took 87 walks in 702 plate appearances and scored 99 runs in an All-Star season.

The fans were stars of their own. Proving once again that Toronto sports fans will rabidly support a winner, attendance jumped to 3,392,099, a 21.4 percent increase over the prior year. No other AL team drew as many fans, and, in fact, only the Dodgers and St. Louis Cardinals filled more seats in the entire MLB.

77 Canadians on the Jays: Position Players

Brett Lawrie is intense, skilled, and just a wee bit aggressive. The Langley, British Columbia native is also quickly establishing himself as the best Canadian hitter ever to play for the Blue Jays. After coming to the team in a trade for starter Shaun Marcum, Lawrie's taken the league by storm.

The level of baseball talent coming out of Canada has escalated steadily during recent years to the point that players from north of the border have become household names. Larry Walker (Maple Ridge, British Columbia) will likely be remembered as one of the best players *not* to earn enshrinement in the Hall of Fame. Several other players from north of the border have entrenched themselves as valuable contributors. Ontario natives Joey Votto (Etobicoke) is an established as major league All-Star. Justin Morneau (New Westminster) and Jason Bay (Trail) have proven British Columbia to be an emerging hotbed of baseball talent, with dozens of minor leaguers from the province close to making their own impact.

The Blue Jays have had their share of Canadian position players throughout the years, highlighted in recent years by East York, Onatario's Russell Martin, and Langley, British Columbia's Brett Lawrie. Toronto's 2016 roster had another pair of northerners, with Michael Saunders of Victoria, British Columbai, and Dalton Pompey of Mississauga, Ontario. Many of the other Canucks to wear Toronto's uniform were part-timers, but a few made fairly significant contributions to the team's success.

Dave McKay was the first Canadian to play for the Jays, taking the field on Opening Day 1977 as the team's third baseman. After putting up rather meagre offensive performances with Toronto and later the Oakland A's, McKay seemed destined to fade into obscurity. Instead, he moved into the coaching world and established himself as Tony La Russa's first-base coach in both Oakland and St. Louis. So far, he's been part of six pennant winners and three championship teams—the 1989 A's and the 2006 and 2011 Cardinals.

The pride of Cambridge, Ontario, Rob Ducey, was the first Canadian to play for both the Blue Jays and the Montreal Expos. With a memorable uppercut swing and a warm smile, Ducey became a fan favourite as a role player on the talent-laden Toronto teams of the late '80s and early '90s. His career would stretch over 13 major league seasons and was followed by a post-retirement stint in the Jays scouting department.

Paul Hodgson of Montreal joined the Jays as an undrafted amateur free agent in 1977. He surfaced in the major leagues just long enough for a *tasse de café* (cup of coffee for those who didn't pay attention in French class), playing all of his 20 career games for Toronto. He can always savour his home run off Baltimore Orioles stud pitcher Dennis Martinez—a shot which was his first and last in the bigs.

The brother duo of Rob and Rich Butler each served as backup outfielders for Toronto, with Rob also acting as pinch-hitter during

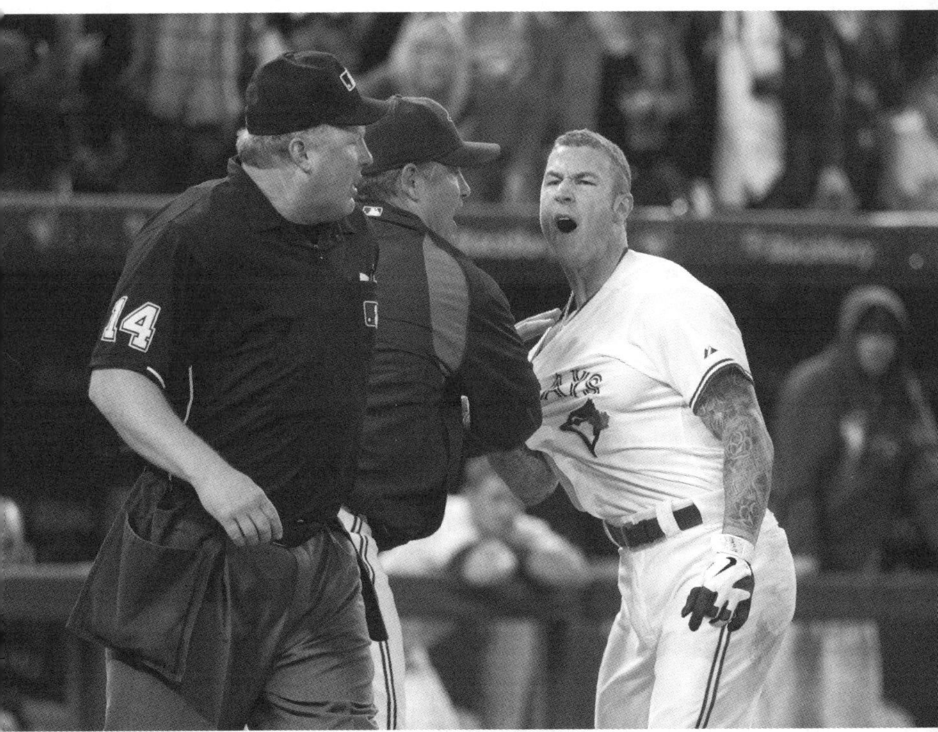

Blue Jays manager John Farrell restrains British Columbia native Brett Lawrie, who protests umpire Bill Miller's called third strike. Lawrie's helmet-throwing demonstration earned him a four-game suspension.

his time on the Jays. Following their departure from Major League Baseball, the pair joined fellow Canadian and former Blue Jays pitcher Paul Spoljaric on the semipro Toronto Maple Leafs of the Intercounty Baseball League.

General Manager J.P. Ricciardi had high hopes for Corey Koskie after signing the free agent to a three-year, $17.5 million contract prior to the 2005 season. Unfortunately the third baseman from Anola, Manitoba, suffered a number of injuries during his time in Toronto and failed to live up to Ricciardi's lofty expectations. He was traded away to the Milwaukee Brewers just more than a year after signing with the Jays.

Adam Loewen of Surrey, British Columbia, was once a top-rated pitching prospect, but the Blue Jays converted him to the outfield. He surfaced as a September call-up and struggled, hitting .188 with one homer and four RBIs in 32 at-bats. Mark Teahen, a Canadian citizen, fared almost identically to Loewen, hitting .190 with a homer and three RBIs in 42 at bats as a Blue Jay. Teahen, though, had more success with other teams, including the Kansas City Royals. North Vancouver, British Columbia's Simon Pond hit just .163 with one homer in 56 plate appearances for Toronto.

New Brunswick's Matt Stairs earned a reputation as one of the most fierce-looking players in the big leagues and enjoyed productive seasons for Toronto in 2007 and 2008. Known for his strong locker room presence, Stairs also earned his stripes as a clutch pinch-hitter. Those two factors certainly helped him earn the distinction of playing for more teams (12) than any other position player in baseball history. He also holds Major League Baseball's all-time record for home runs by a pinch hitter with 23—three ahead of former Jay, Cliff Johnson.

78 Canadians on the Jays: Pitchers

For years Fergie Jenkins has had very little competition for the title of Canada's greatest all-time pitcher. Although none of the Canadians pitching in the majors right now will likely ever come close to challenging Jenkins for that crown, a number have established themselves as high-calibre chuckers.

Ontario's John Axford (Simcoe) has earned repute as a fearsome closer, while starters James Paxton (Richmond, British Columbia) and Jameson Taillon (St. Andrews West) offer hope for future returns. (Taillon was born in the United States but is a Canadian citizen.) Ryan Dempster (Gibsons, British Columbia) retired after a successful career as an MLB starter, while Erik Bedard (Navan, Ontario) and Rich Harden (Victoria, British Columbia) were filled with talent but fell a bit short of expectations due to battles with the injury bug.

A number of Canadians have taken the mound for the Blue Jays throughout the years. Left-hander Denis Boucher was a Montreal kid who worked his way through the Jays system. As a 23-year-old, Boucher started seven games for the team, going 0–3 with a 4.58 ERA. After being packaged with Glenallen Hill and Mark Whiten in the trade that brought Tom Candiotti and Turner Ward to Toronto, Boucher played three more seasons in the big leagues. Most notably, he also played for the Expos—one of four men ever to play for both teams. He's currently employed as a New York Yankees scout.

Nova Scotia's Vince Horsman appeared in just four games for the Blue Jays, leaving Toronto with a perfect 0.00 career ERA. Steve Sinclair of British Columbia wasn't so lucky. He gave up 14 earned runs in 20⅔ innings, finishing his Blue Jays tenure with an ERA in excess of 6.00.

North Vancouver, British Columbia's Scott Richmond took a circuitous route to his Toronto Blue Jay life. Undrafted as a 25-year-old graduate of Oklahoma State, he joined the independent Northern League and produced rather pedestrian results. But during an open tryout, he caught the eyes of Blue Jays scouts who saw a raw talent they believed they could mould into a big-league-calibre arm.

Shawn Hill of Georgetown, Ontario, made four starts for the Blue Jays in 2010, going 1–2. He was credited with a win in his only appearance for the Jays after being called up from Las Vegas late in the 2012 season. Fellow Ontario native Paul Quantrill was certainly one of the most talented and underrated

Canadians to play for Toronto. His contributions to the game of baseball weren't as flashy as those of some of his star teammates, but Quantrill quietly established himself as one of baseball's better workhorses. He led the league in appearances on four different occasions, pitching in an amazing 80 games for Toronto in 2001. During that All-Star season, he produced a stellar 11–2 record, a strikeout-to-walk ratio of almost 5-to-1, and a WHIP (walk plus hits per innings pitched) of just 1.18. After the season, general manager J.P. Ricciardi shipped him, along with Cesar Izturis, to the Los Angeles Dodgers for Chad Ricketts and Luke Prokopec. Neither Ricketts nor Prokopec made an impact in Toronto, while Quantrill continued to skillfully ply his trade for four more seasons, and Izturis collected a Gold Glove and All-Star appearance for L.A. Scott Diamond, the pride of Centennial CVI in Guelph, Ontario, (the author's alma mater) pitched just one inning for Toronto in 2016.

Blue Jays fans hope that some of the Canadian pitchers currently dispersed throughout the team's minor league system might someday make a few All-Star appearances of their own.

79 Bobby Mattick, Al LaMacchia, and Don Welke

If Paul Beeston and Pat Gillick can be characterized as architects of the Blue Jays' success, perhaps Bobby Mattick, Al LaMacchia, and Don Welke were the foremen. One of the Blue Jays' first hires, Mattick joined the team in 1976 as the scouting supervisor and assisted general manager Peter Bavasi with player selections in the expansion draft. A second-generation major leaguer (his dad, Wally Mattick, played in the 1910s), Bobby had a brief playing career, but his scouting career lasted for decades. He's the scout who discovered Frank Robinson, Gary Carter, Gorman Thomas, Rusty Staub, Curt Flood, and Don Baylor, amongst so many others.

With the Blue Jays, Mattick signed players such as Dave Stieb, Jesse Barfield, Jim Clancy, Alfredo Griffin, Lloyd Moseby, Willie Upshaw, Ernie Whitt, Damaso Garcia, Barry Bonnell, and Luis Leal. After two seasons as a scout in Toronto, he took on the role of player development director and then transitioned to manager of the Blue Jays for two seasons. "I don't know where this organization would be without him," Paul Beeston said of Mattick. "I'll tell you this, they would not have been the team of the decade. No chance." Mattick passed away in late 2004. To celebrate his achievements, the Blue Jays renamed their spring training facilities, the Bobby Mattick Training Centre at Engelbert Complex.

Al LaMacchia's scouting was equally prodigious. Consider players he found: George Bell, Cito Gaston, Dale Murphy, Stieb, Upshaw, Rocco Baldelli, David Wells, and Andre Ethier. LaMacchia was a former big leaguer himself, pitching for the St. Louis Browns and Washington Senators during the 1940s. With the Blue Jays, he not only served as a scout, but also as one of Pat Gillick's most trusted advisors. The pair had a long-standing respect for one another from previous scouting adventures. Once he was promoted to the role of Toronto's GM, Gillick used LaMacchia's negotiation skills to initiate dialogue with other clubs and lay the groundwork for potential trades. "Al was a unique character in this business, for sure," said Howard Starkman, the Jays' longtime public relations director, "And he was certainly a vital part of our success." After suffering a stroke, LaMacchia died on September 15, 2010 at the age of 89.

Don Welke's contributions to the Jays are slightly less celebrated than Mattick's and LaMacchia's, though they might have been just as crucial to the team's success. Behind the scenes he quietly contributed to the scouting of a number of major league stars. "Don has an ability to take one look at a guy and decide quickly if he's a player worth following or if he needs to move on," Gillick said. "Few guys can make that decision as quickly and correctly as Don can."

With the Blue Jays, he insisted LaMacchia and Mattick take a good, hard look at some guy named Dave Stieb. He followed it up by recommending the Jays select Jim Abbott, who they didn't draft, and later John Olerud, who they did. Welke left Toronto for the Texas Rangers, and is credited with bringing them Josh Hamilton and Neftali Feliz. Don Welke knows talent. Kevin Goldstein, the ESPN prospect guru who became the Houston Astros pro scouting coordinator, said Welke was more appreciated by those within the game than by fans. "If you went to the Blue Jays game with 28,000 people there, and you asked the crowd if they knew who Don Welke is, maybe 17 of them would know," he said. "If you went to a few hundred scouts, and you said 'Don Welke,' every one of their eyes would light up, and they would say, 'Legend.'

"This guy's been in the business forever. He's helped so many teams get better and he's seen more baseball than you and I could ever dream of seeing. He has an eye for evaluating players and he's closing in on 50 years of doing it. He played a very big role in Toronto for a very long time. He's slowed down a bit, but he's still the kind of guy who shows up at a ballgame and sees a player he likes...GMs go out and sign that player."

Mattick, LaMacchia, and Welke might not be the highest-profile founding fathers of the Blue Jays, but their contributions quietly poured the foundation for the franchise's success.

80 Award-Winning Arms

If the Blue Jays have a singular baseball identity, it's likely as an offensive powerhouse. Throughout their existence, Toronto lineups have featured more than their share of big boppers, and they have ruined many a pitcher's evening. But the Blue Jays' history also includes a number of highly acclaimed pitching studs.

It started, of course, with Dave Stieb, Toronto's first legitimate baseball star. Over the course of the 1980s, Stieb won 140 games—second to only Jack Morris, who would pitch for the Jays in 1992 and 1993. Although he never won a Cy Young Award, Stieb was named the *Sporting News'* American League Pitcher of the Year in 1982, when he won 17 games and pitched 19 complete games. Stieb also had the league's best ERA (2.48) in 1985 and earned seven All-Star appearances.

Jimmy Key might have never earned the league-wide esteem of Stieb, but his talent was undeniable. The left-hander collected an ERA title of his own in 1987 with a 2.76 mark while also leading the league with a WHIP (walks plus hits per innings pitched) of 1.057. In 33 starts in 1989, Key walked just 27 batters—less than one per start. He was selected to four All-Star teams in his career and finished second in Cy Young voting on two separate occasions. The *Sporting News* twice named him AL Pitcher of the year—in 1987 and again in 1994.

Signed as a free agent by the Blue Jays prior to the 1992 season, Morris produced a MLB-leading 21 wins, helping to propel the team toward its first championship. Because his other stats weren't as impressive as his win total, Morris finished fifth in Cy Young voting. In fact, no Blue Jays pitcher would win the award until 1996, the year Pat Hentgen took home the hardware as the AL's

Before getting traded to the Philadelphia Phillies, pitcher Roy "Doc" Halladay won a Cy Young Award with the Blue Jays.

premier pitcher. That year, Hentgen won 20 games for Toronto and served as the team's workhorse with $265\frac{2}{3}$ innings pitched. He led the league with 10 complete games, three of which were shutouts. Oddly enough, he failed to make the All-Star team in his

Cy Young season, but Hentgen made up for it with selections to the team in three other seasons.

The Cy Young Award stayed north of the border for two more years, as the "Rocket" Roger Clemens produced arguably the two most dominant seasons in Toronto Blue Jays history. In 1997 Clemens won 21 games for Toronto to go along with a 2.05 ERA. He struck out a stunning 292 batters over the course of 264 innings pitched and threw nine complete games. He ran away with the Cy Young voting that season and even earned consideration for league MVP, finishing 10th. There was no letdown in 1998 as the Rocket slayed opponents to the tune of a 20–6 record and 2.65 ERA. His strikeout total was again staggering, with 271 over 234⅔ innings. During his time in a Toronto uniform, Clemens averaged an ERA of 2.33, a WHIP of 1.061, and 10.2 strikeouts per nine innings. His WAR (wins above replacement) of 11.6 in 1997 suggests that the finest season of his career took place as a Blue Jay.

While Clemens was in the midst of his sparkling seasons in Toronto, a young pitcher by the name of Roy Halladay was working his way up the Blue Jays minor league system. Despite early struggles, Halladay made the necessary mental and physical adjustments to become one of the most dominant pitchers in baseball. His finest moment as a Blue Jay came when he collected the 2003 AL Cy Young Award. "Doc" Halladay went 22–7 that season, throwing nine complete games and amassing 266 innings pitched. He led the league in strikeout-to-walk ratio with a stellar rate of 6.38. While in Toronto, Halladay made six All-Star appearances and won 148 games. He also left a lasting impression as a humble ambassador of the game.

Several other pitchers hold a place in Blue Jays history as well. Mark Eichhorn (1.72) and Duane Ward (1.95) are the owners of the two lowest single-season ERA totals in team history. Dennis Lamp (11–0), David Price (9–1), Aaron Sanchez (15–2), J.A. Happ

(20–4), Paul Quantrill (11–2), and Juan Guzman (14–3) will be remembered as the Blue Jays pitchers with the highest single-season winning percentages.

The list of 20-game-winners in Blue Jays history is relatively short. Halladay (twice), Clemens (twice), Morris, Hentgen, David Wells, and Happ remain the only members of this exclusive club. Stieb holds the Jays' all-time record with 175 wins, while Tom "the Terminator" Henke's all-time leading total of 217 saves has never been threatened. Henke's ERA of 2.48 through 563 innings pitched is exactly 0.70 lower than his nearest contender, Ward.

Clemens, A.J. Burnett, Halladay, and Brandon Morrow are the only Blue Jays pitchers to exceed 200 strikeouts in a season. All of those stats and facts are impressive, but only the most hard-core of Blue Jays fans would know the team's all-time leader in games pitched.

Jason Frasor with 505.

81 Managers Through the Years

Former Blue Jays manager Cito Gaston is beloved by fans and past players for his firm yet approachable style. Gaston has a heart of gold but could probably gut you with his bare hands if you gave him any lip. The native of San Antonio, Texas, is the Blue Jays' all-time leader in managerial wins with 894 and total games with 1,731. His name will remain in the history books in perpetuity, as he was the first African American manager to win a World Series. But for some reason, that same name never seems to pop up in the discussion of the all-time greats. "In the end, people are going to look up and see what kind of job I did," Gaston said. "I'm pleased and proud about it, and hopefully one of these days, they will, too."

Gaston was a bit of a reluctant manager, replacing Jimy Williams in 1989. He served for a run of 12 seasons, with just a brief interruption due to back pain. (Gene Tenace filled in for him for the 33 games he missed.) He was fired in 1997 but returned to the Blue Jays from 2008 to 2010. Fans fondly wished him farewell as he headed into retirement after 2010 as Toronto's only World Series-winning manager.

Considered one of the formative members of the Blue Jays managerial pantheon is Hall of Famer Bobby Cox. Although he earned much of his prestige while managing the Atlanta Braves, it was in Toronto where Cox launched his career. His most memorable year as Blue Jays manager was unquestionably 1985, the year he led Toronto to its first division title. He earned the American League Manager of the Year Award for his efforts, the only time a Blue Jay has won it. Cox ranks second all-time with 355 wins as Jays manager.

Williams and John Gibbons are the team's next-longest-tenured leaders. Although Williams was often portrayed as a buffoon by local media, few could question his 281 wins and .538 winning percentage. His strategic moves were often unconventional, but he produced results. Gibbons wasn't always given enough credit for his in-game management, but with a patchwork roster during his first go-round in Toronto, he could hardly be blamed. Rehired for the 2013 season, Gibby was given a second chance to surpass Cox's win total and he capitalized. The even-keeled manager has now accumulated 644 wins versus 614 losses, heading into the 2017 season.

It's hard to quantify the performance of Roy Hartsfield or Bobby Mattick in wins and losses. Each took the helm of pretty horrid teams and produced results accordingly. If they weren't

History of Blue Jays Managers

Name	Years	Games	Wins	Losses	Win Percentage
Roy Hartsfield	1977–1979	484	166	318	.343
Bobby Mattick	1980–1981	268	104	164	.388
Bobby Cox	1982–1985	648	355	292	.549
Jimy Williams	1986–1989	523	281	241	.538
Cito Gaston	1989–1991	417	235	182	.564
Gene Tenace	1991	33	19	14	.576
Cito Gaston	1992–1997	902	448	454	.497
Mel Queen	1997	5	4	1	.800
Tim Johnson	1998	162	88	74	.543
Jim Fregosi	1999–2000	324	167	157	.515
Buck Martinez	2001–2002	215	100	115	.465
Carlos Tosca	2002–2004	382	191	191	.500
John Gibbons	2004–2008	610	305	305	.500
Cito Gaston	2008–2010	412	211	201	.512
John Farrell	2011–2012	324	154	170	.475
John Gibbons	2013–	648	339	309	.523

leading teams reminiscent of the Bad News Bears, they surely would have won many more games.

Then there was Tim Johnson. He coaxed 88 wins out of the 1998 Blue Jays but was famously dismissed for lying about serving in Vietnam. Buck Martinez and Carlos Tosca both managed to basically break even as managers. Martinez was 15 games under .500, and Tosca dead-on at .500. Their sample sizes weren't as large as Cox's or Gaston's, but both showed flashes of the positive and negative in terms of tactics and strategy. John Farrell was introduced as the Blue Jays manager prior to the 2011 season. The former Boston Red Sox pitching coach led the team to an 81–81 record in his first year and went 73–89 in 2012 before moving on to serve as Red Sox manager.

Cito Gaston was asked if he ever saw himself returning someday to manage the Blue Jays. "I don't think so," he said, leaving just the tiniest smidgeon of possibility. Cue Lloyd Christmas from *Dumb and Dumber*, saying, "So, you're telling me there's a chance!"

82 2015 Postseason Run

Entering the 2015 postseason, the red hot Blue Jays seemed unstoppable. They had chips on their collective shoulders and 22 years of pent-up fan frustration adding fuel to the fire in their bellies.

ALDS Game 1

Pitching on 11 days' rest, ace David Price took the mound in the series opener to face the less steady hand of Texas Rangers pitcher Yovani Gallardo. Although Gallardo was certainly not the Rangers' best starter, he was the only one who solved the Jays' prolific offense in the regular season, winning twice. The move proved wise, as he surrendered just two runs in five innings. Keone Kela, Jake Diekman, and Sam Dyson followed, allowing just one run amongst them.

Manager John Gibbons was quick to defend Price, who gave up five runs in seven innings. "He wasn't getting hit around. It was just a couple of key hits at some key times that made the difference," Gibbons said.

Result: Texas Rangers 5, Toronto Blue Jays 3 (Texas leads ALDS 1–0)

ALDS Game 2

During a heart-pounding battle royale stretched over 14 innings in the Rogers Centre, starters Marcus Stroman and Cole Hamels dueled over seven of those innings before the Stro Show was pulled for Brett Cecil. As the goggled reliever had done so many times earlier in the season, Cecil coughed up the lead. Fast forward to the 14th inning, where a two-out rally put the Texas Rangers ahead 6–4 and the Blue Jays on the brink of elimination. "The task at hand is pretty simple: we have to win or we go home," said Jays third baseman Josh Donaldson. "That being said I like our chances just for the fact of the team we have in here."

Result: Texas Rangers 6, Toronto Blue Jays 4 (Texas leads ALDS 2–0)

ALDS Game 3

With their proverbial backs against the wall, Toronto's Marco Estrada and Troy Tulowitzki came up big for the Jays. Estrada held the Rangers to just one run over six and a third innings on 89 pitches. He allowed just five hits, while striking out four and walking none.

But perhaps the Jays' batters were squeezing their bats a bit too tightly, knowing that a loss would send them home for the season. The team wasted a number of opportunities to score, while hitting into four double plays in a postseason game. The Jays clung to a 1–0 lead. Stepping up to the plate hitless in the ALDS, Tulowitzki drilled a Martin Perez pitch to right field for a three-run homer.

Result: Toronto Blue Jays 5, Texas Rangers 1 (Texas leads ALDS 2–1)

ALDS Game 4

In a series filled with gut-twisting tension, this was a reprieve. The Blue Jays scored seven runs in the first three innings to take a commanding lead. R.A. Dickey cruised to a 7–1 lead with two out in the fifth inning, when he was somewhat controversially pulled for Game 1 starter David Price. While Price surrendered three runs over three innings, the Jays cruised to victory. With the series returning to Toronto, momentum had clearly swung back in Toronto's favour.

Result: Toronto Blue Jays 8, Texas Rangers 4 (ALDS tied 2–2)

ALDS Game 5

In one of the great games in MLB history, Game 5 was a wild mix of emotion for fans and players of both teams. It would later become the subject of documentaries, literary essays, extensive television coverage, and a chapter of its own in the book you are holding. The Blue Jays would emerge victorious and head to the American League Championship Series against the Kansas City Royals.

Result: Toronto Blue Jays 6, Texas Rangers 3 (Blue Jays win ALDS 3–2)

ALCS Game 1

The Kansas City Royals struck first in the series, shutting out the Jays behind the pitching of Edinson Volquez. It was a typical grind-it-outs Royal performance with opposite field hits and solid base running. Marco Estrada took the loss on the day, noting that he didn't have his best stuff. "To be honest with you, I wasn't really locating my fastball today," Estrada said. "I don't know why."

Result: Kansas City Royals 5, Toronto Blue Jays 0 (Royals lead ALCS 1–0)

ALCS Game 2

What began as a stellar pitching performance by David Price quickly devolved into one of the season's most painful defeats. Heading into the sixth, Price was cruising, having retired 18 consecutive batters. The Jays were up 3–0 when Ben Zobrist hit a catchable ball to right field. Miscommunication between Ryan Goins and Jose Bautista led to the ball falling between them. Lorenzo Cain and Eric Hosmer followed with back-to-back singles to push the first run across. Next came a Kendrys Morales ground-out which cashed in Cain. A Mike Moustakas single would tie the game 3–3. Price managed to collect another out, but Alex Gordon smoked a run-scoring double. "David was so good tonight, it's a shame it had to end that way," John Gibbons said. "It was unfortunate. You really can't pitch a better game, to that point anyway."

Result: Kansas City Royals 6, Toronto Blue Jays 3 (Royals lead ALCS 2–0)

ALCS Game 3

Troy Tulowitzki, Josh Donaldson, and Ryan Goins homered off Royals starter Johnny Cueto to stake the Jays to a commanding lead. Marcus Stroman battled to hold the Royals to four runs before handing it over to the bullpen, which allowed a late rally by Kansas City, but the Blue Jays' prolific offense was the story of the day. "We desperately needed that breakout," said a relieved Blue Jays manager John Gibbons. "You look at how the game finished up, those runs really came in handy."

Result: Toronto Blue Jays 11, Kansas City Royals 8 (Royals lead ALCS 2–1)

ALCS Game 4

There was no such thing as a home-field advantage on this day. Facing the Royals at home in Toronto, the Jays found themselves trailing 5–0 in the second inning. It was one of those games in which R.A. Dickey's knuckler just wasn't working, as dejected fans struggled to replicate the crowd noise that had buoyed the team so many times this season. It got so ugly that Cliff Pennington was brought in to pitch in the ninth inning. He coughed up two more, as shortstops are known to do whilst pitching.

Result: Kansas City Royals 14, Toronto Blue Jays 2 (Royals lead ALCS 3–1)

ALCS Game 5

In a reversal of fortunes, the Jays annihilated Kansas City to force a sixth game in the ALCS. With the Rogers Centre crowd on edge, knowing full well the magnitude of this elimination game, the Toronto bats came to life. Chris Colabello smacked a solo shot in the second inning off Edinson Volquez, putting the Jays in motion. But the majority of the offense came in the sixth inning, when Troy Tulowitki crushed a bases-loaded double to cash in three.

Meanwhile, Marco Estrada held the Royals to just one run on three hits.

Result: Toronto Blue Jays 7, Kansas City Royals 1 (Royals lead ALCS 3–2)

ALCS Game 6

On the 22nd anniversary of Joe Carter's World Series-winning home run, Jose Bautista did his best to recreate history. Joey Bats slugged a pair of home runs on the day, and the second one propelled the Jays to a 3–3 tie in the eighth inning. Prolonging the suspense was a 45-minute rain delay midway through the eighth inning, which led Toronto to bring closer Roberto Osuna into the game. The normally steady Osuna gave up a walk to Lorenzo Cain, who was driven in by Eric Hosmer. The Royals took a lead they would never relinquish. Bautista was left standing in the on-deck circle as Josh Donaldson made the final out of the ninth against Royals closer extraordinaire, Wade Davis. "I'm definitely proud of our team," Toronto manager John Gibbons said. "We put up our best fight today."

Result: Kansas City Royals 3, Toronto Blue Jays 2 (Royals win ALCS 4–2)

83 Evolution of the Jays' Draft Philosophy

There was a lot to like about the Alex Anthopoulos era in Toronto. During his tenure, perhaps the most exciting development was a return to the team's core philosophies. The rejuvenation has involved more than just getting rid of the hideous Angry Birds-style logo to bring back the iconic team uniforms of the past.

Anthopoulos also has brought hope back to fans in Toronto by reviving the team's commitment to scouting, player development, and shrewd acquisitions. His moves were reminiscent of those made by another aggressive team architect, former Blue Jays general manager Pat Gillick—the man who took a flimsy expansion roster and transformed it into a baseball powerhouse in the '80s and '90s. Gillick focused his drafts on athletic, young position players and high-upside arms, entrusting his staff to develop them.

After Gillick's departure and under Gord Ash's watch, the Jays had a number of successful drafts, selecting the best player available rather than placing an undue focus on positional need. J.P. Ricciardi, on the other hand, invoked a rogue draft strategy upon arriving in Toronto. He was a strong-willed contrarian, and his draft style fit with his demeanour. Influenced by his apprenticeship under Billy Beane in Oakland, Ricciardi adhered almost exclusively to a philosophy of drafting projectable college seniors. He and his staff pored over college statistics to identify safe, conservative selections of players whose performances seemed the most predictable.

But, like any inflexible philosophy, this strategy had its share of flaws. By almost completely ignoring high schoolers, Ricciardi's plan reduced the available talent pool by roughly half. And since those safe picks generally lack the upside of risky picks, they ironically present more risk. The problem with that uber-conservative draft strategy, said Kevin Goldstein, the Baseball Prospectus baseball guru who became the Houston Astros pro scouting coordinator, is that, "even when you get big leaguers, they tend not to be stars."

Not long after being hired in Toronto, Ricciardi notoriously cleaned house in the scouting department, letting go of many of the industry's most respected talent evaluators. Instead he focused on what he believed was cutting-edge talent evaluation—the assessment of players through statistical analysis. Goldstein, considered one of the foremost contemporary experts on the Major League Baseball draft and minor league player evaluation, said the test of time has proven that good old-fashioned scouting (mixed in moderation with statistical analysis) trumps studying numbers on a page. "You just can't base everything on a spreadsheet—you just can't," he said. "You just can't look at statistics alone when evaluating college players, because they're not playing Major League Baseball. There are skill sets that hold up really well in college—and even in the minor leagues—that aren't going to work in the big leagues."

Ricciardi's drafts yielded modest success, with Ricky Romero, Brett Cecil, Aaron Hill, Adam Lind, and J.P. Arencibia standing out as his best selections. But Goldstein said Ricciardi's approach to the draft helped lead to his undoing. "If you have one bad draft, that's fine—everybody has a bad draft. If you have a few in a row, all of a sudden your system's in trouble," Goldstein said.

When Ricciardi was dismissed in 2009, he left the cupboard in Toronto's farm system practically bare. "That ultra-conservative approach to player selection played a role, certainly," Goldstein said. But the resilient Blue Jays rebounded with the appointment of Anthopoulos and scouting director Andrew Tinnish—fresh-faced Canadian kids who lived, ate, and breathed baseball. The new approach was aggressive...really aggressive. "If the Blue Jays were any more aggressive," Goldstein tweeted during the 2011 Draft, "they'd be punching somebody with every pick."

Anthopoulos stockpiled pick after pick of high-upside talent, many of whom were considered unsignable by more conservative teams. Going against the grain, he grabbed high schoolers who had committed to colleges, studs coming off injuries, and elite athletes of all shapes and sizes. The results impressed Goldstein. "Their talent is incredible. It's a fantastic farm system. It's just completely loaded, and I think it is a tribute to what Anthopoulos has done in scouting, player development, and international signings."

In particular, Goldstein liked the way Toronto has accumulated callow arms. Remnants of the AA era are guys like Aaron Sanchez, Marcus Stroman, Sean Reid-Foley, and Conner Greene. "There's not another team in baseball that has amassed as much really exciting young pitching talent as the Blue Jays," he said. "There's no question about it."

With just one draft under their belt, the draft philosophy of Ross Atkins and Mark Shapiro is yet to be clearly understood. In the 2016 draft, they selected T.J. Zeuch in the first round and Bo Bichetter and J.B. Woodman in the second.

84 Harbour Sixty

Depending on your budget, as well as your appetite for a scrumptious cut of USDA Prime beef, you may need to plan a pregame visit to the renowned Harbour Sixty Steakhouse.

Just a five-minute stroll from the Rogers Centre, this Toronto landmark serves up some of the finest beef in the area. While there, keep your eyes open—you might just see visiting players or Hollywood moguls.

Front Street Meat

If there's a common complaint amongst Toronto fans, it's the lack of creative in-stadium food options at the Rogers Centre and the hefty price tags accompanying the generic offerings. A pleasant side effect has been the proliferation of "street meat" trucks lining Front Street, just a moment's walk from the ballpark.

There are tight local regulations on food safety, so the variety of food served isn't exactly enthralling. The stationary food trucks lining Front are basically limited to hot dogs and sausages, and only non-refrigerated toppings are allowed under local bylaws. But these vendors offer as many creative toppings as they're allowed under the law. Consumers can line their tube steaks with corn relish, Sriracha sauce, mushrooms, and bacon bits, in addition to the standard mustards, pickles, onions, and sauerkraut. There are enough toppings to draw away your attention from disturbing mental images of what spare parts of the pig/cow might have been ground up to create the masterpiece in hand. Thick-cut french fries are a tasty choice from the vendors, usually slathered with gravy or plentiful amounts of ketchup—or both.

But for every bylaw there's a loophole. Sure enough, local regulations allow mobile food trucks to be exempted from the non-refrigeration restriction, creating an army of high-calibre gourmet food trucks with more interesting options.

Among the most popular are Kal & Mooy's sabaya wraps, Gourmet Gringo's burritos, Me.n.u's roti tacos, Fidel Gastro's pad thai fries, Smoke's poutine, Food Cabbie's cheesesteaks, Blue Donkey's souvlaki, Buster's Sea Cove's lobster rolls, and Caplansky's deli sandwiches.

The steakhouse is housed in Toronto's Harbour Commission building, which is nestled just north of the city's Queen's Quay waterfront. It's not entirely snooty, but you might want to take off your Troy Tulowitzki jersey before entering. Most patrons are dressed in smart-casual style. The atmosphere and service are everything you'd expect from a world-class steakhouse.

Prior to heading over to the Blue Jays game, you can dine on a traditional meal, with a Caesar salad, perfectly prepared New York strip, and a glass of wine to wash it down. Or, if you're more adventuresome, you can try beluga caviar, Kobe beef, and the uniquely Canadian foie gras poutine. Be sure to order their famous campfire s'mores dessert—the perfect finish to a delicious meal—with fine chocolate, marshmallows, and crisp graham crackers. You'll appreciate the short walk to the stadium as juicy morsels of beef, potatoes au gratin, and delicious dessert settle in your belly.

Zagat rates Harbour Sixty as "extraordinary" on their rating scale, an honour reserved for just a handful of stadium-area establishments. Their review of Harbour Sixty is glowing, while pointing out the obvious fact that food at this place doesn't exactly come cheap. "For an extravagant experience, professional athletes, moneyed men, and other carnivores head to this special-event Harbourfront steakhouse offering generous portions of top-of-the-line fare; the wood-accented old-world environs are complemented by superb service, just bring two credit cards because you might max one out."

85 An Upper Deck Shot

Former Blue Jays pitcher DeWayne Buice just wanted some chicken chow mein. Instead, he found himself in the midst of a chance encounter that led to an opportunity worth millions. Buice had a middling career, pitching just seven games for Toronto in 1989 while posting a 1–0 record with a 5.82 ERA in 17 innings pitched. But what happened two years prior to his arrival in Toronto was much more crucial to his pocketbook.

Buice found himself walking through Yorba Linda, California, looking for Chinese food one evening. He stopped into a baseball card store called The Upper Deck and asked the staff for a restaurant recommendation. The owner, Bill Hemrick, recognized Buice, who was then pitching for the California Angels, and not only referred him to a good Chinese restaurant but also invited him back to the store for an autograph signing. Hemrick later mentioned that his ambitions far exceeded the bounds of a backstreet baseball card store. Instead, he wanted to form his own baseball card brand, which he would name Upper Deck.

But he needed Buice's help.

At the time the baseball card world was an oligopoly run by Topps, Donruss, and Fleer, the three companies licensed by the league. Hemrick saw Buice as the insider he'd need to crack into the high stakes game. He offered the pitcher a 12 percent share in his company, conditional on Buice helping to secure a license with the league. Buice took the deal and arranged meetings with Major League Baseball Players Association officials to land the license, even though he never intended to get into the business. "The only thing I ever wanted to do with baseball cards is to have my picture on one," Buice said. "It was my main goal."

On December 23, 1989, the MLBPA granted a license to Upper Deck. Hemrick and his crew were in business—literally. At the end of 1989 season, Buice retired from the Blue Jays, putting an end to his professional playing career. Meanwhile, the Upper Deck company had sold out the entire stock of its product and presold the 1990 season's supply well in advance. Cash was rolling in.

During this heyday Upper Deck paid Buice more than a million dollars in recognition of the role he played in landing the MLB contract, but the now-retired reliever believed he was being shortchanged. He sued his former business partners, and that led to a settlement in his favour for more than $17 million, which was to be paid out like an annuity. "Every month on the profit and loss statement, 'the Buice Payment' was a line item wedged under gross sales and returns," said a former executive of the company.

Buice has long since been paid off, and he got his money at the right time. Upper Deck, while a major card company during the '90s, declared bankruptcy on February 12, 2012.

86 A Game Full of Strange Memories

The Blue Jays' 5–4 victory against the Atlanta Braves on October 18, 1992 marked the first time a Canadian team won a game in the Fall Classic. But it wasn't just the historic Game 2 win that made this one of the most memorable nights of baseball in Blue Jays history.

During the contest, an entire nation was disrespected, an announcer successfully predicted the future, a singer flubbed the national anthem, an American League ace morphed into a successful hitter, and a player nicknamed after a Greek god stirred controversy by mocking fan tradition.

How's that for an interesting ballgame?

Even before the game started, some of the most iconic moments in team history were being authored. It began with a U.S. Marine Corps colour guard official carrying the Canadian flag upside down as he marched across the field. You could almost hear Canada's headline writers running to their keyboards to document the indignity. Clever Toronto vendors also seized the opportunity to make a buck by selling upside down U.S. flags outside SkyDome before Game 3.

Popular Canadian singer Tom Cochrane took to the microphone at Atlanta's Fulton County Stadium for the Canadian national anthem and proceeded to butcher the lyrics. Not only did he substitute a verse which hadn't been part of the anthem in decades, but he also sang the lyrics out of order, further frustrating uptight patriots.

Once the game began, the weirdness continued, as umpire Mike Reilly flubbed a potentially game-changing call in the fourth inning. Heading home on a passed ball, Roberto Alomar was called out at the plate by Reilly, though replays clearly showed the Jays star had touched home before the tag.

Not one to let a blown call get him down, Jays starting pitcher David Cone rapped a base hit in the fifth inning to drive home Pat Borders. The hit was the second of the game for Cone, which was all the more memorable because those two singles equalled the total number of combined hits by AL pitchers since the designated hitter rule was first used in the 1976 World Series.

With future Pro Football Hall of Famer Deion Sanders contributing on offence and on the base paths, the score stayed in Atlanta's favour for nearly the entire game. The outfielder/cornerback had skipped the Atlanta Falcons game versus the San Francisco 49ers to play in the championship contest. The decision paid off, as the speedster got on base three times, stole a pair of bases, and contributed to Cone's removal from the game in the fifth inning.

Heading into the top of the ninth inning, the Blue Jays trailed Atlanta 4–3. Braves closer Jeff Reardon—the all-time saves leader in baseball history at the time—issued a free pass to Derek Bell, putting the tying run on first base. Backup infielder Ed Sprague stepped up to the plate for Toronto. That's when Tom Cheek, the Jays' longtime announcer, became baseball Nostradamus. "Watch him hit a homer," said Cheek to the Canadian audience.

And that's exactly what Sprague did. He crushed a low fastball over the fence in left field, putting the Jays ahead 5–4. Cheek's prognostication became a lasting Blue Jays memory.

Jane Fonda, the wife of Braves owner Ted Turner, was caught on camera praying (perhaps to the baseball gods) for a rally in the bottom of the ninth, but Tom Henke closed out the Braves and put a bow on the Jays' first victory in a World Series game. Yet strange events continued even after the final play.

After catching the pop-up which ended the game, Jays third basemen Kelly Gruber mocked the Braves' Tomahawk Chop as he ran off the field. That slight of Atlanta fans' signature—albeit racist—tradition infuriated the Braves faithful, and Gruber became a prime target for jeers and insults throughout the remainder of the series.

87 The 2016 Postseason in Haiku

Inspired by Fangraphs' NotGraphs features and the website Box Score Haiku, the following is a half-assed attempt to describe the indescribable events of the 2016 playoffs.

AL wild-card

Edwin E walks off
Zach Britton sits in the 'pen
Bonehead Showalter

Explanation: The Blue Jays won the wild-card game on the strength of a memorable three-run blast off the bat of Edwin Encarnacion. Baltimore Orioles manager Buck Showalter was roundly criticized for failing to bring his star reliever Zach Britton into the game in such a crucial circumstance, opting to put his team's season on the line with the subpar pitching of Ubaldo Jimenez instead.

Result: Toronto Blue Jays 5, Baltimore Orioles 2 (Toronto wins wild-card)

ALDS Game 1

Jays bats deliver
Estrada stifles Rangers
Face punch to Texas

Explanation: With expectations of retaliation and anarchy, Toronto instead tidily destroyed the Texas Rangers in a 10–1 drubbing. Troy Tulowitzki cued the offense with a three-run triple in the third, and Marco Estrada allowed just one run through eight and a third innings. Jose Bautista added the icing on the cake with a three-run shot in the ninth inning. Not to be forgotten were Josh Donaldson's four hits and two RBIs. Even Melvin Upton Jr. contributed to the offensive onslaught with a solo shot.

Result: Toronto Blue Jays 10, Texas Rangers 1 (Toronto leads ALDS 1–0)

ALDS Game 2

This is not like Yu
Happ-y days are here again
Tight game, Blue Jays win

Explanation: Starter J.A. Happ battled his way through five innings without his best stuff in a game that saw the subsequent pitcher, Francisco Liriano, take a liner off his head. Texas Rangers starter Yu Darvish struggled against the vaunted Toronto offense. Troy Tulowitzki socked a two-run homer in the second inning. The unlikely duo of Kevin Pillar and Ezequiel Carrera followed those with solo shots in the fifth inning against Darvish. Not to be outdone, Edwin Encarnacion walked the parrot after another bases-empty bomb.

Result: Toronto Blue Jays 5, Texas Rangers 3 (Toronto leads ALDS 2–0)

ALDS Game 3

Double-play grounder
Donaldson dashes from third
Poor little Rougie

Explanation: In another instant classic, the postseason pressure got to Rougned Odor once again. A routine double-play ball was fed from the hand of Elvis Andrus to Public Enemy No. 1, who fired a low throw to first. With Texas Rangers first baseman Mitch Moreland unable to dig it out of the dirt, Josh Donaldson began to charge home from third base. Moreland scooped the ball up and threw it home with all his might, but Donaldson beat the throw by a hair. Jays teammates raced onto the field to celebrate the victory—and series sweep—with Donaldson and Russell Martin. One fan's sign, which captured the mood, read: "I'd rather be punched in May than knocked out in October."

Result: Toronto Blue Jays 7, Texas Rangers 6 (Toronto wins ALDS 3–0)

ALCS Game 1

Marco was brilliant
With one minor exception
Damn you, Frank Lindor

Explanation: Marco Estrada pitched magnificently for much of the game, but his performance was interrupted by a Francisco Lindor two-run homer on an 0–2 pitch in the sixth. Estrada intended to throw his signature change-up in the dirt but yanked it and left a centre-cut meatball for the young Cleveland Indians shortstop to smash out to right-centre field. Corey Kluber danced around several pressure situations to stymie the Toronto bats. Relievers Andrew Miller and Cody Allen shut the door, as Cleveland went on to take Game 1.

Result: Cleveland Indians 2, Toronto Blue Jays 0 (Cleveland leads ALCS 1–0)

ALCS Game 2

Anxious Jays batters
Yikes, here comes Andrew Miller
He's good at baseball

Explanation: Josh Tomlin had a solid start for the Cleveland Indians, but J.A. Happ held up his end of the bargain, allowing just a pair of runs over five innings. This game, however, might ultimately be remembered as the one in which the baseball world became enlightened to a new way to utilize late-inning relievers (hat tip to the Kansas City Royals for a similar model). For the second night in a row, Cleveland manager Terry Francona went to his lights-out reliever Andrew Miller for multiple innings, and for the second night in a row, he completely dominated the Jays. Toronto hitters looked utterly helpless against the lanky lefty, who struck out five of the six batters he faced. Cleveland's offensive star on the night was once again the newly crowned Blue Jays nemesis Francisco Lindor, as he drove in the game-winning run for the second consecutive night.

Result: Cleveland Indians 2, Toronto Blue Jays 1 (Cleveland leads ALCS 2–0)

ALCS Game 3

Trevor gushes blood
Cleveland's drone-fixing buffoon
Miller deals, again

Explanation: In one of the most fantastically stupid stories you'll ever hear about a professional athlete in the midst of a playoff run, Cleveland Indians starting pitcher Trevor Bauer had injured the pinky on his pitching hand repairing a toy drone. Team doctors did their best to protect the wound from opening up for their Game 3 starter, but steady drips of blood began to fall from his finger in the first inning. Manager John Gibbons informed the umps that gushes of hemoglobin were steadily dripping onto the Rogers Centre mound, and the pitcher was forced to leave the game. While this seemed to be an event that would work in favour of Toronto, the parade of relievers that followed kept the Jays in check. Summoned to patch together a bullpen game, Dan Otero, Jeff Manship, Zach McAllister, Bryan Shaw, and Cody Allen limited Toronto to two runs. Then, of course, it was Miller time, and his legend would only grow, as he struck out three of the five batters he faced. It was another multi-inning appearance and a save for the great Andrew Miller.

Result: Cleveland Indians 4, Toronto Blue Jays 2 (Cleveland leads ALCS 3–0)

ALCS Game 4

Jays bats come to life
Josh and Sanchise deliver
We beat the Klubot

Explanation: Fighting to stay alive in the playoffs, the Jays came up big against ace Cleveland Indians Corey Kluber. Josh Donaldson, who had arranged a closed-door team meeting prior to the contest, helped break a team-wide slump with a solo shot in the third inning. It was the first time the Jays had scored first in the series and the first time they had held a lead of any sort. In the fourth inning, Kluber issued consecutive walks to Troy Tulowitzki and Russell Martin to start the inning. Tulo scrambled home on a blooper by Ezequiel Carrera, and the Jays led 2–0. Edwin Encarnacion delivered a grounder up the middle to cash in two, and Carrera scored on a sac fly by Zach Pillar. Aaron Sanchez was dealing for the Jays, giving up just two doubles in six well-pitched innings.

Result: Toronto Blue Jays 5, Cleveland Indians 1 (Cleveland leads ALCS 3–1)

ALCS Game 5

Baffled by curveballs
Seventy-one miles per hour
Who are you, Merritt?

Explanation: It was a rather disappointing way for a great offense to go out. Ryan Merritt, a relatively unknown Cleveland Indians pitcher, was pressed into service and delivered a gem. In keeping with its series-long struggles, Toronto was really never able to mount much of an attack on the rookie. Like in every other game in its series, Jays pitching kept them in this one, but the hitting was once again feeble. "You can point the finger at us and say we didn't do a good job," Russell Martin said. "Or you can point the finger at [Cleveland]. To get us out, you have to pitch well—you have to. And they did."

Result: Cleveland Indians 4, Toronto Blue Jays 1 (Cleveland wins ALCS 4–1)

88 World's Fastest Grounds Crew

Granted, their nickname has not been confirmed by the folks at the Guinness Book of World Records. But we'll go along with Tom Cheek, who coined the term "the world's fastest grounds crew" to describe Toronto's field maintenance corps. Don't run to the concessions stands at the start of the fifth inning or you'll miss one of the signature events of a Jays home game.

As the fifth inning approaches, members of the grounds crew prepare to sprint from a gate in left field. Carrying their rakes and other field equipment, they swoop in at full speed, do their thing, and head back to the gate. It's a remarkable feat for a group of individuals to run from the outfield fence to the infield, smoothly rake the dirt, and retreat behind that same outfield fence in 30 seconds or so.

Allen Ford, a former member of the grounds crew, shared his thoughts on The 500 Level Blog about the experience of working for the renowned clean-up gang. "There was always an informal race to see who got off the field first," wrote Ford, now a graphic designer. "Usually the guy taking the second-base screen won, since he had the shortest distance to run to the left-field entrance,"

Being a member of the world's fastest grounds crew is more rewarding than simply being a great way to burn a few calories. The group has opportunities hardly any other members of the public would ever get to experience. Before the game a select few are lucky enough to be given the plum assignment—batting cage duty. Once the clock hits 6:45 PM, the chosen ones head to the cage and wait for the final few minutes of batting practice. While the players take their last cuts, crew members can lean against the cage, alongside players and coaches, and watch some of baseball's greats from an unprecedented vantage point. "For those three minutes there was no cooler place in the world," Ford said. "Listening to the players shoot the shit, hearing the smack of the ball from six feet away, and admiring the arc of it as it sailed way into the bleachers, was everything you could imagine it to be."

The crew's quality of work never suffers despite their alacrity. They do such a thorough job that pitchers have said the mound at the Rogers Centre is among the best-kept in the majors.

89 Attend a Canada Day Game in Toronto

Canada Day at the Rogers Centre is an indulgence only those of us from north of the border can truly appreciate. On July 1 the Blue Jays always dress in red jerseys to honour the birth of our country and have the names on their shirts replaced with one unifying word: CANADA.

Perhaps more than any game of the season, Canada Day is as much about the people in the stands as it is about the players on the field. Superfan Peyton Ekralc dressed in red to commemorate the day 2012's Canada Day. "I've been coming to Canada Day games almost exclusively since 1997," Ekralc said. "It's a day to celebrate the two greatest things in the world—this Blue Jays team and the great country of Canada."

Prior to the game, fans partake in events surrounding the stadium, including live music, family entertainment, games, and food. Once fans enter the stadium, they'll witness a pregame ceremony in which members of the Canadian Forces are joined by the Royal Canadian Mounted Police. They present the colours and unfurl a massive Canadian flag.

The Blue Jays upped the patriotic ante in 2012 by inviting 14 members of the Canadian Olympic Team to participate in the pregame festivities as well.

Jays players have been known to take to their Twitter accounts to send their wishes to fans. "Happy Canada Day to all our Blue Jays fans across the GREAT country!" wrote Jose Bautista. Similar sentiments were expressed by J.P. Arencibia, Casey Janssen, Ricky Romero, and, of course, Canadian star Brett Lawrie. Despite the well wishes, the Los Angeles Angels defeated the Blue Jays 10–6.

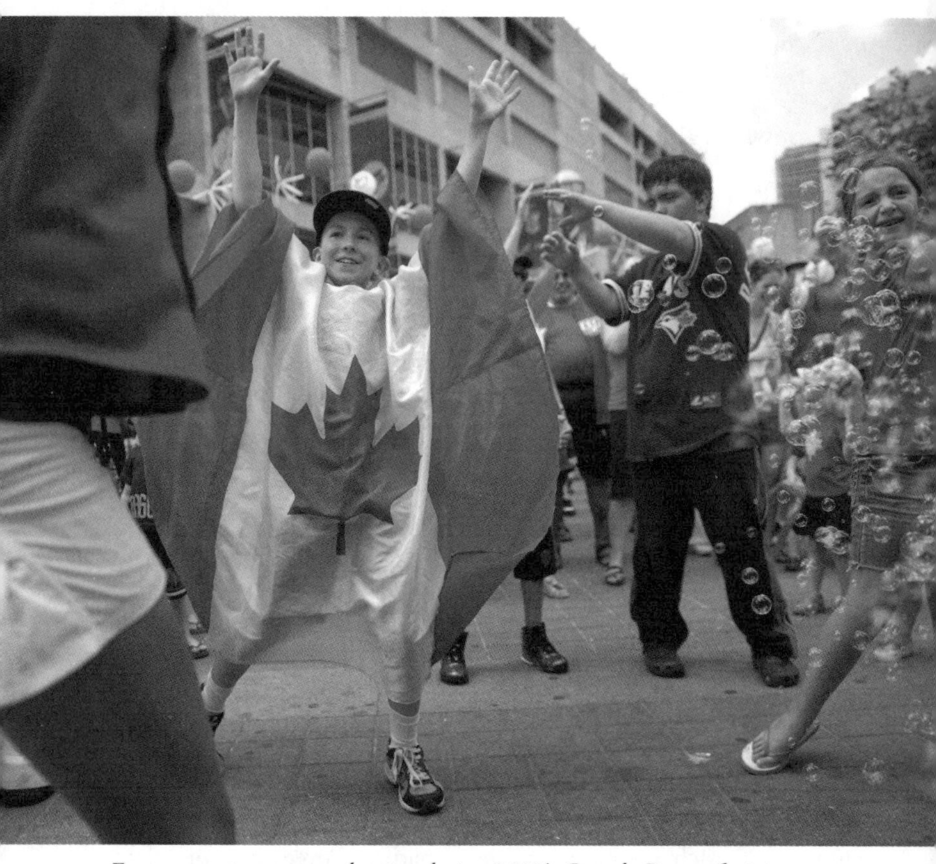

Fans engage in pregame dancing during 2012's Canada Day, a festivity featuring red colours and Canadian flags to honour the country's birth.

Regardless of the outcome, the games typically carry a festive feel, almost reminiscent of the playoff atmosphere Toronto experienced long ago. Blue Jays fans would be remiss if they didn't scratch this uniquely patriotic experience off their bucket list. It's fun, it's joyful, and it's uniquely Toronto.

90 Today's Attendance: 746

The Jays had a pretty incredible attendance streak in the early 1990s. They drew 3.89 million fans in '90, breaking the all-time major league record held by the Los Angeles Dodgers. The next year, they became the first team to ever draw in excess of 4 million. Again, in '92 and '93, they surpassed each record total, peaking at 4.06 million fans on their way to the World Series.

But for a team with such an incredible history of attracting fans, they couldn't draw flies one April day a few years later in Chicago. A grand total of 746 fans attended the Jays-White Sox matinee on Wednesday, April 9, 1997.

Fans of the Jays during their glory days can probably recall beer vendor lines with larger congregations. But it was a bitter cold day in the Windy City, with a gametime temperature near freezing. The 1:07 PM weekday game didn't appeal much to fans who could sit comfortably near their fireplace and watch the game on the tube...or actually have to work.

The Sox did what they could to drum up interest in the game, offering a couple of gameday specials. "Tickets are $5. Parking is $5," Rob Gallas of the Sox's marketing department told Steve Rosenbloom of the *Chicago Tribune*, "and I'll come to your house to wash your car."

But just 746 brave souls bundled up to watch the game in person. If someone was so inclined, they could have literally counted every single person in the stadium and check their math before the next inning. The only thing that could have thrown off the calculations was the occasional disappearance and reappearance of a guy who drank too many Budweisers and had to make a run for the ballpark urinal. Rosenbloom saw the bright side to the tiny crowd: "No one had to leave early to avoid traffic."

Transportation convenience aside, the fans in attendance got to see a gem—albeit a loss for their Sox. The Jays' Roger Clemens dominated Chicago, allowing just a pair of hits to go along with seven strikeouts in 5⅔ innings. Jays relievers allowed just one more hit as they defeated the Sox 5–0.

Commenting on the bargain $5 tickets and parking, Rosenbloom said, "If you wanted to sit in freezing weather to watch the Sox pile up three hits and wait until the ninth inning to get the leadoff man aboard, it was a pretty good deal."

91 Gillick and LaMacchia Meet the Upshaws

Pat Gillick wasn't always a top-level baseball executive. Long before he became known as a Hall of Fame-bound general manager, he was an area scout, pounding the pavement to find baseball talent. Sometimes, it made for odd bedfellows among the bird dogs. "I was trying to land an 18-year-old strapping first baseman from Blanco, Texas, population 200. His name was Willie Upshaw," said Gillick during his enshrinement speech. "It turned out there were only three scouts who knew about Willie—Dave Yocum and I working for the Yankees, and Al LaMacchia from the Atlanta Braves.

"Al and I played every trick we had, and in the end luck was on my side, and the Yankees got Willie in the fifth round of the draft. But he wasn't sure whether he wanted to play baseball or football." Upshaw was a two-sport star and the cousin of Pro Football Hall of Famer Gene Upshaw. Scouts scrambled to try to get him to choose baseball. "Dave [Yocum] spent three days trying to sign Willie without any luck," Gillick said.

All signs pointed toward a career on the gridiron for Upshaw. Knowing that it was down to the Yankees or football, Gillick called on an old rival to help his cause. "I called Al LaMacchia to see if he would go with me to Blanco, Texas, to help convince Willie's family that baseball was the right decision," Gillick said. "Remember, Al and I had been fighting tooth and nail over Willie and the draft, but he said he'd be happy to help. We sat in the living room, two scouts from rival teams, and talked with Willie and his family about the pros and cons. Willie chose baseball. I don't think a scout from one team would help another nowadays.

"Can you imagine that happening today? A rival scout taking time out of his schedule to go to the middle of nowhere to help a competitor and help a young man make the right decision for his future? That's just how we operated back then. We fought like heck for every player and every advantage, but we knew we were part of something bigger than ourselves. To me, that is what baseball is all about. I hope it is always what baseball is all about."

When Gillick arrived in Toronto's front office in 1976, one of his early moves was to grab Upshaw in the following season's Rule 5 draft away from the division rival Yankees. Upshaw played 10 years in the big leagues, peaking during the Blue Jays run of success throughout the mid-1980s. He collected 123 home runs, 88 stolen bases, and 528 RBIs during a decade of baseball. "Willie ended up having a great career," Gillick said.

Another of Gillick's earliest moves was to hire a respected rival to join his upstart Blue Jays team. "I called Al at the Braves and offered him the job [of special assistant]," Gillick said. "He was one of our vice presidents when we won the World Series in 1992 and 1993. Baseball is about talent and hard work and strategy, but at the deepest level it is about love, integrity, and respect—respect for the game, respect for your colleagues, respect for the shared bond that is bigger than any one of us."

92 The Dreaded Curfew

You wouldn't think curfews would affect professional baseball, but the Blue Jays have had more issues with them than a defiant teenager. In hindsight, these incidents serve as strange, humorous memories. At the time, though, they were infuriating.

Perhaps the most memorable moment in Blue Jays-related curfew history came in April of 1979, when Toronto and the Montreal Expos battled for the Pearson Cup. Entering the bottom of the 11th inning, Dave McKay stepped into the batter's box for the Jays, looking to break a 4–4 tie. McKay never saw a pitch, as umpires announced that the game was complete and would end without determining a winner.

The teams had agreed in advance to a 5:15 PM curfew in order to ensure the Expos could catch their 6:50 commercial flight to Chicago, where they would play a game the next day. Even though the game was an exhibition, fans were furious. The primary source of their angst was that Montreal players appeared to deliberately delay the game. Fans booed and shouted at the Expos, who dragged their heels for roughly three minutes prior to the start of the 11th inning to force the game's termination.

Riot police with helmets and batons were called to the stadium to control the angry masses. Fans shouted for refunds, and some even suggested the crowd "mob the players." An embittered throng lingered around the ballpark for roughly 30 minutes after the unannounced curfew was enforced. Jays president Peter Bavasi took some responsibility for the ugly scene. "We should have made the announcement earlier, but we didn't expect anything like this to happen," he said.

Dick Williams, feisty manager of the Expos, was unapologetic. "My catcher had a little trouble getting his equipment on, and then the ball got by my second baseman," he explained, perhaps a little tongue in cheek. He told reporters that he had plans for a further delay if those moves weren't enough. His next ploy was to pull his pitcher and send in a reliever to warm up for as long as possible.

Blue Jays manager Roy Hartsfield said he could hardly blame Williams for his actions and said he was "kind of laughing" when the pair walked onto the field for the trophy presentation. "At one time, [Williams] was quite popular in Toronto, but he agrees that situation no longer exists," Hartsfield said.

On Aug 28, 1980, the Jays and Minnesota Twins played to a 5–5 tie in 14 innings, with the game being halted at the early hour of 5:00 PM. What made this game particularly odd was the nature of the curfew. The players had to pack their bags and leave the stadium to allow workers at Exhibition Stadium time to prepare for a concert by the group, The Cars.

With that debacle still fairly fresh in their memories, the Blue Jays refused to allow a curfew on their September 21, 1985 game, despite the fact a Bryan Adams concert was booked for that very night. The contest went into extra innings, forcing the concert to end at 2:21 AM. Blue Jays public relations man Howard Starkman said the game would be played to completion "no matter what." This time, the concertgoers and their parents became the angry mob. Many of the teenaged audience were unable to travel home on city transit, stranding roughly 1,500 at the stadium.

On another occasion, with a 1:00 AM curfew looming on July 29, 1980, Dwayne Murphy, then of the Oakland A's, rapped a 12th inning single to beat the Blue Jays—just three minutes before a curfew would have ended the game in a tie. Murphy, who would later go on to prominence as the Blue Jays hitting coach and the man who helped transform Jose Bautista from role player to superstar, gave the A's a 5–4 lead they wouldn't relinquish. A's manager Billy Martin seemed in favour of a curfew. "This game is getting too long when it interferes with your drinking," said Martin in typical style.

Cam Norton, a Blue Jays season-ticket-holder who suffered through all the losing, the curfews, and the ban on alcohol sales at Exhibition Stadium, may have summed up Jays fans sentiments best. "If they'd sell us beer, we wouldn't drink it," he said. "We'd probably cry in it."

93 Visit the Site of Toronto's First Ballpark

Thankfully the history of baseball stadiums in Toronto runs much deeper than the "mistake by the lake" known as Exhibition Stadium and the much-maligned mausoleum known as the Rogers Centre. Long before the Blue Jays were a twinkle in Paul Godfrey's eye, high-quality baseball was being played in the Ontario capital. Past generations of Hogtown residents tell tales of sluggers like Babe Ruth and Hall of Fame managers like Sparky Anderson, who graced the stadiums of Toronto.

The Toronto Baseball Grounds may not look like they did a century ago, but fans of baseball in Toronto owe it to themselves to visit the site of the city's first baseball field. Head just past the intersection of Queen Street East and Carroll Street in the Riverside District and you'll find a Toyota dealership, a few boarded up buildings, and The Edwin, which rents rooms by the day, week, or month.

You'll also find a plaque, which pays tribute to the original home of Toronto baseball—the only visual evidence that the ballpark ever existed at this location. The Heritage Toronto plaque attached to this building at 655 Queen Street East, west of Broadview Avenue reads:

"Sunlight Park" was constructed in 1886 as the Toronto Baseball Grounds. The smell of baked potatoes and cigars greeted fans filing in to the park through an avenue of workers' cottages called "Baseball Place." The stands, four storeys high and surrounded by a 4m wooden fence, sat 2,250 paying customers. Admission was 25 cents. The grounds became known as Sunlight Park after William Hesketh Lever opened Sunlight Soap Works south of the park in 1893.

Toronto won its first professional baseball title here on Saturday, September 17, 1897. The hero was rising superstar pitcher/outfielder Edward "Ned" Crane, nicknamed "Cannonball" for his long distance throwing feats. Over 17,000 fans witnessed the first two games against Newark, New Jersey to decide the International League champion.

Crane pitched Toronto to a 15–5 win in the morning game and, to the delight of fans, pitched all of the second game (even though he severely sprained his ankle in the fourth). After hitting a base-clearing drive in the eighth to send the game to extra innings, he hit a home run in the eleventh to steal a 5–4 Toronto victory (the roar of the crowd was heard as far as Yonge and King).

Crane returned to the park Sunday, with sore ankle and shoulder, and pitched Toronto to another victory (22–8).

Today, Eastern Avenue cuts across the old infield of Sunlight Park. The site of the wooden structure lies just to the south of Queen Street, just to the south east of this plaque. Sunlight Park Road traces the southern edge of the field.

"'There is still something about the site of this first stadium that is magical," [Toronto-area baseball historian Dr. Bruce] Meyer said, "beyond the buzz of the city's traffic, beneath layers of concrete and years that have buried the old green field. It is still possible to stand here and imagine what it must have been like, what that crowd fifteen deep in the outfield must have felt, what it was to go home a winner.'"

94 The Ones That Got Away

Roster management ain't easy. Baseball general managers are required to make significant decisions at the drop of a hat and live with the consequences. Some decisions will work out in their favour; others might lead to their dismissal. And some deals simply fall apart on the negotiating table, leaving fans to wonder what could have been.

The Blue Jays have had their share of near-misses—many of which have become public knowledge over the years. The first close call was engineered by Pat Gillick, who was then assistant to GM Peter Bavasi. He reached an informal agreement with the

New York Yankees to swap right-handed pitcher Bill Singer for "Louisiana Lightning" Ron Guidry. Bavasi vetoed the deal, quashing the opportunity to pair Guidry with Dave Stieb in a potentially fearsome rotation for the expansion team. Guidry went on to win 170 games for the Yanks (with a .651 winning percentage) and collect an American League Cy Young Award to complement his four career All-Star Game appearances. Singer was released by the Jays in December of 1978.

A few years later, the Jays aggressively pursued Carlton Fisk when he became a free agent following the 1980 season. "The papers were full of breathless reports on the possibility of the Red Sox star coming to Toronto," wrote Alison Gordon in her book, *Foul Balls*. Likewise, the Jays worked overtime in an attempt to land closer Goose Gossage for the 1984 season. The Jays were a team on the cusp of contention but needed to improve their sloppy bullpen, which featured the hapless combination of Joey McLaughlin and Randy Moffitt. Gossage rejected the opportunity, and instead Dennis Lamp took Toronto's money and headed to the bullpen.

Keith Law, formerly Toronto's assistant GM under J.P. Ricciardi, now serves as an ESPN baseball analyst. When asked in an ESPN online chat whether rumours were true that the New York Mets attempted to trade David Wright to the Jays for Jose Cruz Jr., Law confirmed that the future All-Star third baseman was offered to Toronto. "I've been asked about that trade rumour for three years but never answered while Ricciardi was still GM," he said. "The offer was made, though; I was there when the call came in. It was the first time I'd heard of Wright, since I wasn't with Toronto in 2001, nor had I followed the draft when Wright was in it. J.P.'s reaction was, 'I'm not trading a major league player for some guy in the Sally League.' And that was pretty much that."

Law mentions that another All-Star was also offered to Ricciardi for Cruz. "We had a chance to trade Cruz after that for Rafael Soriano," he said, "but J.P. refused to do it unless [the

Seattle Mariners] included Clint Nageotte, who at the time was a pretty hot prospect." Ricciardi also turned down the opportunity to ship out a middling starter for one of baseball's preeminent sluggers. "The Phillies called about a Ryan Howard-Ted Lilly deal," he said, "[But] Ricciardi said he won't trade Lilly."

Another deal, which was rumoured to be extremely close to completion, would have shipped Alex Rios to San Francisco for a long-haired pitcher named Tim Lincecum, who would go on to win two Cy Young Awards. Ricciardi was reportedly close to pulling the trigger, but he walked away when San Francisco also asked the Jays to throw in catcher Robinzon Diaz.

It wasn't a total loss for the Jays. In 2008, they finally did consummate a deal involving Diaz, trading his rights to the Pittsburgh Pirates. Their return on swapping the backup catcher?

Just some guy named Jose Bautista.

95 John McDonald Hits One for Dad

A seemingly ordinary marketing idea—a Father's Day Contest spearheaded by Blue Jays shortstop John McDonald in 2010—ended up as the ultimate tribute. Fans looking to enter the contest were required to submit an essay about what their father meant to them. Winners of the contest, along with their papas, would get a close-up view of batting practice, meet McDonald and his father, and then take in a game at the Rogers Centre.

McDonald's idea had its roots in Cleveland, his former big league home. "[My] dad thought it was a good idea, thought it would be fun. We figured, 'What a great way for a father and son, or father and daughter, to celebrate Father's Day—coming to the ballpark.'"

But it became increasingly clear Jack McDonald, John's father, wouldn't be able to travel to Toronto for the event. He was critically ill and suffering from the latter stages of cancer. Yet no matter how serious his condition, the elder McDonald insisted his son get his butt back to Toronto for Father's Day. "No matter what happens, you have to go back for the event," Jack said.

Third-base coach Brian Butterfield congratulates John McDonald after he hit a home run, honouring his dad's dying wish, on Father's Day.

Sadly, the McDonald family lost Jack on June 15, 2010 at the far-too-young age of 60. John McDonald attended his father's funeral services, but fulfilled his dad's wishes by returning to Toronto in time to rejoin the Blue Jays for the Father's Day event the pair had planned together. His teammates on the Jays were humbled by what John had gone through, leading up to that Sunday, June 20 event. In an act of unity, they presented him with a Blue Jays jersey signed by each member of the team. On the back of the jersey was the No. 25—the uniform number his father wore as an umpire in East Lyme, Connecticut.

That former umpire, while on his death bed, had made another request to his son. Jack told John, "Hit your next homer for me."

The Father's Day game was shaping up to be a bit of a disappointment for the Jays, as they trailed 9–3 to the San Francisco Giants heading into the ninth inning. Manager Cito Gaston subbed McDonald in as a defensive replacement at second, setting up McDonald to bat in the bottom half of the inning. McDonald watched the first pitch from the Giants' Jeremy Affeldt zip past him for a called strike. Catcher Eli Whiteside fired the ball back to Affeldt, and both pitcher and batter readied themselves for the second pitch. Affeldt wound up and delivered a breaking ball. McDonald's eyes lit up, and the light-hitting second baseman swung with all his might.

Making solid contact, he socked the ball toward left field, where the ball managed to sail over the fence for a home run. "It just barely got over," McDonald said with a laugh.

As he touched home plate, Johnny Mac pointed two fingers to the sky, paying tribute to his dad. Filled with emotion, he headed to the dugout tunnel. Teammates Aaron Hill and Vernon Wells wrapped their arms around him. "We cried on each other's shoulders for 30 seconds," Wells said. "When it went out, it was instant goose bumps. That was one of the most special moments I've seen in this game. That's the happiest loss any of us encountered in our pro careers."

"All that kind of coming together at one moment up in the tunnel," McDonald said. "Yeah, I think I needed somebody to cry with at that point. My teammates, the guys we have on our club, they've been fantastic. They made it really easy not to have to go through that grieving process by myself."

Scott Downs helped out, as well. Since the ball was hit into the Jays bullpen, the reliever was able to scoop it up and give it to McDonald after the game as a memento.

McDonald was asked what was going through his mind as he ran the bases. "Probably that I couldn't call my dad after the game," he told the media scrum. But days later, Johnny Mac said the homer turned some of the sadness in the McDonald household into joy, serving as a tribute to Jack. "It seems after the day I hit the home run, it was more of a celebration. What a way to celebrate your father's life. You just got to talk about so many positive things, so many good things that my dad did."

96 The Trade II

It started out rather humbly, when Miami Marlins general manager Larry Beinfest contacted Toronto general manager Alex Anthopoulos on November 8, 2012 to suggest a swap of catchers—John Buck for Jeff Mathis.

Over the course of the next few hours, the proposed transaction expanded to include stud pitchers Josh Johnson and Mark Buehrle. Then, Jose Reyes, the four-time All-Star shortstop and former

National League batting champ, was thrown into the package proposed to head north.

In his inside look at the transaction, the *Toronto Sun*'s Bob Elliott reported that the Marlins jokingly asked Anthopoulos, "What is this, one-stop shopping?"

When all was said and done, the proposal included a franchise-altering bounty: Johnson, Buehrle, Reyes, Emilio Bonifacio, and Buck (who previously played with the Blue Jays in 2010).

Heading to Miami would be much-maligned shortstop Yunel Escobar, Henderson Alvarez, Adeiny Hechavarria, Jeff Mathis, plus minor league standouts Jake Marisnick, Justin Nicolino, and Anthony DeSclafani. Completion of the deal, however, hinged on Rogers Communications' willingness to allow the team's payroll to increase significantly.

Anthopoulos excitedly called team president Paul Beeston to seek approval to pull the trigger on the deal which added more than $42 million to the team's annual outlay. "Let me get on the phone in the morning and make some calls," Beeston told his GM. Days later, with Rogers' blessing, the deal was consummated.

Ken Rosenthal of Fox Sports began to break the story shortly after 6:00 PM on November 13. First, we learned that Johnson was Toronto-bound...then Buehrle...

Buster Olney of ESPN followed up with even more details. "The Blue Jays-Marlins trade is done...This is going to be one of the all-timers, with Reyes, Johnson, Bonifacio, Buck, Buehrle... holy crow," he said via his Twitter account.

"Just about any [Marlins] player making money is going to Toronto," a source told ESPN.

Marlins star Giancarlo Stanton, perhaps the last legitimate star remaining on Miami's roster after the deal stripped the team of its best players, jumped on Twitter to share his thoughts on the deal. "Alright, I'm pissed off!!! Plain & Simple," he tweeted.

Marlins fans took to the phone lines to voice their disdain for the team's salary dump. "If it wasn't raining," said a caller to The Ticket 790 AM, "I'd be outside right now burning my Marlins jersey."

Public outcry against the salary dump was so strong in the Miami area, it led commissioner Bud Selig to carefully review details of the transaction before ultimately allowing it. "This transaction, involving established major leaguers and highly regarded young players and prospects, represents the exercise of plausible baseball judgment on the part of both clubs [and] does not violate any express rule of Major League Baseball and does not otherwise warrant the exercise of any of my powers to prevent its completion," Selig said in a statement. "It is, of course, up to the clubs involved to make the case to their respective fans that this transaction makes sense and enhances the competitive position of each, now or in the future."

"The Marlins gave the Jays a gift," said a scout who joked that Marlins owner Jeffrey Loria, former owner of the Montreal Expos, "was apologizing to ball fans in Canada."

97 Consolidating the Rogers Empire

Three certainties of life: death, taxes, and complaining about one's expensive Internet/cell phone provider. Rogers Communications may receive their share of scorn, but they certainly are thriving. The nearly 90-year-old corporation is entrenched as one of the world's largest media empires. At the end of 2011, the company's assets were reported to be $18.32 billion with an annual gross revenue of more than $12 billion.

In September of 2000, Ted Rogers Jr. joined the fraternity of media moguls who own Major League Baseball teams. Rogers paid $112 million to Belgian brewery consortium Interbrew to acquire 80 percent of the club; Interbrew retained the other 20 percent. "We didn't buy the team to skimp on the lightbulbs," Rogers memorably said. Asked if Toronto's baseball team was in good hands with Rogers, Bud Selig said that they were one of the only groups to ever purchase a major league team with cash.

Selig laughed at the suggestion that Major League Baseball would leave the Toronto market in the foreseeable future. But there was one remaining problem: the team didn't own or operate its stadium. In fact, the Blue Jays were the only MLB team in such a position. Rogers bought the team without having any control over concessions, parking, or any of the various revenue sources typically associated with big league ownership. That changed when Rogers Communications purchased the SkyDome in late November 2004 from Sportsco International, a Chicago-based group of investors, for $25 million. "A very fair price," said Blue Jays CEO Paul Godfrey.

Sportsco took a massive hit on the sale, having paid $80 million to buy the SkyDome out of bankruptcy court in April 1999. The stadium was built for roughly $600 million and had also previously sold for $151 million in 1994. Godfrey said the price was well in line with "the cash flow it can generate. It's not [based] on what [it] cost to build it."

At the press conference announcing the transaction, reporters asked if naming rights would be sold to boost revenues. "We're going to try to take a fresh approach on that," Godfrey said. That so-called "fresh approach" turned out to be the branding the former SkyDome as Rogers Centre.

Because it now owned the facility, the team had the ability to address some of the stadium's issues, such as its uninviting atmosphere. "At some point in the future we would feel a lot better if we could diminish the concrete look of the building," Godfrey said. "Over the longer term, we expect to improve the way the fans experience the game." Rogers now owned the team, the ballpark, and the lucrative television rights to distribute Blue Jays games and specials throughout the country.

In 2008 Rogers purchased the remaining shares from Interbrew, now called AB InBev, to firm up complete ownership. Later that year, Ted Rogers Jr., the man largely responsible for the creation of one of the world's biggest media conglomerates and the owner of the Jays, passed away at the age of 75. His surname remains emblazoned on cell phones, high-definition receivers, Internet modems, television networks, radio broadcasts, and office towers throughout Canada.

And his name should remain attached to the stadium for years to come.

98 Learn From Jays Legends

Not many kids will get a chance to learn how to turn two from Robbie Alomar, how to gun down a base runner from Jesse Barfield, or how Rance Mulliniks deftly manicures his hardy moustache. But for less than the cost of a PlayStation 3, kids aged 10 to 16 across Canada can participate in a Honda Super Camp, a three-day training camp with Blue Jays legends. It's a real-life experience which surpasses any joy their gaming system might provide.

In exchange for a couple hundred bucks to register, participants have the opportunity to receive high-calibre instruction on hitting, pitching, and fielding from former baseball pros. Often, it's personalized advice from a former Jay like Alomar, Barfield, Mulliniks,

Duane Ward, Lloyd Moseby, Paul Quantrill, Homer Bush, or Frank Catalanotto. (If, as a 12-year-old, the author of this book was presented with the opportunity to receive personalized instruction from a Blue Jays legend, he might have sold a vital organ to pay the registration fee.)

Much of the coaching is provided by Baseball Canada-authorized instructors, with the former players assisting in the process. "There really is no other similar partnership in professional sports providing this quality of instruction with this many major league and national team-quality instructors to kids across an entire country," said Stephen Brooks, the Blue Jays vice president of business operations.

Kids will enjoy a fairly intensive training experience, but the former players know this event is far more than just a baseball boot camp. "We're just trying to have fun with these kids," said Alomar, the two-time World Series winner and Baseball Hall of Fame member. "And we're trying to let them know that with hard work they can do the same thing we do—play baseball."

Registration is limited to 150 for each event, and all bookings can be made through BlueJays.com/camps. A certain number of kids will have their registration fees covered by the Jays Care Foundation and the Toronto chapter of the Baseball Writers Association of America.

In recent years participants left the event with a Blue Jays hat and T-shirt along with a 12-inch, leather pro model Roberto Alomar Series baseball glove, not to mention a whole pile of baseball knowledge.

Sadly, due to demand, Mulliniks moustache-grooming lessons are not guaranteed.

99 Barfield Wants Booty

In the April 8, 2008 installment of his CBC blog, Jesse Barfield took a stance on a crucial issue facing modern baseball. The time was right. The time was now. Baseball players needed to stand up, be proud, and make a change.

They needed to show their butts more clearly.

The man who crushed 40 home runs for the Blue Jays in 1986 and collected 162 career outfield assists chose to devote his energy to the troubling lack of ass-hugging pants in Major League Baseball.

No, seriously…he did.

"What ever happened to the fashion police in baseball? Have you guys seen these uniforms some of these guys are wearing today? Some of them look like the old Negro League uniforms," Barfield wrote.

He knew those particular uniforms well, since his uncle, Albert Overton, played for the Cincinnati Clowns of the Negro Leagues decades earlier. "Those were some ugly, baggy uniforms. So, have we gone retro?" Barfield said. "Can you believe that some of the guys have their uniform pants made like their street jeans? Come on now! Let's get out of the music videos and on to the field.

"Some of you may think I am joking, but I am serious. Let's keep the integrity of the game," he wrote. "Take it from me, I love to style—my family calls me the Style Master—but it's with taste on and off the field. What's funny is you may think these guys are trying to cover up bad bodies, but they're not. Most of these guys have sculpted bodies under all that fabric. Take it from me, they better enjoy having a young, athletic body while they can, because time does take its toll."

The Style Master pondered an important consequence of the less-revealing pants. "Can the baggy uniforms be the reason that female attendance has gone down a bit?" he asked. Yeah, it might be that. Or it could be the fact the Jays were then a rudderless ship en route to a series of mediocre seasons. Tough call.

Barfield poetically reiterated his comments, regarding the opinions of the fairer sex, to the style publication, PeaceMagazine.com. "They can't see the booties," he said. "Chicks may dig the long ball, but if the uniform isn't fitting, in the baseball stands, the chicks ain't sitting."

100 Rising Stars

The 2017 season is a new beginning for the Blue Jays, and there are plenty of reasons to be optimistic. Despite some obvious re-shaping, the Jays have a pitching staff that rivals any other in the American League and an exciting collection of offensive contributors.

There is no bigger reason for optimism than meteoric starter Aaron Sanchez. After adding muscle to his frame, he emerged as the team's new ace with a stellar 2016 season. Selected with the 34th overall pick of the 2010 draft, Sanchez made a steady climb through the Toronto organization before debuting on July 23rd, 2014 in relief. Sanchez entered the 2016 season in the rotation, though with the team-issued caveat stating that he would be on an innings limit and would transition to the bullpen at some point. He responded by going 9–1 with 2.97 ERA in the first half. When Boston Red Sox reliever Craig Kimbrel bowed out of his spot on the All-Star Game due to injury, Sanchez got the call. In addition to the honour of being named an All-Star, Sanchez led the AL with a 3.00 ERA, winning 15 games along the way against just two losses.

Sanchez's pal, Marcus Stroman, electrified fans in his rookie season and then beat the odds in his sophomore season to come back from a spring training knee injury. The Stro Show injected the 2015 squad with life, winning all four of his September starts when Toronto needed them the most. The excitable Stroman is not only a fantastic follow on social media, but his unorthodox hairstyles are a source of endless entertainment.

During the later parts of the Anthopoulos era, prospects were promoted aggressively through the system to test their abilities on bigger and bigger stages. Sometimes, it didn't work perfectly. The (still incomplete) cases of Miguel Castro and Dalton Pompey come to mind. But the promotion of a young Roberto Osuna proved to be incredibly fortuitous for Toronto. On April 8, 2015, the Mexican righty became the youngest pitcher to appear in a game for the Jays. Since that date Osuna has compiled 56 saves with 2.63 ERA and a 0.93 WHIP. Osuna left school at age 12 to start work picking vegetables to support his family. Just a few years later at the tender age of 16, he was pitching in the professional Mexican League, where the Blue Jays first spotted him. When asked how it was possible that such a young man could have such composure in high-pressure, late-inning situations, former teammate LaTroy Hawkins said, "He's comfortable being uncomfortable, growing up where he grew up."

Who will be the next young pitcher to burst onto the scene for Toronto? The smart money is on Sean Reid-Foley, Conner Greene, T.J. Zeuch, Justin Maese, or Jon Harris—all of whom appear on prospect watch lists throughout the industry.

Jays fans have reason to be optimistic about some rising offensive stars as well. Of all of the bats in the Blue Jays system, no one has turned more heads than the offspring of former All-Star outfielder Vladimir Guerrero. "[Most] of the organization's top prospects from a year ago took a step forward in 2016, none more so than Vladimir Guerrero Jr.," wrote *Baseball America*'s John Manuel. "The son of the ex-big leaguer debuted impressively in the rookie level Appalachian League, showing a polished hitting approach for his age and prodigious power potential." Manuel and the *BA* staff project Guerrero's power to grade at a 70 on the 20/80 scouting scale, a rating that is normally reserved for sluggers such as Edwin Encarnacion and Jose Bautista.

There are other intriguing prospects as well, including Rowdy Tellez. Nicknamed "Rowdy" before birth for moving around endlessly in the womb, Tellez has outplayed his draft slot to emerge as a potential first division major leaguer. "It's one thing to be an excellent contact hitter like Tellez. It is quite another to have the patience and pitch recognition to work a pitcher for walks. His eye-hand coordination are well above average, and he hunts pitches he can drive," wrote former scout Bernie Pleskoff on TodaysKnuckleball.com. "I am very bullish on the future for Rowdy Tellez. I believe he is just beginning to tap the tremendous power and hitting potential in his game. He could fashion a solid batting average to accompany 25 to 30 home runs once he is established as a big league player."

Another prospect, Anthony Alford, played in the 2016 Fall Stars Game in the Arizona Fall League. "I would classify Alford as a very good candidate to play some center field in Toronto at some point in 2018. At this point I would say he is rather 'raw' as a player. He needs the extra plate appearances and at-bats he is getting in Arizona during the Fall League," Pleskoff said. "The fact Alford plays center field increases his viability as a top-flight prospect capable of carving out a big league career. His speed and athletic ability are highlighted with him being the focal point of the outfield."

Shortstop Richard Urena has opened eyes in the Jays minor league system, and some scouts place him above Tellez and Alford when speaking of long-term potential. "He's always had all-around ability," Gil Kim, the Blue Jays' director of player development, told Sportsnet's Shi Davidi. "But this year his work ethic and ability to focus from pitch-to-pitch every single pitch of the game, he's made big strides there."

Sources

When I was 13 or 14 years old, my grandmother, Rita Muir, gave me one of the most thoughtful gifts I've ever received. Knowing how much I loved the sport of baseball, she gave me a collection of second-hand books she'd gathered, ranging from Jim Bouton's *Ball Four* to Bob Uecker's *Catcher in the Wry.* Reading through my new treasures, my appreciation for baseball expanded from a simple love of the game into a love of baseball literature. A few years later, with some encouragement from my mom, Linda, a dyed-in-the-wool educator and writer in her own right (and advocate of quality juvenile literature), I volunteered to do some writing for the student-run *Western Gazette* and later latched on with several online publications. I can't thank my nana and mom enough for sparking this love of baseball reading and writing.

Although the events discussed in a significant portion of the book are hardly proprietary in nature, a number of print and web sources served as invaluable resources during my research of the book.

Among the many papers, publications, television stations, and websites I researched for this book are the *USA TODAY, The Sporting News, Toronto Star,* Baseball Prospectus, *The New York Times, New York Daily News, Newsday,* the *Toronto Sun, The Globe and Mail, Chicago Tribune, Los Angeles Times, San Francisco Chronicle,* the *National Post, St. Petersburg (Florida) Times, The Montreal Gazette, The Seattle Times, Baseball Digest, Baseball America.* Also *Sports Illustrated*, ESPN.com, *Time* magazine, *People,* MLB.com, BleacherReport.com, radio network Sportsnet 590 The Fan, Baseball-Reference.com, Retrosheet.org, JoePosnanski.com, Fox Sports, MLB Network, Fangraphs, the *2016 Official Rules of Major League Baseball,* and the Toronto Blue Jays Media Guide.

I'd like to especially offer my thanks to the cutting-edge bloggers who devote so much time and energy to covering Toronto's baseball team. They served a unique purpose during my research, answering questions about the more obscure details of the team's history.

Whenever I was faced with a question like "how many ballparks did Rick Bosetti desecrate with his urine?," I knew I could probably find the answer at any or all of the following: DrunkJaysFans.com, BlueJayHunter.com, TaoOfStieb.com, MopUpDuty.com, JaysJournal.com, DirkHayhurst.com, Kevin Gray's Gray Matter, JaysProspects.com, BattersBox.ca, BluebirdBanter.com, BlueJays.com, Sportsnet.ca, cbc.ca, BacktoBaseball.com, CanadianBaseballNews.com, and many more.

Audio and video clips of memorable Blue Jays moments by broadcasters Tom Cheek, Jerry Howarth, Buck Martinez, Pat Tabler, Alan Ashby, Mike Wilner, and many others were key components of the research process.

The information and quotes in several books were extremely helpful throughout the process. The books I consulted include:

Baseball Prospectus team of Experts. *Baseball Prospectus Annual.* Hoboken.

Wiley, 2010. New York: Plume/Penguin. 2007-2009.

Gruber, Kelly with Keith Boland. *Kelly: At Home on Third.* Toronto: Viking/Penguin, 1991.

Martinez, Buck. *The Last Out.* Toronto: Fitzhenry & Whiteside, 1986.

Stieb, Dave with Keith Boland. *Tomorrow I'll Be Perfect.* Toronto: Dell/Doubleday, 1986.

Whitt, Ernie with Greg Cable. *Catch: A Major League Life.* Scarborough: McGraw-Hill Ryerson Limited, 1989.